North Carolina Day
Hiking for Every Body

North Carolina Day Hiking for Every Body

What to Know and Where to Go from the Blue Ridge to the Beaches

Whitney Harris Wallace

Jefferson, North Carolina

All locations mentioned are in North Carolina unless otherwise indicated.
All images are author photographs unless otherwise indicated.

ISBN (print) 978-1-4766-9725-3
ISBN (ebook) 978-1-4766-5788-2

LIBRARY OF CONGRESS CATALOGING-IN-PUBLICATION DATA

Library of Congress Control Number 2025032818

© 2026 Whitney Harris Wallace. All rights reserved

*No part of this book may be reproduced or transmitted in any form
or by any means, electronic or mechanical, including photocopying
or recording, or by any information storage and retrieval system,
without permission in writing from the publisher.*

Front cover images: (top, left to right) Rhododendron in the Great Craggy
Mountains (Sean Pavone); stone bridge and waterfall in Reynolda Gardens
in Winston-Salem (Bryan Pollard); wild horses on the beach at Corolla
(Jeffery Scott Yount); background image by Tim Mainiero
(all photographs from Shutterstock)

Printed in the United States of America

Toplight is an imprint of McFarland & Company, Inc., Publishers

*Box 611, Jefferson, North Carolina 28640
www.toplightbooks.com*

To North Carolina trail maintenance volunteers, state and national park staff, local search and rescue team members, and all the others who put so much work into keeping these beautiful trails available and safe: I'm a big fan of your work and especially thankful for all who have done so much to reopen trails after Hurricane Helene.

To Travis:
I love the trails we have hiked together, both actual and metaphorical, even when they are steep and rocky. I wouldn't want to follow them with anyone else. All my love.

To Nathaniel:
You have taught me that some of life's greatest rewards are found in following the blue blazes. I love you and am proud of you.

To Elliott and Quinn:
Our state's natural spaces are left in your hands. I hope you'll continue the family tradition of loving them and wanting to protect them. Don't forget to live a little wild every now and then.

Author's Notes

The information and tips shared in this book are based on my training, research, and experiences as a day hiker and hiking group leader on a variety of trails across North Carolina. You should not take my words as gospel, however. In all things related to hiking you should find what provides the safest experience for your individual needs and abilities. Feel free to take this book as a starting point, but please do your own research when needed.

Trail conditions and availability change frequently—sometimes daily. For Western North Carolina, Hurricane Helene in September 2024 brought a stark reminder of that. Roads can close because of weather conditions. Small parking lots can fill up quickly. Trails can become incredibly muddy after lots of rain or overgrown from sparse use. Easy creek crossings can become difficult. Trails can be rerouted as a result of overuse, making them more or less difficult. Sections of trail or even entire routes can be closed for extended periods of time due to damage or lack of staff available to safely oversee the land. Part of hiking is doing your research and being prepared but also holding things with a very open hand. You may have to change hiking plans at a moment's notice for a variety of reasons.

A word about names: Name capitalization and spelling can vary between sources and change over time. Different names can even be used to refer to the same place or thing. For example, cottonmouth and water moccasin refer to the same snake. In this book I have used the most common, current names, capitalizations and spellings.

Acknowledgments and Appreciations

My hiking experiences, and therefore this book, would not have been possible without the support of many people. First and most of all, I want to thank my husband, Travis. Whatever I set my mind on accomplishing, he's right there beside me. He has been encouraging and understanding as I have not only spent hours in front of my laptop writing but more importantly spent even more hours on the trail. I would not have been able to experience all the hikes I have, much less write this book, if he hadn't backed me up in those endeavors. Next is our son, Nathaniel. He's a fantastic young man and inspires me to pay more attention to all the amazing diversity in our world, both on and off the trail. You'll also get to enjoy some of his beautiful photography over these pages.

Thank you to my other friends and family who have encouraged me along the way as well, even when they maybe thought I was a little strange for wanting to spend this much time traipsing around in the woods, in all kinds of weather, often alone. I'm especially appreciative of those who have joined me on the trail from time to time. Equally important has been the online community I've met through my hiking Instagram, @whitneygoeshiking, and my hiking Facebook account, Whitney Goes Hiking. Their comments, laughs, trail and gear recommendations and inspirational pictures have been invaluable, even though I've met very few of them IRL! I'd also like to thank my fellow hikers in the Piedmont Plus Size Hikers group. Thank you for being willing to step out of your comfort zones while giving me the chance to get out of mine and lead you. Come as you are, do what you can, and happy trails!

Thank you to Bill Sanderson, co-director of the Carolina Mountain Club Search and Rescue team and volunteer with Haywood County Search and Rescue, for his review of Part II of the text. Mr. Sanderson also happens to have been my biology teacher 30 years ago in my senior year of high school. He taught me about native North Carolina plants and wildlife in that class and much of it has stuck with me all these years. His thorough feedback and many helpful suggestions for this book prove that he's still teaching me things!

Thank you also to Matt Kirby from Catalyst Sports in Asheville for talking with me about adaptive hiking and sharing some wonderful resources and to Dawn Bartlett and Ken Hackney for the amazing educational resource they provide through the NC Wild Snake ID and Education group on Facebook and for providing the incredible images of snakes you will see in the text.

Last, thank you to my McFarland friends for giving me the opportunity to see a book from the author side of the desk. I couldn't be more honored and excited to join the distinguished McFarland/Toplight family of authors. Special thanks to Susan, Heather, Jeanette, Lisa and Mark. You make me look good.

Table of Contents

Author's Notes vi
Acknowledgments and Appreciations vii
Preface 1
    What You'll Find in This Book 5

Part I. Background and Context   9

1. An Introduction to Hiking 10
    What Counts as a Hike? 10 • *How Long Has Hiking Been Around?* 12 • *What Are the Benefits of Hiking?* 15 • *How Frequently Should I Hike?* 20 • *The 20/5/3 Nature Pyramid* 21 • *How Fast Should I Hike?* 23

2. An Introduction to the Natural Features of North Carolina ... 24
    The Mountains 25 • *The Piedmont and Foothills* 30 • *The Coastal Plain* 36

Part II. Safe and Enjoyable Hiking   43

3. Know Yourself and Trust Your Gut 44
    Know Yourself and Honor Your Limits 44 • *Trust Your Gut* 49 • *Personal Safety on the Trail* 51

4. Do Your Research: Understanding Trail Information and Weather Forecasts 53
    Get Trail Information from More Than One Source 53 • *Know How to Read Basic Trail Guide and Map Information* 55 • *Check Reliable Weather Forecasts and Know Typical Weather Patterns* 62

5. Trail Accessibility and Adaptive Hiking 69
    Features of an Accessible Trail 69 • *Adaptive Hiking Equipment and Programs* 71 • *How Else Might a Trail Be Accessible ... or Not?* 72 • *Transportation to Trails* 72 • *Finding Information About Accessible Trail Options* 73

6. The 10 Essentials 75
    The 10 Essentials 75 • *Water* 77 • *Food Appropriate for the Length*

Table of Contents

    and Difficulty of the Hike 78 • *Taking Care of Your Feet* 79 • *Appropriate Clothing* 82 • *A Way to Navigate (and Another Way to Navigate)* 84 • *Sun Protection and Heat Exposure* 86 • *A Source of Light* 87 • *A Basic First Aid Kit* 89 • *Other Essential Items* 91

7. Beyond the 10 Essentials   93
    Insect and Tick Repellents 93 • *Trekking Poles* 94 • *Chafing Prevention and Treatment* 96 • *Extra Phone Battery* 97 • *A Hiking Journal* 98 • *Extra Health and Safety Items* 99 • *Don't Lose Your Stuff* 100 • *Where to Buy Gear* 102

8. How Not to Get Lost: And What to Do If You Do Anyway   104
    Have More Than One Way to Navigate 104 • *Tell Someone Where You Are Going* 105 • *Learn How to Follow Trail Blazes* 105 • *Pay Attention* 107 • *What to Do If You Do Get Lost* 107 • *30-60-90 Walk* 108 • *Carry a Whistle* 110 • *Don't Believe the Internet* 110

9. Wildlife Encounters: Sharing the Trail with Other Species   112
    Insects and Arachnids 113 • *Reptiles and Amphibians* 118 • *Mammals* 122

Between pages 126 and 127 are 12 color plates containing 17 photographs

10. Be a Good Trail Citizen: Sharing the Trail with Other Humans   127
    Trail Etiquette 127 • *Leave No Trace* 130 • *Hiking with Pets* 133

11. Mindful Hiking   136
    Setting the Stage 136 • *Mindful Moments* 138

Part III. Finding Trails   145

12. National Park Sites   146
    National Seashores 146 • *National Historic Sites* 148 • *National Military Sites* 148 • *National Historic Trails* 150 • *National Memorial Site* 152 • *Great Smoky Mountains National Park* 152 • *Top Recommended National Park Hike* 155

13. National and State Forests   157
    Pisgah National Forest 158 • *Nantahala National Forest* 159 • *Uwharrie National Forest* 161 • *Croatan National Forest* 163 • *State Forests* 164 • *Top Recommended National Forest Hikes* 165

14. The Blue Ridge Parkway   171
    Blue Ridge Parkway History 171 • *Hiking and the Blue Ridge Parkway* 173 • *Top Recommended Blue Ridge Parkway Hike* 175

Table of Contents

15. State Park Sites 178
Different Types of State Park Sites 178 • *Hiking at State Park Sites* 181 • *Top Recommended State Park Hikes* 183

16. Land Trusts and Conservancy Organizations 189
Hiking on Protected Lands 190 • *Top Recommended Land Conservancy Hikes* 192

17. County and Municipal Parks and Privately Owned Lands 195
The Benefits of Trails in Communities 195 • *Hiking at Local Parks and on Privately Owned Lands* 197 • *Top Recommended Local Park and Privately Owned Land Hikes* 199

18. Long-Distance Trails 205
The Appalachian Trail 205 • *The Mountains-to-Sea Trail* 206 • *Top Recommended Long Distance Trail Hikes* 208

Epilogue 213
Appendix I. Most Recommended Hikes by Region 217
Mountain and Foothills Region Trails 217 • *Piedmont Region Trails* 218 • *Coastal Plain Region Trails* 220

Appendix II: North Carolina Every Body Hiking Challenge 222
Chapter Notes 225
Additional Resources 235
Index 239

Preface

Hello! It's nice to meet you. My name is Whitney, and I'm so excited to explore North Carolina's trails together. Whether you are a long-time admirer of North Carolina's many wonderful paths or a newcomer to hiking, you are welcome here.

I was born in North Carolina—the sixth generation, at least, on my dad's side of the family. And, aside from the six and a half years I spent in exile living in Miami in the early 2000s (I kid, South Florida), I have lived here my entire life. I've had the opportunity to live in all three regions of the state—the Mountains, the Piedmont and the Coastal Plain—calling Asheville, Boone, West Jefferson, Jefferson, Charlotte, Kannapolis, Winston-Salem, Lexington, and New Bern home at different points along the way. I've also had the wonderful opportunity to explore all three regions through hiking.

Hiking and the nature connection that often comes with it are not new but rather rediscovered passions for me in my 40s. I was going to start this off by saying I wasn't an "outdoorsy" kid growing up, but that would be a lie. I wasn't athletically outdoorsy. I wasn't athletic, period. Ever. In any way, shape, or form. I tried out many sports and other activities—dance,

This picture is from one of my favorite hikes ever, the three balds hike at Roan Highlands. It was a glorious day in May 2021 and the weather was perfect.

soccer, field hockey, martial arts—and I was never very good at any of them. I was the proverbial kid picked last in gym class.

I wasn't athletic, but I loved the outdoors. You might say it was in my blood. My paternal great-grandfather was a private ranger for the Vanderbilts (of Biltmore House fame) and then the first federal park ranger for Pisgah National Forest when it was formed primarily from land bought from the Vanderbilts. My father is an avid fly fisherman, and he would take me along fishing, hiking and camping. My maternal grandmother would take me for long rides on the Blue Ridge Parkway where we would stop at overlooks and picnic areas to admire the views and take short hikes. During our annual family trips to the beach at Thanksgiving she would walk with me on the sand, and we'd admire the shells, the birds, and everything else we could see.

I spent hours exploring the creek across the road from our house looking for cool rocks and the critters that lived under them. Often as soon as I arrived home from school, I would head outside to climb trees or take a walk to a nearby lake. I learned to recognize mountain laurel and rhododendron and eastern box turtles and lots of different kinds of birds and butterflies. Like most kids, I didn't think of hiking in terms of how much distance we covered or what mountains we climbed. I enjoyed what we saw and learned along the way, remembering the fog rolling across the mountains,

My grandmother (oldest girl, fourth from left, circa 1928) and five of her eight siblings, all of whom lived in my great-grandfather's ranger housing in the Pisgah National Forest. Part of my great-grandfather's duties included raising fawns orphaned in the forest, a task that became a family affair. One such fawn can be seen being bottle-fed in this image.

the seashells found in the surf, the old homestead discovered or the field full of wildflowers.

While the time I had to spend enjoying the natural world decreased as the years went by, I never lost my love of outdoor spaces. I majored in biology in college and spent three spring semesters working as a lab assistant for the botany field

My maternal grandmother, Becky, and I enjoying a day exploring the beach in November 1985.

I've been spending time on the trail most of my life. Here I am, at five years old, enjoying a hike near Chimney Rock.

lab, wandering around Charlotte-area fields, forests and preserves studying and identifying local plants. As the demands of work, married life and motherhood increased, I still enjoyed finding points of connection with nature. It was something I found myself drawn back to time and again.

Then came the year that would never end: 2020. Covid-19 began wreaking havoc, we faced a tempestuous election cycle, and my only child turned 18 and started his senior year of high school. Life seemed to become more than a little topsy-turvy. In the fall of that year I decided that I had to start getting out of the house and, more importantly, out of my head. I felt claustrophobic in my own mind.

So I decided one October afternoon to go on a hike by myself. I had never really hiked alone, but I needed some time away from others. We lived in Ashe County at the time and after doing a little research I picked a trail that I thought wouldn't have many people on it that afternoon. It also happened to start with half a mile or so straight uphill. Not very smart on my part, quite frankly. I realized quickly that I wasn't going to be able to just run up that mountain. I honestly wasn't even sure I was going to be able to walk up it. So I started counting my steps … 1, 2, 3, 4, 5 … until I would get to 100. I told myself that I would go just 100 more steps and then I'd let myself turn around and go back down to my car. But when I reached the end of those 100 steps, I'd say, "I think I can do 100 more," and sure enough, I could. Little by little, 100 steps at a time, I made it up that steep incline and was greeted with … no view at all. The clouds were really socked in, and I couldn't see a thing. But I still felt like I had accomplished something

The non-view at the top of that first hike. You would never know there are lots of mountains out there. The lack of view didn't matter, though. I still had a wonderful hike.

and, despite being tired and winded, I felt a lightness in my step—and my head—that I hadn't felt in a while.

My pictures from that hike also hint at something else that would come to define my hiking journey. There were lots of small details—plants and animals and rocks that caught my eye along the way. As I would stop after each set of 100 steps to catch my breath, I would take a few moments to look around and notice what I could see, hear, and smell. I reached out and touched different textures on the trees and picked up rocks and looked at them from all angles. I watched the low clouds play through the almost-bare trees and listened to the quiet they carried along with them. I looked around trying to catch sight of the birds I could hear singing. My pictures include the details of a fallen orange leaf, a red newt and some purple flowers. After I got home I spent time looking up some of the things I had seen and was interested to read more about the different species. I left that hike not only feeling energized from the physical work of the journey but also a connection to the place I had been that was more relational than transactional. And I felt like maybe, just maybe, there was a little more order and beauty to the world than appeared through all my doomscrolling on social media and 24-hour news sites.

That hike, October 25, 2020, started a journey that I had no idea would lead me to so many places across this amazing state I call home and others nearby. Hike after hike I've discovered beautiful things and hard things on the trails I've traversed, as well as within myself. In many ways that first hike also exemplified the type of hiking I will share about in this book, one that very much resembles my nature explorations during my childhood. It was not a long hike—less than three miles. It represented a bit of a physical challenge, but not an overwhelming one, and I respected my limits and completed it safely and in a way that worked for me. It was a trail that was perhaps a little less well known. And I spent almost as much time noticing and appreciating the land around me as I did putting one foot in front of the other and moving up the mountain.

Since then, I have completed more than 250 hikes on over 200 unique stretches of trail. The fact that I continue to hike on average at least once per week five years later is a testament to all the things that hiking has brought into my life. These go way beyond accomplishing some athletic feat. I can truthfully say that I am a different person than I was when I started. In this book I hope to help you discover the enjoyment, positive challenge and life enrichment this particular approach to hiking can bring and I hope to help you see how this can happen even with limited available time. I hope especially to encourage those who might be new to hiking or who do not feel like they fit into outdoor spaces as they are typically presented.

What You'll Find in This Book

When I first got back into hiking, I looked for a how-to book that matched my kind of hikes. I'm a busy, sandwich generation, plus-size wife and mom who has a job and interests and responsibilities outside of hiking *and* someone who loves to spend quality time on the trail connecting with nature. I am not a long-distance hiker or backpacker, and a lot of books were for those folks. I wanted a book that focused less on backpacking skills and long, often quite difficult, trails, and more on the kind of hiking that was doable for most people in an afternoon. A book that discussed how to be safe and how to be a good trail citizen. A book that offered some great ideas on where to find good trails and maybe taught a few tips and tricks along the way. I wanted a book that acknowledged people could be out there hiking with physical or mental considerations that might impact their experience on the trail. A book that embraced hikers of different fitness levels, body sizes and disability statuses. A book that acknowledged that hikers sometimes have chronic illnesses or mobility challenges. A book that did not assume that everyone was hiking to accomplish the same types of goals and that valued the benefits of hiking beyond the physical. A book that approached hitting the trail from a "stop and smell the roses" perspective. I didn't find that book, so I decided to write it.

Since 2020, in addition to my hours spent day hiking, I have also completed wilderness first responder, associate in wilderness medicine, and forest therapy guide certification programs. The knowledge I gained through these (along with being a bit of a nerd about natural history and a researcher by nature) makes up the text you are reading. This book is for anyone who has been interested in hiking but is a little hesitant to make it a regular part of their life. For anyone who is overwhelmed by all the information, gear, and terminology out there. For anyone who likes the idea of hiking alone but is afraid to try it for safety reasons. For anyone who's ever looked at most people on the covers of hiking books or in the social media posts of outdoor influencers and thought, "Well, if I have to look like *that* to hike, then I'm out." For anyone who is maybe returning to hiking after not hitting the trails for a while. For anyone who might be new to hiking and wonders how their disability or chronic illness might impact their experience. For anyone who would perhaps like to experience North Carolina in a different way. I have been all these people!

I hope this book will prove to be a go-to resource that shares about hiking, especially North Carolina day hiking, in a way that is helpful and approachable for hikers of all kinds. For every body. In addition to providing information on how to hit the trail safely, I hope this book will encourage you to approach your hikes in a somewhat different manner. I want to help you consider that a successful hike might have less to do with how many miles you cover or how many mountains you climb and more to do with your journey along the way. The things you notice, the flora and fauna you share the land with, your sensory experiences and what you learn about yourself. Alongside the more typical hiking how-to information, we're also going to talk about mindfulness and fostering a connected relationship with the natural world. The physical benefits of hiking are great and many, but so are the mental ones, and we're going to spend just as much time focusing on those.

One of the inspirations for this book was a woman I met while out hiking one day in June 2022. I was almost back to the parking area from one of the longest hikes I've ever completed, and she was sitting on a bench with a friend about a tenth of a mile down the trail. I said hello as I approached them, and she asked me a question about the trail ahead. We started talking, and I learned that they were resting on the bench because the six or seven steps up from the parking area and the section of trail past that had been exhausting for her. I also learned that she had not been in the outdoors for any length of time in more than two years. She shared that she was ashamed of her condition and how her body looked and that, even with the encouragement of her wonderful friend, coming to this trail that day had taken all of her courage. I told her how happy

I was for her that she was out enjoying the trail and that I hoped it would be the first of many hikes for her. I shared a couple of tips with her, like how using trekking poles had helped me, and about a couple of trails in the area that I thought she might enjoy as she got started. And we spent a lot of time talking about the many benefits of just being

A beautiful golden-hour hike on the Bluff Mountain Trail off the Blue Ridge Parkway in July 2021. What interesting and wonderous things do you think lie just down the trail? Let's find out!

outside, no hiking required. I think about her often and hope she has continued to enjoy time on the trail and found a supportive hiking community to be a part of.

So, while this book is written for day hikers of all kinds, I especially hope this text feels like advice and encouragement from a good friend for this hiker and others like her. For those who find the hiking world to be intimidating or even a bit unfriendly, I hope to educate and cheer you on from the viewpoint of someone just a little further down the trail, and after you finish reading, I hope you will feel empowered to get out there and discover the joys and benefits of hiking in a safe, enjoyable, mindful way.

One more note: this book is not exactly a trail guide, at least not like most trail guides you may have seen. At the end of each chapter in Part III, I'll share more detailed information about some of my favorite hikes and in Appendix I you'll find some additional information about the 15 hikes from each region that I would most recommend. I also mention my experiences on lots of other trails throughout the text. But, for the most part, you won't find location-by-location listings of trails, complete with maps, elevation profiles, or directions to trailheads. This book will highlight a general picture of North Carolina day hiking—the whole state, not just the mountains or a specific region or city—and lots of resources on where to find the kind of detailed information you'll need about a particular trail before heading out. (Don't forget to check out the Chapter Notes and Additional Resources list for sources of reputable information.) Much of the advice that I offer in Part II of this book will be applicable to hiking in other locations, especially in the southeast United States, but the specific suggestions, stories, and trail highlights I share will focus on North Carolina. I hope that wherever you are in the state, you'll discover (or rediscover) wonderful natural spaces right in your own community. As we explore together through these pages, I hope that you'll feel inspired to get out and experience this beautiful, amazing state we share. Let's go. Let's get hiking! Wonderful things are just around the bend.

Part I

Background and Context

We'll start by spending a little time getting to know hiking as an activity and North Carolina as a state from a natural history perspective. Having this information can provide some context to the specifics that follow as well as help you connect to the land you'll be visiting as you hike.

1

An Introduction to Hiking

> Two roads diverged in a wood, and I—
> I took the one less traveled by,
> And that has made all the difference.
> —Robert Frost, "The Road Not Taken"

For most of human history a walk in the wilderness was something everyone did. This was true even once people started living in community with one another. Connection to nature was part of everyday life and the rhythms of that life were very much guided, if not outright dictated, by the natural world. What you ate was often determined by the seasons. When you slept and when you didn't was driven by the setting and rising of the sun each day. You were familiar with the blooming, growing, and harvesting patterns of the plants you saw around you and could identify many of them by local names. You knew how to watch for signs of changes in the weather and what animals, threatening and friendly, could be found on the land around you. There are many places in the world where this intimate connection to nature is still a feature of daily life. Our Western, especially American, lives are generally not among them. Statistically, we spend precious little time outdoors. As a result, hiking as a distinct recreational activity is a predominantly Western endeavor. Many would argue that we were better off when spending time with nature wasn't considered something that had to be scheduled into our days.

What Counts as a Hike?

So how are we defining hiking? The good thing about hiking is that, in many ways, this answer is entirely up to you! When I first started hiking and attempted my first 100-hike challenge, I decided that my hikes needed to be at least 1.5 miles long and on a mostly natural-surface trail in a "natural area" as opposed to a paved walking track around developed playgrounds and ball fields in a park. Let me be clear: *these rules were completely arbitrary, and I made them up myself.* For me, they were what just "felt" like a hike. And I've even broken my own rules sometimes when deciding what counted!

Merriam-Webster defines a hike as "a long walk especially for pleasure or exercise." Oxford Languages adds to this definition: "a long walk, especially in the country or wilderness." "Long" can be quite a subjective term. What is "long" to me might not be "long" to you at all. And what is "long" to me today might not feel "long" next week,

1. An Introduction to Hiking

What counts as a hike? One time I was out with my then three-year-old nephew at the Beaver Lake Bird Sanctuary in Asheville (pictured). We were enjoying the boardwalks and short trails (definitely less than a mile) when I said, "Isn't this a nice walk?" He looked at me and said, "No, Aunt Whitney! We're on a *hike*!" Well, of course, we were! We were outside enjoying the fresh air and sunshine, walking, and spending time observing the birds, turtles, bugs, squirrels, trees and flowers we could see. Who am I to argue with the kid?

depending on a variety of factors. So, for our purposes, we're going to define hiking as "walking or rolling (in the case of those who use adaptive hiking gear) in woods, wilderness, countryside or other areas of less human development, for pleasure."

How Long Has Hiking Been Around?

It's hard to determine when hiking, as we have defined it above, first became a distinct activity and the pastime's history is not without its controversies and problems. While there are scattered earlier references in literature, hiking first emerged as a leisure activity in Europe in the 1700s; most of the earliest documented hikes for pleasure and recreation occurred there, specifically in the UK, Germany, and Switzerland. The concept of walking for pleasure was popularized by writers from Europe, including the likes of William Wordsworth, John Keats, Robert Louis Stevenson, and Johann Gottfried Seume.[1] American authors such as Ralph Waldo Emerson and Henry David Thoreau also contributed literature that fostered an appreciation of the outdoors and exploration of natural spaces. This helped spread the popularity of hiking, although it remained mostly an activity of the well-off. Spending time walking in nature for fun required time and resources that weren't equally accessible to all.[2]

Hiking was first officially recognized as a recreational activity at the end of the 19th century.[3] Outdoor clubs and hiking groups began in many parts of the United States, inspired by similar organizations in Europe. "Early clubs included the Alpine Club in Massachusetts (1863), the White Mountain Club in Maine (1873), the Rocky Mountain Club in Colorado (1873), and the Sierra Club in California (1892)."[4]

Yellowstone became the first national park in 1872, and many areas of the park could only be seen when traveling by foot, often on trails that had been previously established by Indigenous people in the area.[5] This utilization of traditionally Indigenous lands and trails for recreation by non–Indigenous people was, and still is, a common practice. In recent years this practice, land acknowledgments, and reparations have been growing topics of conversation in the outdoor community and beyond.[6] This is an important and complex discussion, and I encourage you to inform yourself on these topics through sources more qualified to speak on them than I am. Please remember and respect that the lands on which we hike have long, rich, diverse histories, much of which occurred well before Europeans showed up on the scene.

The earliest hiking club and first state and national parks in North Carolina date to the early 1900s. The Carolina Mountain Club (CMC) has its roots in the Appalachian Mountain Club (AMC), one of the first and oldest outdoor clubs in the United States still in existence. The AMC was formed in January of 1876 in Boston and membership grew rapidly over the next four decades.[7] By 1920 it had several thousand members and four chapters in the northeast United States, in addition to the original chapter in Boston. These chapters built and maintained trails, shelters, and cabins to benefit hikers in the region.[8]

In North Carolina, the first state park was established in 1915 at Mount Mitchell to protect this landmark peak from destruction resulting from poor logging practices.[9] Five years later, on June 11, 1920, a meeting was held in Asheville and a Southern Chapter of the Appalachian Mountain Club was formed. This new chapter was officially recognized in May 1921. Much like their northern counterparts, the members of the Southern

Hikers climbing the Sunset Trail near Asheville in 1912 (Library of Congress).

Chapter focused their attention on maintaining cabins and shelters for use by hikers. The Carolina Mountain Club, still in existence today, formed in July 1923 in Asheville when this Southern Chapter of the AMC split from the northern organization; this split was in protest over membership funds from Southern Chapter members being used to exclusively build and maintain trails in the northeast, rather than those right in here in North Carolina.[10]

Three years later, the dedicated efforts of a number of groups and individuals, mostly based in Knoxville, Tennessee, and Asheville, led to the founding of Great Smoky Mountains National Park in southwest North Carolina and eastern Tennessee. In May 1926, President Calvin Coolidge signed a bill that established Great Smoky Mountains National Park and Shenandoah National Park in Virginia. Great Smoky Mountains National Park was formally dedicated by President Franklin D. Roosevelt in September 1940 at a ceremony hosted at Newfound Gap on the North Carolina/Tennessee border.[11]

Five years after the formation of the national park, in late 1931, the dwindling membership of CMC joined forces with the more vibrant Carolina Appalachian Trail Club (CATC). This group focused on routing, marking, measuring, and maintaining unfinished sections of the Appalachian Trail (AT). It also hosted regular hikes and outings and was interested in putting together a hiking guidebook. When the two groups merged, the CMC took on these focuses and somewhat moved away from the maintenance of cabins in the area.[12] Not long after, construction of the Blue Ridge Parkway

President Franklin D. Roosevelt dedicates Great Smoky Mountains National Park at Newfound Gap, September 1940 (State Archives of North Carolina).

Mount Mitchell State Park parking lot, circa 1955 (North Carolina Division of State Parks).

began in September 1935. This scenic roadway provided access to some of the great hiking locations in the North Carolina mountains. All but 7.7 miles of the Parkway were completed by 1966.

The exclusivity of hiking as a pastime in the United States began to change somewhat in the 1900s with outdoor-focused youth organizations like the Boy Scouts and Girl Scouts of America. They introduced young people to many outdoor activities, including hiking and camping, and by the mid–1900s hiking became a popular hobby for millions of Americans. Changes in labor practices, the greater availability of reliable transportation, and a wider focus on physical activity and spending time outdoors increased the accessibility of hiking and its desirability—at least for some portions of American society.[13]

Since the formation of the Carolina Mountain Club, Mount Mitchell State Park, and Great Smoky Mountains National Park in the 1910s and '20s, hiking has increased in popularity across North Carolina, not just in the mountains. Numerous other hiking clubs, trail building organizations, land conservancy agencies, and other groups focused on hiking and outdoor recreation can be found in almost every corner of the state. North Carolina is now home to 41 state parks, 10 national park sites and four national forests. And in addition to the more than 200 miles of the Appalachian Trail that travel along the North Carolina/Tennessee border (more than 90 miles are exclusively in North Carolina), the state also now boasts another long-distance trail—the Mountains-to-Sea Trail. Hiking as a pastime is alive and well in the Old North State and there are plenty of places to get out and enjoy it, regardless of where you live or are visiting. In fact, hiking and other types of outdoor recreation are so popular in North Carolina that 2023 was designated the North Carolina Year of the Trail. The Great Trails State Coalition and their partnering organizations spent the year celebrating "North Carolina's vast network of trails, greenways, and blueways which showcase [the state's] diverse landscapes—grand mountain vistas, quiet rivers, vibrant urban greenways, coastal forests and the rolling hills of the piedmont."[14]

What Are the Benefits of Hiking?

The joys and benefits of hiking are many. Most people think about the physical benefits of hiking—granted, these are important—but there are just as many mental benefits as physical ones.[15]

The Physical Benefits of Hiking

The physical activity of hiking works your entire body in ways that can even benefit you off the trail. First, hiking can help strengthen your bones and muscles. Walking in general helps maintain or even improve bone density and prevents or slows bone loss as it is a weight-bearing exercise, but you're adding to this effect if you carry a pack, even a day pack, because you are loading additional weight onto the spine. Hiking can also increase muscle strength as it is a whole-body activity, especially if you are using trekking poles. Hiking by foot especially works the legs and glutes. Traversing trails using a wheelchair strengthens the upper body and both kinds of hiking work the back and core muscles. Hiking uphill and downhill work different sets of muscles, thus contributing to an overall strengthening. You'll also call on additional muscles to work as you navigate obstacles on the trail. More difficult hikes can even include rock scrambling or climbing ladders. The Profile Trail at Grandfather Mountain is famous for its ladders!

Grandfather Mountain's Profile Trail isn't the only trail where you'll find ladders. Boone Fork Trail at Julian Price Memorial Park on the Blue Ridge Parkway has some of its own. Sections of this trail can be challenging but you'll also be treated to the Hebron Colony Falls and some beautiful views along the way.

Hiking can also improve your balance and coordination by strengthening stabilizing muscles in your core and legs. These muscles are forced to work a little harder as you hike because you are often moving across uneven terrain or on softer ground. Crossing a creek on slick, moss-covered rocks works these stabilizing muscles too. In addition, traversing uneven terrain can help improve your proprioceptive sense. Proprioception is the sense of where your body is in space and how your body is moving.

Hiking on different surface types works your body in different ways. You might find that different muscles are tired after hiking on a sandy path than on a trail with a harder surface. This sandy trail awaits you on Ocean Isle Beach.

The strengthening of your stabilizing muscles and your proprioceptive sense can help prevent falls on *and* off the trail.

The use of so many muscles and the weight-bearing nature of hiking can also help increase cardiovascular fitness, especially if uphill portions are included in your hike. In fact, you can achieve higher heart rates with hiking than with some other types of physical activities, even though it is a slower and lower-impact activity comparatively.

Hiking can also contribute to increased immune system function and better sleep which are important to our overall well-being. Numerous studies in recent years have looked at how spending time outside, in green spaces and especially in the forest, can boost our immune systems. When we breathe in the fresh air in the forest, we are also breathing in phytoncides. These airborne compounds are what give the forest that "forest" smell. They are given off by all plants but especially by evergreen trees. Plants give off phytoncides to protect themselves from insects; they also have antifungal and antibacterial properties. When we breathe in phytoncides, our bodies respond with an increase in the activity and number of natural killer cells, a type of white blood cell. These cells attack virus-infected and tumor cells in our bodies.[16]

Sleep is not just a time of rest for our bodies but also a time of repair for everything from our blood vessels to our immune system to our brain, and consistently deficient sleep or poor sleep quality can make us more prone to illnesses, both acute and chronic.[17] Hiking can help improve your sleep in a few ways, even if you aren't snoozing away out under the stars in a sleeping bag. First, the physical activity of hiking helps raise your body temperature and the drop in it after the hike can help you fall asleep faster. Also, exposure to Vitamin D from sunlight helps control your sleep-wake cycle, and you're getting good doses of it even if you're hiking on a cloudy day. Hiking has also been shown to reduce stress which can improve sleep quality.[18]

The Mental Benefits of Hiking

The benefits of hiking extend beyond the physical, however, and many people—myself included—find that what keeps them coming back to hiking regularly are the mental benefits even more than the physical ones. Hiking can boost your mood, focus, and memory as well as reduce stress and anxiety and lower your risk for depression. A 2010 study from the University of Essex showed that just five minutes of physical activity in a green space can do this, so just think what a whole hike might do! While there are certain aspects of our super-connected society that are positive, the constant exposure to information and drama and always being accessible to others has been shown to increase our stress levels. Hiking can help you unplug and provide balance to these times of high technology usage.

Hiking can also increase your confidence and self-esteem. Our confidence grows when we accomplish a goal, especially a challenging one such as a more difficult hike—however you define "difficult" for yourself—or completing a certain number of hikes. Also, hiking requires problem solving and being able to adapt and improvise, skills that can translate to other areas of your life too. Hiking can help you feel more independent, capable and stronger both mentally and physically.

Spending a few minutes in a peaceful spot such as this can help you unwind and de-stress. The sound of flowing water is often considered especially relaxing. This wonderful location is along the hike to Carter Falls near Elkin.

Other Hiking Benefits

Beyond these physical and mental health benefits, hiking can help us engage with our surroundings in new ways. First, hiking helps you explore your local area in a different way. You might visit communities that hadn't caught your eye before to check out a new trail or find an amazing spot that you can't drive to but only experience as you hike. You might even experience a familiar place in a new way, noticing new details that weren't apparent before. Hiking also gives you a chance to learn more about the natural and human history of your area. Quite a few times I have come home with questions to look up about a cool plant I saw or an old homestead I came across.

Hiking helps you tune more into the natural rhythms of life and the land around you. You start to pay more attention to the typical weather patterns in your area. You begin to notice sunrise and sunset times and how those change over the course of the year. You might find that you become more aware of the seasonal changes in local plants and animals, such as when certain flowers bloom or if autumn is lasting longer than it usually does.

Hiking can also increase your sensory experience and mindfulness. Even though we feel like we are constantly being bombarded with sensory experiences, they are often not healthy or even that varied throughout our day. Hiking can help you tune into your senses in a different way: feeling a cool breeze on your face, smelling spring wildflowers or the mustiness of fall leaves, hearing birdsong, savoring the cold water you brought or some yummy trail mix.

Also, since hiking requires us to use our bodies and brains in so many different ways, many people feel they can be more focused on the present moment when hiking than when doing other types of activities. This sense of mindfulness, when we are fully engaged in the present moment—neither ruminating on the past or worrying about the future—has been shown to decrease stress levels and help with focus and mood. It's a bit like meditation and, indeed, some people see aspects of hiking as a type of walking or movement meditation.

Last but not least, hiking can offer the opportunity to meet new people, make new friends and even strengthen current relationships. There are lots of hiking groups in North Carolina and organizations such as state parks and land conservancy agencies that host group hikes. One of the main reasons I co-founded the Piedmont Plus Size Hikers group was to meet other people in our region who wanted to hike but maybe had not felt comfortable in other groups. Our group is just one example of the variety of those available for all kinds of hikers. I have also hiked with friends and family and found that these experiences added new elements to our relationships.

Some years have an especially large crop of acorns, and you might notice a detail like this when you spend time in an area across seasons and years. I found these large chestnut oak acorns on an October 2022 hike on the Purgatory Mountain Trail at the North Carolina Zoo along with many, many others of at least five different species of oaks. All were left for the wildlife to enjoy.

How Frequently Should I Hike?

As mentioned at the top of this chapter, most of us spend very little time outside. According to the Environmental Protection Agency, on average, Americans only spend

10 percent of their time outdoors.[19] As Wayne R. Ott, a professor with Stanford University who worked on the National Human Activity Pattern Survey (NHAPS) study, stated, "In a modern society, total time outdoors is the most insignificant part of the day, often so small that it barely shows up in the total."[20]

Some scientists, physicians, and mental health professionals are beginning to recognize the benefits of being outdoors that we've discussed and are even starting to write prescriptions for time spent in nature to encourage more of it.[21] The truth is, despite all the documented reasons to prioritize time spent outdoors, we don't often take this time for a variety of reasons. Our lives are often filled with ever-greater numbers of distractions and demands, and these aren't always within our control. Especially if you are just starting out hiking—and perhaps still trying to convince yourself it's worth it—you naturally may want some guidelines on how much time to spend out on the trails. Perhaps a goal to shoot for. The 20/5/3 Nature Pyramid can be one way to approach this question.

The 20/5/3 Nature Pyramid

Dr. Rachel Hopman-Droste, a neuroscientist formerly of Northeastern University, studies the science behind the mentally restorative aspects of spending time in nature. Her work was reported on in a *Prevention* magazine article from July 2021 by Michael Easter[22] (as well as in his book *Comfort Crisis*), and she shared about the concept of the "nature pyramid." The nature pyramid makes recommendations on how much time to spend engaged with different types of natural settings, such as local parks, state parks, and backcountry locations.

20 Minutes

This is the recommended amount of time to spend outside, like at a neighborhood park or even in your own yard, if you have one, three times a week. This time is ideally spent in a place with grass, trees, birds, sunshine and shade, not necessarily a more remote or undeveloped natural space. Greenway trails through neighborhoods and local public gardens would also fit the bill. Hopman's research showed that a 20-minute walk in these types of locations could boost memory and increase feelings of well-being. Interestingly, she also found that people who used their cell phones during such walks experienced none of the same benefits.

5 Hours

This is the recommended amount of time to spend per month in semi-wild locations. This might include a state park, a more remote nature preserve, or even a remote beach. Hopman's research showed that the time spent in wilder places offered even more benefits, and other studies have supported this conclusion. People who spent at least five hours in these types of locations per month were more likely to be less stressed and happier in their everyday lives, not just while they were out in nature.

3 Days

Three days appears at the top of the pyramid and is the number of days research recommends spending once or twice a year "off grid" in nature. This might be a camp-

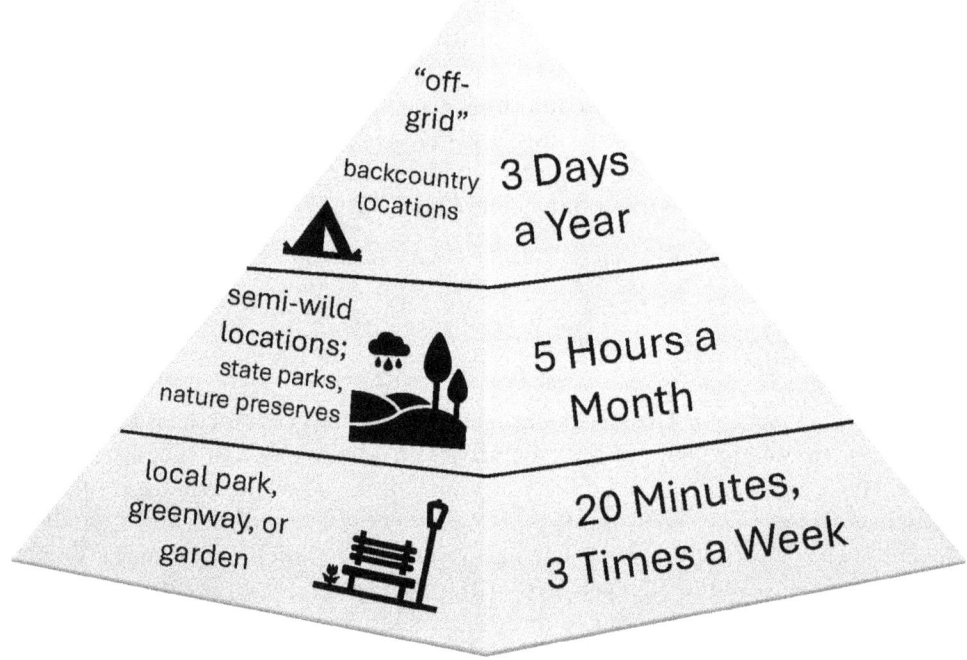

The 20/5/3 Nature Pyramid, developed by Dr. Rachel Hopman-Droste, provides guidelines on amounts of time to spend in different natural settings (graphic by author).

ing trip in a backcountry location or renting a remote cabin. This time is ideally spent in a location where you can really unplug and experience the rhythms of nature around you. This extended time up close and personal with nature in these wilder locations is a bit like an extended meditation retreat and our brains and bodies react as such.

The type of hikes we'll be talking about in this book fit nicely into the 20-minutes-three-times-per-week or the five-hours-a-month categories of the pyramid. We'll be talking about hiking in locations that are fairly easy to reach but that offer some opportunities to step away from the hustle and bustle of life for a few hours. Locations that give you the chance to experience reduced traffic noise and increased birdsong, reduced pollution and increased fresh air. Places that feel a bit wilder but maybe don't feel so remote as to be intimidating to explore. While North Carolina certainly has many places that would fit more into the "3-days" level of the pyramid, there are still lots that are perfect "20-minute" and "5-hour" locations as well. And, of course, you're welcome to spend as much time out hiking and in nature as you want—no need to limit yourself to the 20/5/3 guidelines if more time fits with your schedule and resources.

How Fast Should I Hike?

The short answer is "As fast as you want and can do safely." There truly is no right answer here. When hiking alone or with one other person, you can hike as slow or as fast as you want as long as you're not pushing yourself in such a way as to be unsafe. One of the joys of hiking alone is that you get to set your own pace, and no one can tell you it should be something different. Hiking alone also gives you the opportunity to determine your typical, comfortable hiking speed on different types of terrain without the pressure to go a certain pace by a group.[23]

Some people challenge themselves to see how fast they can finish a hike, but I would encourage you to intentionally slow your pace a bit, at least occasionally. Doing so gives you more of an opportunity to notice the small details of the land around you as well as to enjoy all those sensory experiences mentioned previously. Once I was hiking at the Piedmont Environmental Education Center in High Point and I was moving at a fairly slow pace, as is typical for me. I glanced into the woods and saw a doe. I stopped for a moment to watch her and noticed she wasn't alone. Not far off were also a buck and a small fawn. I've seen lots of deer while out hiking but never a buck, doe and fawn together. It was very special. I have no doubt that if I had been moving at a faster pace, I would not have noticed them. The soft sounds they were making easily blended in with the other surrounding noises and they were moving slowly through the woods.

If you are considering hiking with a group, check out what hike pace the leader has advertised to make sure that you will be comfortable hiking at that speed. If that information isn't provided, feel free to ask for it. Some groups publish how they categorize hikes based on pace, distance and elevation gain—what they consider a casual, easy, moderate or strenuous hike. Being a slower hiker is perfectly fine; if you find yourself hiking with a group that consistently makes you feel like you have to go faster or that, somehow, you're not a "real" hiker if you move more slowly, you might look for a new group with which to hike.

Now that we've had a brief introduction to hiking, let's spend some time learning a little about the natural wonders to be found along North Carolina's hundreds of trails.

2

An Introduction to the Natural Features of North Carolina

"Quite simply, there are very few relatively small geographic areas on Earth that can compare with North Carolina in geologic, climatic and ecological diversity."

—Tom Earnhart, *Crossroads of the Natural World*

There are so many amazing natural spaces across North Carolina. What an awesome place where you can be standing at 6,684 feet on Mount Mitchell—the highest point east of the Mississippi River—overlooking the glorious Appalachian Mountains and eight hours later be standing on the beach in the Outer Banks gazing out at the Atlantic Ocean! And let's not forget all the beautiful, interesting places in between. One of the joys of hiking is getting to engage with these natural spaces in a different, more intimate way.

To get the lay of the land and a preview of some of these special places we might visit on hikes, let's spend some time exploring the three major regions in the state—the Mountains, Piedmont and Foothills, and Coastal Plain—and some of the natural features in each.[1] You'll see some differences in counties included in each region depending on the source you're using, and these regions, of course, don't have distinct physical

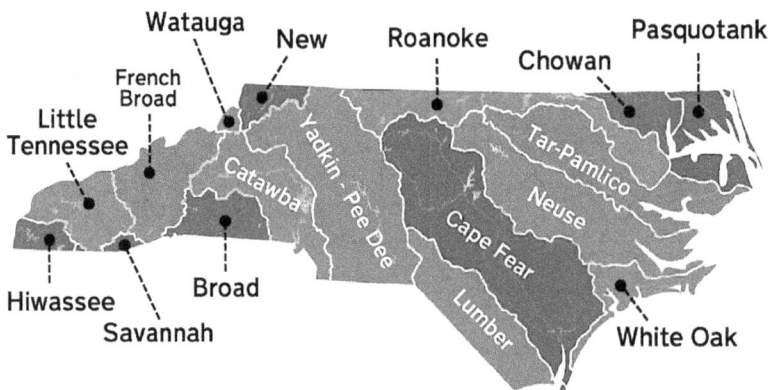

The river basins in North Carolina often extend across regions—they're just one example of how the three regions in the state are closely connected (North Carolina Office of Recovery and Resiliency).

boundaries between them. The physical barrier created by the mountains can impact the weather in the Piedmont and Coastal Plain and a hurricane landfall in the Coastal Plain can impact the entire state. Rivers don't recognize regional boundaries, and something tossed in a river in the Piedmont can eventually end up in a sound in the Coastal Plain. And, obviously, wildlife and plants don't understand these regional distinctions. If you're hiking in counties at the edges of regions you can expect to occasionally see flora and fauna from the neighboring area.[2]

The Mountains

The Mountain region of North Carolina is characterized by high peaks (at least by eastern U.S. standards), deep valleys, rocky rivers, waterfalls and grand vistas. This region earns its nickname "Land of the Sky." Twenty-three counties are considered part of the Mountain region and approximately 15 percent of the state's population lives in this area. The mountains also contain about 16 percent of North Carolina's landmass.[3] In some sources you will find this region further divided into the Southwest Mountains, Central Mountains and Northern Mountains.

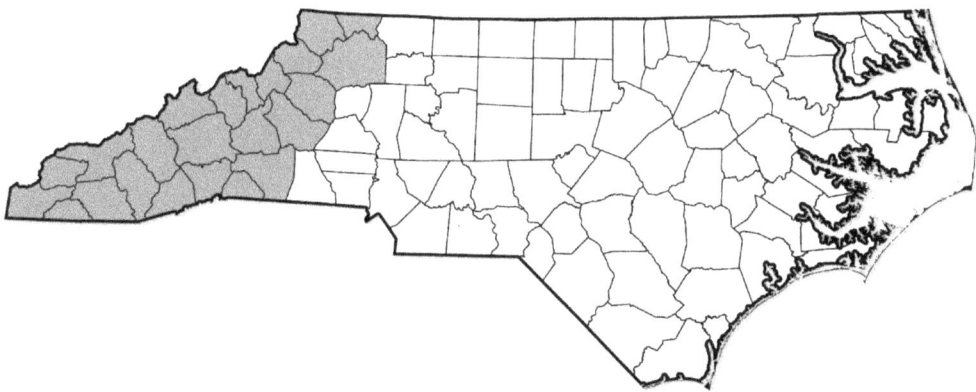

The Mountain region includes Alleghany, Ashe, Avery, Buncombe, Burke, Caldwell, Cherokee, Clay, Graham, Haywood, Henderson, Jackson, Macon, Madison, McDowell, Mitchell, Polk, Rutherford, Swain, Transylvania, Watauga, Wilkes, and Yancey counties (North Carolina Office of State Archaeology, 2022).

The Land

As the name of the region implies, the mountains are the defining natural feature of the area. These mountains are all a part of the Appalachian Mountains range, specifically classified as the Southern Appalachians.[4] The Appalachian Mountains range is at its widest in North Carolina. This region, the Blue Ridge Mountains, starts in northwest South Carolina and northeast Georgia and extends through North Carolina, Tennessee, Virginia, West Virginia and Maryland and then into southern Pennsylvania. Sometimes the term "Blue Ridge" is used to refer only to the front range of the Appalachian Mountains, but the geographical definition of this region extends westward and includes several other subranges and clusters of mountains that are also part of the

Southern Appalachians. In southwest North Carolina are the Great Smoky, Nantahala, Snowbird, Balsam and Newfound Mountains. Continuing north you'll find the Bald and Black Mountains, Roan Mountain and the region known as the High Country. You'll also find the Iron, Pisgah, Stone, and Unaka ranges in the Mountain region. East of the

This view from the hike to Whitewater Falls in Transylvania County shows the rapid change in elevation along the Blue Ridge Escarpment. Land with much lower elevation can be seen just in the distance.

Blue Ridge, the Brushy Mountains and South Mountains are often considered "spurs" of the Blue Ridge.

The Appalachian Mountains are also at their highest in elevation in North Carolina. As mentioned previously, Mount Mitchell, a peak found in the Black Mountains, is the highest east of the Mississippi at 6,684 feet and the High Country area has the highest average elevation in the state.[5] North Carolina has at least 40 peaks that reach 6,000 feet or more and another 100 that rise to between 5,000 and 6,000 feet.[6] The abrupt rise of these mountains from the foothills is known as the Blue Ridge Escarpment and it can rise as much as 1,500 feet from the surrounding land. If you've ever driven I-40 from Old Fort to Black Mountain or I-26 near Sylva, you've experienced the quick elevation changes that happen along the Blue Ridge Escarpment.

The Blue Ridge Mountains also form the Eastern Continental Divide. Rivers on the western side of this divide flow to the Mississippi River and those on the eastern side flow to the Atlantic Ocean. As a result of the topography, hikers should expect significant elevation changes in many hikes in this region, even in ones considered "easy" or "moderate."

Bodies of Water

The rocky, swift rivers in the Mountain region also attract many visitors to the area. Whitewater rafting and tubing are popular summer pastimes here and the 3,000 miles of trout streams[7] in the area draw anglers from across the country.[8] It is not unusual for hikes in the Mountain region to feature multiple creek crossings, so come prepared as footbridges are not always available on more backcountry trails.

Several major rivers and their tributaries flow through the mountains of North Carolina and the headwaters of many rivers that travel across the state and eventually to the Atlantic Ocean are found in the Mountain region.[9] Nine river basins are found in the Mountain region, and some of the major rivers include the New, Watauga, Little Tennessee, Hiwassee and French Broad.[10] The French Broad River Basin, for example, is well known as the home to almost 4,000 miles of streams and Asheville, the largest city in the region.[11] The Catawba River Basin begins on the eastern slopes of the mountains in McDowell County and extends to the Piedmont. It includes the Linville River which flows over Linville Falls and bisects the Linville Gorge, known as "the Grand Canyon of the East."[12] Also found in the Mountain region is the New River Basin, which extends well into Virginia. Its namesake river, the New, is thought to be one of the oldest rivers in the world. The New begins as two streams, the North Fork and South Fork. These converge along the Ashe/Alleghany County line after which the New loops along the North Carolina/Virginia border before finally heading north into Virginia.[13]

Thanks to the sharp changes in elevation of the Blue Ridge Escarpment, the mountains are home to many impressive waterfalls alongside smaller ones found in most rivers and streams. The highest waterfall in North Carolina is also the highest waterfall east of the Rockies. Whitewater Falls is located in the Nantahala National Forest, on the Whitewater River, right on the North Carolina/South Carolina border. Upper Whitewater Falls, found on the North Carolina side, plunges 411 feet, while the lower falls, found in South Carolina, tumbles another 400. Upper Whitewater Falls is far from the only waterfall to visit in the mountains, however. It's estimated that there are more than 1,000 waterfalls in the Mountain region with, for example, 250 found in Transylvania County alone.[14]

There are also many lakes of varying sizes to be found throughout the Mountain region. West of the I-95 corridor in the eastern part of North Carolina most large lakes are man-made, created when rivers were impounded for flood control, drinking water reservoirs or hydroelectric power plants. One of the most notable examples, the Fontana Dam,

A view of Fontana Dam from near the visitor center. While the road across the top of the dam is currently closed to vehicular traffic, you are more than welcome to hike across it. We'll discuss this hike in more detail later in the book.

impounded the Little Tennessee River, creating Fontana Lake which covers more than 11,000 acres and reaches depths of 150 feet. The tallest dam east of the Rockies, Fontana Dam was built in record time. Laborers worked 24 hours a day, seven days a week from January 1942 to November 1944 to construct the 480-foot-tall dam and hydroelectric facility that supplied power to the top-secret Oak Ridge National Laboratory. Today, the Appalachian Trail crosses Fontana Dam and thru hikers have named the nearby shelter the "Fontana Hilton" since it's one of the few AT shelters with hot showers close by.[15]

Weather and Climate

The weather in the Mountain region is characterized by cold, snowy winters and mild summers. Locations along the North Carolina/Tennessee border can experience significant snowfall amounts, but most areas in the mountains see at least some snow most winters. The average yearly temperature in the mountains is 48 degrees, so hikers should be prepared for cooler temperatures year-round and freezing temperatures, ice, and snow much later into the spring and earlier in the fall than in other parts of the state. Spring tends to come late and fall tends to come early in the mountains. The region is popular in the summer for the cool temperatures, in the autumn for the beautiful fall colors, in the winter for snow sports like skiing, and in the spring for wildflowers.[16] Truly there is something to enjoy along the trail in every season in the Mountain region.

Flora and Fauna

The Mountain region is home to a wide variety of plants and animals. "From high, windy, boreal forests to protected gorges which harbor subtropical species, the Blue Ridge mountains and foothills of North Carolina sustain some of the greatest biodiversity in North America."[17] For example, check out these statistics from the Blue Ridge National Heritage Area:

- More species of plants can be found in the mountains of North Carolina than in any other area of similar size in North America.
- Botanical studies have documented more than 4,000 species of plants, 2,000 species of fungi, and 500 species of mosses and lichens in the region.
- The North Carolina mountains are home to more species of salamanders than any other place in the world.
- More old-growth forest stands survive in the mountains of North Carolina than in any other Southern Appalachian state.
- The Great Smoky Mountains boast more than 1,400 varieties of flowering plants and 100 species of trees (more species of trees than the whole of Europe).[18]

The Blue Ridge Mountains get their name from the blue color seen when one looks out across the range, and the biological diversity of the area is the reason the Blue Ridge is blue. The thick vegetation of the Blue Ridge Mountains, especially the conifers (a.k.a. trees that produce cones like pine, spruce, and fir), release a class of organic compounds called terpenes. These molecules react with other molecules already in the air and form new particles that scatter blue light, giving the mountains their hazy blue color. The Cherokee were the first to refer to this blue color in their name for these mountains— Shaconage, or "the land of the blue smoke."[19]

A specific set of mountains in northwest North Carolina features some unique flora and fauna, and it's all because of the rock that's found beneath them. Three Top Mountain, Elk Knob, Snake Mountain, Bluff Mountain, Paddy Mountain, Phoenix Mountain and Mount Jefferson, found in Watauga and Ashe counties, are amphibolite mountains. The mineral-rich rock found here erodes into a non-acidic soil (compared to the other mountains in the state) and supports species of plants, and by extension, animals, rarely found in other parts of this region.

A Word About Hurricane Helene

The remnants of Hurricane Helene, which made landfall in the Big Bend area of Florida on September 26, 2024, devastated parts of the Mountain region on the morning of September 27. The storm was preceded by several days of heavy rainfall, leaving the ground saturated and the rivers swollen. Then the storm hit, dropping even more rain. Rainfall totals for the region for September 24–28, 2024, ranged from 12 to more than 30 inches. Wind gusts between 45 mph and the upper 80s were common in the area, and Mount Mitchell recorded a gust of 106 mph.

The very topography we've discussed here contributed to the heartbreaking impacts of Hurricane Helene in the mountains and portions of the foothills. Lots of water, saturated soils, high winds, and the wind direction, added to the steep landscapes, especially along the eastern-facing slopes, led to catastrophic tree damage, landslides, and record-breaking river levels. According to state officials, Hurricane Helene caused "1,400 landslides and damaged over 160 water and sewer systems, at least 6,000 miles of roads, more than 1,000 bridges and culverts, and an estimated 126,000 homes."[20] The Forest Service estimated that more than 820,000 acres of timberland received some level of damage from Helene. The worst damage was found in a six-county region with Buncombe and McDowell counties receiving the heaviest impacts.[21] More than 100 people lost their lives in the storm in North Carolina and countless others lost livelihoods and homes as structures suffered extreme tree damage, were filled with water or mud, or were swept away. Descriptions of the damage included such words as "biblical" and "apocalyptic."

Many of the hiking locations in the mountains that we'll discuss in this book were also damaged in the storm. In the late days of September and early days of October 2024, Pisgah and Nantahala national forests, all state parks west of I-77, and all sections of the Blue Ridge Parkway in the state were closed. Slowly but surely, dedicated state and federal staff, volunteers, and military personnel worked to clear, repair and reopen these areas and others, but many locations will not be the same for years, if ever. Hikers should exercise extra caution in the affected mountain areas for the foreseeable future.

The Piedmont and Foothills

Most people either think of the western mountains or the eastern coastal areas when it comes to outdoor recreation in North Carolina. The 36 counties of the Piedmont and Foothills region are more often thought of as the population, education, and commercial centers of the state, and this is certainly true. Many of the major and most well-known universities in North Carolina, such as the University of North Carolina at

2. An Introduction to the Natural Features of North Carolina

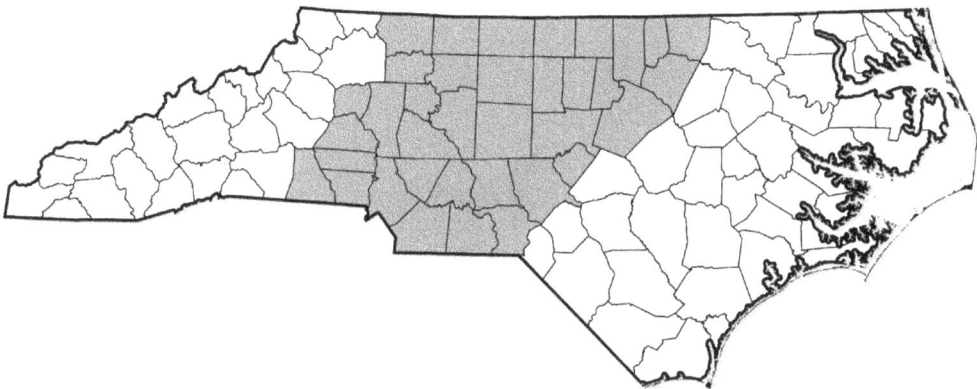

The Piedmont and Foothills region including Alamance, Alexander, Anson, Cabarrus, Caswell, Catawba, Chatham, Cleveland, Davidson, Davie, Durham, Forsyth, Franklin, Gaston, Granville, Guilford, Iredell, Lee, Lincoln, Mecklenburg, Montgomery, Moore, Orange, Person, Randolph, Richmond, Rockingham, Rowan, Stanly, Stokes, Surry, Union, Vance, Wake, Warren, and Yadkin counties (North Carolina Office of State Archaeology, 2022).

Chapel Hill, Duke University, NC State University, and Wake Forest University, among many others, can be found in the Piedmont. Eight of the top 10 most populous cities in North Carolina are in the Piedmont and a total of approximately 6.2 million people live in this region. (Some sources group the Foothills with the Mountains and some with the Piedmont.)

Aside from some of the larger lakes and the state parks in the area, the Piedmont region is not the area that often first comes to mind when one thinks of hiking or connecting with nature. But regardless of where you are in the state, I hope to persuade you to give the outdoor spaces in the Piedmont a chance. It is a unique area with a lot to offer to the outdoor enthusiast. Despite the higher population density there *are* still places in this region that help you feel like you're away from it all.[22]

The Land

Just as it's located geographically, the landscape of the Piedmont region sits as a midway point between the mountains and the coast. The Piedmont region makes up about 45 percent of the landmass of North Carolina and has an average width of 200 miles. The elevation ranges from 300 feet in the east to five times that in the west. As a hiker you'll find some trails to be quite flat while others can have steep inclines. This area is known for its rolling hills but there are mountains to be found here too. Many of the mountains in the region are monadnocks—isolated hills or mountains consisting of weathering-resistant rock that rise above where softer rock has eroded away over time, creating a surrounding lowland. Some monadnocks are without much vegetation, such as the well-known Stone Mountain, Hanging Rock, Pilot Mountain and Crowders Mountain. Others are covered with forest and perhaps blend in a little more with the surrounding environment. The Sauratown Mountains are located in Stokes and Surry counties and includes Pilot Mountain and Hanging Rock along with several other peaks. The Uwharrie Mountains are found primarily in Randolph, Montgomery, Stanly and Davidson counties. These ancient mountains are home to Morrow Mountain State

The Pilot Mountain Knob is perhaps the most well-known monadnock rock formation in North Carolina. In this image you can see another famous one in the back left—Hanging Rock. These two peaks are part of the Sauratown Mountains, sometimes called "the mountains away from the mountains." Three other peaks are found between Pilot Mountain State Park and Hanging Rock State Park. In this image you can also see some of the Pilot Knob Trail. This trail leaves from the parking area and travels out to and around the famous knob. It includes amazing views of the surrounding Piedmont landscape but also includes lots of uneven stone steps.

Park, Uwharrie National Forest, and the North Carolina Zoo along with many other great hiking locations.

The soil in the Piedmont region tends to be red clay and rocky, soil that is more difficult to farm than the softer clay in the Coastal Plain but easier than that in the Mountain region. The area is also rich in mineral resources.[23] In fact, the first documented gold discovery in the United States occurred in 1799 at a site now known as Reed Gold Mine in Midland (hiking is available at Reed Gold Mine!) and North Carolina led the nation in gold production until it was surpassed by California in 1948.[24]

Bodies of Water

There are many streams and rivers in the Piedmont, even some with rapids and falls, although not nearly as many as are found in the Mountain region. The rivers here tend to be shallow and swift-flowing.[25] The nature of the rivers in the Piedmont made them good power generators for gristmills in earlier times. These mills ground wheat and corn and could be found dotting many rivers in the area. This and other human activities along these waters, including farming and industrial practices, have had a lasting impact on some rivers. For example, the early European settler farming methods churned up the loose soils of the Piedmont, creating lots of erosion. The erosion-creating agricultural practices continued until the Dust Bowl era with cotton and tobacco farming, and this dropped 150 years' worth of sediment into the region's rivers. The effects can still be seen in some of them, including the Yadkin River, also known as the "Mighty Muddy Yadkin" for this very reason. It's believed that it could take another 150 years for this sediment to work its way through the river system.[26]

"The Mighty Muddy Yadkin," pictured here from the historic Wil-Cox Bridge at Yadkin River Park in Davidson County, becomes High Rock Lake at this location. This lake was created when the Yadkin was impounded about 15 miles downstream from this point in the 1920s for hydroelectric power.

As in the mountains, the lakes in the Piedmont are man-made through the impounding of rivers and streams for hydroelectric power, recreation, drinking water reservoirs, and flood control. The major lakes of the region and their associated rivers are:

River	Associated Lakes
Yadkin/Pee Dee rivers	W. Kerr Scott Reservoir; High Rock Lake; Tuckertown Reservoir; Badin Lake; Lake Tillery; Blewett Falls Lake
Catawba River	Lake James; Lake Rhodhiss; Lake Hickory; Lookout Shoals Lake; Lake Norman; Mountain Island Lake; Lake Wylie
Dan River drainage	Belews Lake; Townsend Lake; Farmer Lake; Hyco Lake; Mayo Reservoir
Roanoke River	John H. Kerr Reservoir; Lake Gaston
Haw/Cape Fear rivers	B. Everett Jordan Lake; Harris Reservoir
Neuse River	Falls Lake
Deep River	Oak Hollow Lake

These lakes, along with their smaller counterparts, provide not only many human benefits but also valuable wildlife habitats in the more urban areas of the Piedmont.[27]

Weather and Climate

The average climate for the region is also a middle-ground of the state. While summers are definitely warmer than in the mountains, they aren't as warm as at the coast. The Piedmont also experiences an earlier average first frost and later average last frost than the Coastal Plain. The region does not typically experience the storms, frigid temperatures and heavy winds that characterize winters in the mountains, nor the tropical storms that impact the coast, although severe thunderstorms do occur, especially in the summer, and tornadoes are possible although not common. Summer hikers in the Piedmont should carefully check the forecast and learn to spot these types of storms forming while hiking.

Flora and Fauna

The plant life in the Piedmont now looks very different than it did before European settlers came to the area. While some areas of virgin forest can still be found in the mountains and there are even some old-growth spots in the Coastal Plain, you won't find any in the Piedmont. Almost all has been harvested over the years and the land has been used for development and agriculture. Areas that are now under conservation and no longer subject to further development or harvesting can display a range of plant life, depending on the land's stage of succession.

Ecological succession is the predictable process by which a biological community changes over time without human intervention. During succession, plants follow an established pattern of regrowth. The first stage of succession typically lasts up to 10 years and starts with changes we might not even notice such as growth of microbes, algae, mosses and lichens in the soil. Next, short-lived plants such as ragweed, goldenrod, wild blackberries and sedges appear. Next come perennial grasses and a tall-grass prairie

2. An Introduction to the Natural Features of North Carolina 35

Lake Norman, located in Iredell, Catawba, Mecklenburg, and Lincoln counties, is the largest man-made lake in North Carolina. This peaceful cove seen from the Lakeside Trail at Lake Norman State Park does not portray how busy this lake really can be.

may develop, followed by small shrubs and trees that can tolerate the full sun found in these types of environments.

Between 10 and 100 years, the diversity of plants starts to increase, and larger trees begin to grow. The pines are typically first and then an understory of young hardwoods such as maples, hickories, and oaks being to fill in. The second half of the 100 years represents a transition from predominantly pine forest to predominantly hardwood forest. After 100 years, most areas will be an oak-hickory forest. Of course, this process is not an exact science and the specifics in a particular location can vary depending on the presence of different pests, fire, storm damage and how the land was being used prior to conservation.[28]

As would be expected, many of the animal species found in the Piedmont have become adept at living near humans, so the wildlife you might encounter while hiking in the area are, for the most part, similar to ones you might see around less "wild" areas as well. White-tailed deer, raccoons, opossums, squirrels, and a wide variety of reptiles, amphibians, birds and insects are all common. You might also see bobcats, otters, beavers, coyotes, and even mink. Black bears are not common in the Piedmont, but they have been spotted in certain areas. Many are believed to have migrated from the Coastal Plain and Mountain regions, but sightings of mothers with cubs have been reported in the area which points to the possibility of a resident population being established.

The Coastal Plain

Furthest east in North Carolina you'll find the Coastal Plain region. This area is full of rich history and beautiful landscapes that are just waiting to be explored while you hike. In fact,

> the Coastal Plain of North Carolina is distinguished by unusual geology and the greatest biological diversity along the Atlantic Coast north of Florida. A large variety of habitats have nurtured a multitude of plants and animals, many found nowhere else in the world. The Coastal Plain is a mosaic of barrier islands, estuarine marshes, tidal creeks, sandy pine ridges, pocosins, blackwater and brownwater river corridors.[29]

We often think of visiting the beach during the summer, but this area also makes a great place to hike during the winter if colder hikes aren't your thing.[30]

The Outer Coastal Plain region includes Beaufort, Bertie, Brunswick, Camden, Carteret, Chowan, Craven, Currituck, Dare, Gates, Hertford, Hyde, New Hanover, Onslow, Pamlico, Pasquotank, Pender, Perquimans, Tyrrell, and Washington counties (North Carolina Office of State Archaeology, 2022).

The Coastal Plain is subdivided into the Inner and Outer Coastal Plain areas and occasionally into even more regions depending on the source. The Outer Coastal Plain includes 20 counties. This area is often further divided into the Outer Banks—a chain of barrier islands stretching 175 miles in length along the coast—and the Tidewater. The major islands on the Outer Banks are Hatteras, Ocracoke, and Bodie islands. The Tidewater is defined by its relationship to the tides; the rise and fall of the ocean tides impacts the sounds, bays and rivers in this area. As the tides come in, water flows into these and then recedes when tides go out. The Inner Coastal Plain includes 21 counties. On the southwestern edge of this area and southeastern edge of the Piedmont you'll find the Sandhills. This hilly, sandy region covers portions of Cumberland, Harnett, Hoke, Lee, Montgomery, Moore, Richmond and Scotland counties.

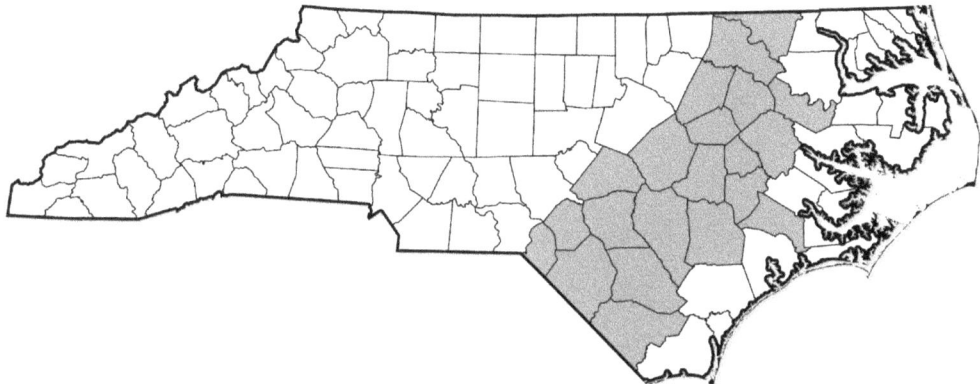

The Inner Coastal Plain region includes Bladen, Columbus, Cumberland, Duplin, Edgecombe, Greene, Halifax, Harnett, Hoke, Johnston, Jones, Lenoir, Martin, Nash, Northampton, Pitt, Robeson, Sampson, Scotland, Wayne, and Wilson counties (North Carolina Office of State Archaeology, 2022).

The Land

The Coastal Plain makes up approximately 45 percent of North Carolina's landmass and covers 21,000 square miles. It is bordered by the Atlantic Ocean on the east, and the western boundary of this region is formed by the "fall line."[31] This imaginary border indicates where the Cape Fear, Neuse, Roanoke, and Tar rivers fall from the hillier Piedmont to the flatlands of the Coastal Plain. And flat it is. The terrain ranges from sea level to approximately 400 feet above at the highest points.[32]

The land in this region tends to be quite fertile and easy to cultivate. It's made up primarily of sandstone, clay and sand, and it is not rocky. The soil does tend to be lacking in minerals, however. Significant sand dunes can be found in the Outer Coastal Plain area; these range in height from two feet to more than 100 feet at Jockey's Ridge located in Nags Head. (This is also home to Jockey's Ridge State Park and the eastern terminus of the Mountains-to-Sea Trail.)[33]

Bodies of Water

In many ways, the Coastal Plain is defined by its bodies of water. Of course, the Atlantic Ocean is the big draw in this region, but there are many others and trails in the area frequently highlight these. North Carolina's barrier islands are separated from the mainland by shallow bodies of water called sounds, giving visitors to these islands the opportunity to enjoy both sunrises and sunsets over the water—sunrise over the ocean to the east, and sunset over the sounds to the west. The largest of these is the Pamlico Sound, and others include the Albemarle, Bogue, Core, Croatan, Currituck, and Roanoke. Inlets in the area provide access to the ocean from the sounds.[34] The Intracoastal Waterway stretches down the coast, traveling through over 300 miles of these sounds, along with rivers, creeks, marshes and man-made cuts.[35]

All of North Carolina's natural lakes (as opposed to its man-made ones) are located in the Coastal Plain region. Many of these lakes are typically referred to as Carolina

Lake Waccamaw as seen from the dock found on the Lakeshore Trail at Lake Waccamaw State Park. This Carolina bay is only about 20 feet deep at its deepest, but it covers almost 9,000 acres.

bays, which is a bit confusing as they are not really bays at all. (The name is thought to have originally come from the prevalence of bay trees that grow along the edges of these bodies of water.) These unique geological formations are oval depressions in the earth's surface concentrated in North and South Carolina, although they can be found as far south as Georgia and as far north as Maryland. Eighty percent are found in North Carolina. These depressions are oriented in a northwest-southeast direction and tend to be quite shallow. For example, Lake Waccamaw is only about 20 feet at its deepest but covers almost 9,000 acres.[36] Lake Mattamuskeet, North Carolina's largest natural lake at 18 miles long, seven miles wide and covering about 40,000 acres, averages only two to three feet in depth.[37]

There are also a number of swamps in this region. Many of these have been drained and used for timber and crop growth over the years, but some still exist.[38] One example is the Great Dismal Swamp, found in northeastern North Carolina and southeastern Virginia. The Great Dismal Swamp, originally as big as 2,000 square miles, now covers an area of approximately 750 square miles.[39] The swamps in the Coastal Plain region occur along rivers and sounds in areas where flooding is influenced by tides—either lunar or wind-driven—and can vary in their saltwater content. This greatly influences the kinds of vegetation you'll find in different locations.[40]

The rivers of the Coastal Plain tend to be flat and straight and flow southeasterly. Those found in this region include, from north to south, the Pasquotank, Chowan,

The Lumber River, a blackwater river seen here from the Princess Ann access point of Lumber River State Park, is considered, predominantly, a bottomland hardwood swamp. Typical swamp species, such as the cypress tree seen in the foreground, can be found throughout the region.

Roanoke, Tar-Pamlico, Neuse, White Oak, Cape Fear and Lumber rivers. The Cape Fear River empties directly into the Atlantic Ocean, while the other large rivers empty into the sounds.[41]

Weather and Climate

Summers in the Coastal Plain can certainly be warm and humid although temperatures are typically not extreme, with highs averaging in the mid to upper 80s and the lows near 70. Of course, heat waves can push temperatures into the triple digits and highs in the low 90s in July are not unusual, especially in the more inland areas that do not benefit from sea breezes and the moderating effects of the ocean. Winters have highs averaging in the mid–50s and lows in the mid–30s. The region receives around 50 inches of rain a year and infrequent snowfall. Hurricane season runs from June 1 to November 30 and the topography of the Coastal Plain region makes it more likely to be hit than other locations further south and north. Hatteras Island sticks out 175 miles into the

This view, seen from a covered overlook off the Fort Macon Nature Trail/Yarrow Loop Trail at Fort Macon State Park, shows both the oceanfront grasses and the slightly more inland shrubs and small trees typical of the barrier islands.

Atlantic Ocean from where the North Carolina coast meets South Carolina at Calabash making it, and other parts of the Coastal Plain, easy targets for northward-moving hurricanes and tropical storms. The concave shape of the coastline can also act like a net for westward-moving storms. Impacts from these storms can be felt well inland, sometimes even into the Piedmont and Mountain regions. On a more daily basis in the summer, warmer air over land and cooler air and moisture from the ocean lead to frequent afternoon showers and thunderstorms. Nor'easters can bring heavy precipitation during the winter months.[42]

Flora and Fauna

As mentioned previously, the Coastal Plain region is quite biologically diverse. For example, the coastal maritime forests of the Bogue Banks area and the pocosins of Croatan National Forest are home to plants found nowhere else on Earth. Trees native to the Coastal Plain include bay, loblolly and longleaf pine, sassafras and oak. Maritime forests are found near the ocean behind sand dunes, on the sound side of the Outer Banks and on barrier islands. The trees typically found in these forests—live oak, red cedar, wax myrtle, and yaupon holly—have a high tolerance for sandy soils, salt spray and strong ocean winds. Many other interesting types of plants can also be found in the Coastal Plain. These include several varieties of iris that are native to the area and the carnivorous Venus flytrap, which only grows natively within a 75-mile radius around Wilmington.[43] Perhaps the most recognizable plant that has come to represent the Coastal Plain is the sea oat. It grows in tall patches along the beachfront and helps create and stabilize sand dunes. This hardy grass can tolerate salt spray, blowing sand, constant breezes, and unrelenting sun.[44]

The variety of habitat types in the Coastal Plain region also supports a diverse mix of wildlife, including some found nowhere else. For example, five counties in northeastern North Carolina are home to the only wild population of endangered red wolves in the world. On the other hand, much more common wildlife make their home in the Coastal Plain, too. Black bears are most often associated with the Mountain region, but the largest concentration of them is actually in a five county area of the Coastal Plain—the same five counties where red wolves are found.

Now that we've got the lay of the land in the Old North State, let's talk about how to hike safely and enjoy it along the way. Ready to hit the trail?

Part II

Safe and Enjoyable Hiking

Believe it or not, you do not have to run out and get a bunch of new gear to start hiking. You also don't have to have any kind of specialized training in wilderness first aid or search and rescue. On the other hand, trouble doesn't just happen on long, remote hikes. You can just as easily sprain an ankle, suffer from dehydration or even get lost on a shorter trail in a nature preserve close to town. Preparedness is the name of the game in hiking. In Part II we'll discuss ways to hike safely, many of which occur before you ever even hit the trail. Safe hiking is also the first step in enjoyable hiking for you and others around you. The goal of this part is to help you feel prepared, not scared, and to empower you with accurate, reliable, trail-tested information. You'll see lots of chapter notes in these pages. The resources they reference will take you to more in-depth information on a variety of topics if you wish to read more.

3

Know Yourself and Trust Your Gut

Before you spend too much time perusing the shelves at an outdoor store or checking out trails online, I would encourage you to first think about what kind of hiker you might be and what you bring to the trail with you—other than the gear you will carry—that might impact your experience.

Know Yourself and Honor Your Limits

I recently watched a video about a challenging group hike on social media and person after person said something along the lines of "You've got to push past your limits." Sure, hiking can involve getting outside your comfort zone and challenging yourself. Lots of times I have hiked farther than I would have guessed I could when I first set foot on the trail. But there is a fine line between challenging yourself in good ways and pushing past your limits in a dangerous way. You're looking for a "just right" challenge. Quite frankly, the "push past your limits" mantra is part of an all-too-frequent refrain in the outdoor recreation world that implies that you're not doing it right if you're not always striving to move further and faster and tackle harder, longer trails. This simply isn't true. None of the benefits of hiking discussed previously are dependent on how far or fast you hike. In fact, some of the benefits would be harder to enjoy. Let's start by getting one thing straight: recognizing your true limits is the first step to an enjoyable and safe hike. There are times you want to challenge yourself, but there is a difference between doing this and being unsafe because you pushed yourself way beyond your capabilities for that day. Your "limits" can even change from day to day. Taking the time to answer these questions while planning a hike can help you get off to a good start.

How often do you hike and how recently have you been hiking?

Even if you have hiked in the past, you may need some time to get back in the groove if it's been a while, especially if you've had any significant physical or mental changes recently. If the last time you went hiking was five years ago, you'll probably feel like you're starting anew. Let's say you went hiking two months ago, but in the meantime you have had a significant illness that has greatly impacted your stamina. You'll likely be able to tell a difference from your last hike.

How often are you physically active in other ways?

Being active in other ways can give you a good foundation for some of the physical demands that can come with hiking but remember that hiking uses your entire body in ways that you might not typically use it. For example, if you regularly take a three-mile walk around your neighborhood or on a paved greenway, having your first hike be a three-mile hike on a rough trail with lots of elevation gain is probably not best. It will feel quite different, and likely more challenging, than your typical walk.

Do you have any medical or mobility concerns?

Because hiking can tax your body in ways it might not be used to, it's good to remember how your body reacts to stress. Does your blood sugar trend low? Does your asthma act up? (Being exposed to allergens outdoors can cause this too.) Do you have migraines that might flare up? Do you have a back injury or a previous knee injury that could act up with lots of stairs or climbing over rocks? Are you on medication that makes you more sensitive to sunlight? None of these things will necessarily prevent you from hiking, but take them into account when picking a trail and when deciding what gear you need to carry with you.

How comfortable are you hiking alone?

Some people really enjoy the solitude and peace that comes with hiking alone (raising my hand here). Some people are not comfortable with it at all. Both are okay. And it's not a completely yes-or-no question. Maybe you don't mind hiking by yourself, but you don't want to hike alone on a less used, remote trail with spotty cell service. Your personal comfort level is the key, and it might change from hike to hike.

Do you react strongly to heat or cold?

Some people are especially sensitive to temperature extremes. This can result from numerous things such as individual body composition, medical and developmental conditions, or even pregnancy or menopause. Certain medications can also decrease your heat tolerance, reduce your body's ability to regulate your temperature, or increase your sun sensitivity. These medications can include varieties of antibiotics, antihistamines, blood pressure medications, decongestants, psychiatric medications (certain classes of antidepressants and antipsychotics) and stimulants such as those used to treat ADHD. A quick online search of your medication's name can typically provide useful information on this topic and your doctor is, of course, a great resource as well. Learning how to dress appropriately for the weather can help, but some people just have some hard temperature limits over or under which they cease to enjoy hiking. For example, I love hiking in the cold. I've got all the gear and, because I tend to run hot, I always warm up nicely as I get moving. I just know my hands and ears will stay cold without adequate covering. On the other hand, no matter how I dress, above a certain temperature, typically the low 80s depending on cloud cover, I am miserable. Fifty-five to 65 degrees is my personal hiking sweet spot. You'll learn your personal hiking comfort ranges as you get out on the trails in a variety of conditions.

Knowing your limits isn't just about advanced planning, though. It's something that continues as you wake up on the day of your hike and hit the trail. Before you head out, consider this:

How are you feeling on the day of your hike?

Did you sleep well the night before? Did you wake up feeling bad or even just "off"? If you are already exhausted or not feeling well, picking an easier trail or even postponing the hike altogether might be best. This can be a *really* hard decision to make if you've planned a hike for a long time, have limited time to squeeze in a hike among your other responsibilities, traveled to hike in a certain location or planned a hike with other people. These situations can make us ignore our instincts and push on with our plans anyway. That might work out okay in other settings, but it can turn very unpleasant or even dangerous on a hike, especially one even somewhat far away from help. You don't have to always be 100 percent to hike, but you should think hard about going on one, especially by yourself, if you aren't feeling well.

My son is a life-long aviation enthusiast, and he shared with me a mnemonic device that some pilots use to judge their readiness to fly on any particular day. I think it's a good device for hikers too, especially if you are planning a longer hike, a hike to a more remote location or a solo hike. The mnemonic is I'M SAFE.

Illness: Have you developed any kind of illness that might make hiking unsafe? Especially consider gastrointestinal illnesses, an illness with a significant fever, or anything that impacts your balance and coordination.

Medications: Are you taking any kind of medication that might affect your balance and coordination, bring on significant side effects, or make you especially susceptible to heat or sunlight? Have you taken prescribed medications as directed?

Stress: The impact of stress and strong emotions on our ability to safely hike can be a bit tricky to judge. Hiking can be a great way to relieve stress and boost your mood. I have found peace, solace and clarity on the trail during some hard and stressful moments. But there *is* such a thing as a level of stress and emotion that could make hiking unwise. The question to ask is, "Are my emotions strong enough right now that they could distract me and prevent me from focusing on this hike in the way I need to stay safe?" We've all had those moments when our emotions are so intense, so raw, that we can't think about anything else. That probably isn't the best time to go for a hike. Spending some quiet time in nature just sitting with the beauty and fresh air might be more appropriate in those moments.

Alcohol: Obviously it is not safe to hike (much less drive to the trailhead) while you're intoxicated. Doing so can greatly impact your physical abilities as well as your ability to make safe decisions. Being hungover can also impact you in these ways as well as contribute to dehydration. It's probably best to leave the brews at home. I've seen the trend of the "summit beer" on social media, where hikers carry a favorite beer to enjoy at the top of the mountain or at some other destination point on the trail. This is probably fine from a safety standpoint. Just make sure to drink some water too! One word of caution, however. Alcohol is not allowed on some state park and national forest lands as well as in some nature preserves. Be sure to check out the rules for where you're hiking.

Fatigue: Did you sleep well enough the night before so you can focus and have the needed energy to complete the hike in a safe manner or is something else contributing to a level of fatigue that might impact your ability to hike? Hiking can be a great way to re-energize but picking an easier or a shorter trail if you're already feeling fatigued might be better. Plus, don't forget the dangers of driving tired if you have a long trip to get to the trailhead.

Eating: We'll discuss packing proper food for your hike in more detail later, but make sure you not only carry enough fuel for your hike but also that you're going into your hike well fed and well hydrated. Also consider how strenuous the hike is going to be, especially in hot weather, if you've had a particularly heavy or large meal as this can impact your comfort level as you hike.

Asking yourself these questions helps you not only decide whether you should hike at all but also can help you pick a trail. I keep a running list of the hikes I'd like to complete, and it is broken down into easier hikes that are perhaps a little closer to home, some medium-difficulty hikes or ones that perhaps involve more travel to reach, and hikes that are a higher difficulty level and/or require a bigger time commitment. When I plan for a hike, I often have a couple of trail options in mind to account for any needs on a particular day.

Hiking also requires some continuous assessment of the circumstances while you're on the trail. If you're like me, changing plans mid-stream can be hard, but asking yourself these questions during your hike can help you decide if some alterations to your plans are needed:

Has anything changed during your hike?

Has the weather changed in unexpected ways? Is the trail a lot harder than it appeared to be on the map or in reviews? As the old joke goes, "Wow, this trail looked a lot flatter on the map!" How are your legs holding up? Are you feeling a blister starting to form? Is the hike taking longer than anticipated and it's starting to get dark? Asking yourself these questions can help you answer the next one:

When is it enough?

Sometimes you've planned everything perfectly, you are carrying all the right gear, and you are hyped for a great hike. And then things just don't go as planned. The weather takes a sudden turn for the worse. You find a huge tree across the trail that would be dangerous to try to climb around. A stream that was supposed to be an easy cross has swollen to dangerous levels with recent rains. You get an uncomfortable vibe from someone hiking around you on the trail. You start feeling sick or are showing signs of heat-related illness or hypothermia.

Knowing when enough is enough is an important skill for everyone recreating outdoors. A successful hike is one you return home from safely. Especially in day hiking, it's not about reaching a certain destination or mileage; it's about getting back to your car in one piece and having an enjoyable experience, even if it is challenging. This can be even harder to judge on an out-and-back hike. You can still be feeling really good as you get further and further away from the trailhead and forget that you have to go all the way back. The handful of times I have fallen on a hike have all happened on the "back" portion of an out-and-back hike. Some of the adrenaline of the hike has worn off, your legs and feet are starting to get tired, and you are passing back over the same trail, so there's typically not as much novelty to keep you alert. It's easy to lose focus and trip and fall. As you're hiking, check in with yourself—and anyone else you're hiking with—and ask, "If I headed back now, would I reach the car with at least 5 percent of my energy left?" I have even been known to turn around and head back the way I came on a loop trail because I've realized that the complete loop was just going to be too much based on the conditions.

I have been on several hikes where I decided to head back a little early based on the conditions or how I was feeling, but one specific hike comes to mind that can illustrate some of the ideas we've discussed here. On a sunny Sunday afternoon in early June 2021, a friend and I decided to go for a hike at Stone Mountain State Park. Earlier that day I had participated in a group hike as a part of North Carolina Trail Days in Elkin—a great event to attend if you ever get the chance. The hike had not been terribly strenuous but hiking with a group I don't know is always a bit draining for me. Also, the day before, our son had graduated from high school. We homeschooled him for most of his K–12 years, so I had planned and hosted his graduation ceremony and the party afterward with many of our friends and family in attendance. It was a wonderful day but also a tiring and emotional one.

My friend and I met for lunch—a fairly heavy meal—before heading out to Stone Mountain State Park. We decided to park at the upper trailhead parking lot and hike on the Stone Mountain Loop Trail clockwise to see Stone Mountain Falls and the Lower Falls and perhaps some more of the loop around the front of Stone Mountain. After a bit on the trail, we hit the 300 steps that parallel Stone Mountain Falls. We were going down the steps; most people would think that going down stairs is easier than going up, but this is not necessarily true. Both can be

Just some of the steps that lead down to the bottom of Stone Mountain Falls at Stone Mountain State Park.

challenging for different reasons. By the time we reached the bottom of the stairs my legs were quite fatigued and a little shaky. We hung out by the waterfall—which is awesome and well worth the hike—for a little while and then continued down the trail toward the second set of falls.

Suddenly everything hit me at once—the heat, the fatigue from the events of the day before and the morning hike, the heavy lunch, the stairs—and I felt terrible. Like the I'm-about-to-be-sick-or-pass-out kind of terrible. I stopped to rest for a minute and drank some water, hoping the feeling would pass and we could keep going. But the feeling didn't pass, and I knew I needed to head back. I'm not going to lie; it was hard for me to say something. I was enjoying my time out with my friend, and I didn't want to be the reason we had to cut our hike short. I knew she wanted to keep going. *I* wanted to keep going. But I also knew that wasn't the smart thing to do and told her that I thought I needed to turn around. She, of course, understood and we started the hike back, stopping for lots of breaks and water along the way. (If you're hiking with someone and they give you lots of grief about needing to turn back, I would think seriously about hiking with that person again.) I recognized that I had hit my limit for the day and respected that. I was back out hiking two days later on another trail with no issues. Remember, a successful hike is one you return home from safe and sound. Being honest about your personal limits, both overall and on any individual hike, can help keep you safe and help ensure that you enjoy your experience and leave the hike looking forward to the next one.

Trust Your Gut

It can be hard to trust our instincts, our "gut." We are often taught that we can't trust our feelings. We are told that they will lead us astray. We are taught to follow our minds, our logical selves, rather than our feelings, in order to make good decisions. Now don't get me wrong; I can be logical to a fault. And sometimes it is good. But I can also think of plenty of times that I have felt something instinctively and *not* paid attention to that feeling and it's gotten me in trouble. Among the many things hiking has taught me is to at least stop and listen to that gut feeling, even if I don't end up following it. Hiking has taught me to honor what that part of myself is trying to say. And doing this can be especially important when you're hiking alone.

When I say "trust your gut" when hiking, I partly mean knowing and honoring your limits as was discussed before. Listen to what your body is telling you about how much you can handle on any given day and trust that it's not lying to you. But I also mean trust your gut when it comes to situations you encounter on the trail. Does something just feel off about the weather? Even if the forecast looks okay, maybe it's time to get off the trail. Does something about the location feel unsafe for any reason? Perhaps it's a trail best left for another day or hiked with another person. Does something about another person's behavior on the trail make you uncomfortable and you can't quite explain why? Unfortunately, just because you're spending time in beautiful outdoor surroundings doesn't mean that people with harmful intentions can't also be sharing that space. And none of us are immune to the possibility of becoming a victim of violence. Those harmed can be any gender, age, size, nationality, race, or ability level. Yes, it is very true that certain groups are statistically *more likely* to be the victims of violence—women, people of color, non-binary and transgender individuals—but *none* of us can assume we get a pass on this subject, and we should all listen to our intuition and learn some basics about how to protect ourselves on the trail. I am not trying to scare anyone away from hiking, even from hiking alone. I predominantly hike alone. I'm simply asking you to pay a little extra attention to the signals your body and your brain are sending you and spend some time thinking, before you hit the trail, about what you would do if you ever felt threatened while hiking.

As the Mountains-to-Sea Trail (MST) passes between the Boone and West Jefferson areas, it includes a fair amount of road walking along the Blue Ridge Parkway. I have loved hiking on the MST, but after my first few hikes in this area I realized that I felt very uncomfortable during the road walking sections. This particular stretch of the Parkway is not as busy as others, and as I walked along the side of the road it was obvious that I was hiking alone. These stretches of trail typically aren't very busy with hikers either. Walking along the road, I felt like it would have been easy for someone to pull up beside me and grab me and I'd be gone before anyone knew it, so I chose to hike stretches of the MST that stayed in the woods and off the Parkway instead. Instinct feelings while hiking can come in a variety of forms and about any number of situations. The important thing is to be open to what they are trying to tell you and at least consider them when making decisions. Your gut may just be trying to keep you safe.

While an empty stretch of the Blue Ridge Parkway does allow for images like this, it can also feel isolated and exposed when hiking along the roadway alone (courtesy Nathaniel Wallace).

Personal Safety on the Trail

Many of the behaviors we'll discuss in the "How Not to Get Lost" chapter will also help you stay safe, but what are some other things you can do to protect life and limb?

First, especially if you are going to be regularly hiking alone—on any kind of trail—consider taking a self-defense class. I took one and it was so valuable. It's amazing what you can learn in just a couple of hours. What I'm sharing here shouldn't be viewed as a substitute for taking an in-person class where you will have a chance to practice some of the hands-on self-defense skills.

Next, be aware of your surroundings as you hike. For a variety of reasons, going on a hike is not a time to "tune out." Pay attention to where you are, where you're going, and what's going on around you. This is true from the moment you pull into the parking lot to the moment you leave it. No need to be hypervigilant or paranoid here; just be aware.

If someone approaches you in a way that makes you feel uncomfortable, don't be afraid to ask questions and don't reveal too much about yourself. If someone says they are with a local trail maintenance, search and rescue, or law enforcement agency, ask for verification of their identity. Don't give information about where you're hiking, who you're hiking with, or what kind of car you drive. This includes on social media in advance of your hike. If a situation makes you really uncomfortable, report it to whatever agency oversees your hiking location.

If someone approaches you aggressively or persistently, or heaven forbid lays hands on you, don't be afraid to make a scene. This is not the time to worry about being rude or too loud. You *want* to draw attention to yourself. Yell. Scream. Make it clear that you do not welcome the person's attention, that you don't want to go with them and even that you don't know them if that's the case. If the person tries to grab you, go limp and make yourself as heavy as possible. You know when a toddler throws a tantrum and basically becomes dead weight that you're trying to pick up? That's what you're going for. Try to face the person if possible and not let them get behind you where you can't see them.

Your safest option in this kind of situation is to get as far away from the other person as possible, not try to fight them off. So, even if they grab you, as soon as you have the chance, run. Don't get loose from their grip and then turn to go toe to toe with them. If you do have to fight them, hit and kick with the heels of your hands and feet, not with your fingers/knuckles or toes, as those are much more likely to break, causing you harm and perhaps making getting away harder. Aim for vulnerable spots on the person's body, such as the groin, the throat, the bridge of the nose and the eyes. Bend their thumbs back, hit or kick the sides of the knees or directly on the kneecap, trying to get the joint to move in the opposite direction than it normally does. Grab the ears and pull the person forward. Bite or claw at them. Your goal here is not to knock the person out or "take them down," which is actually quite hard to do. You're trying to create a split-second window where the person is caught off guard or off balance so you can get away. Go to a safe location as quickly as possible and call 911.

A word about carrying weapons on hikes: Using any kind of weapon to defend yourself takes training and practice. This is not just true for firearms but also for knives or even pepper spray or Mace. Trying to use such weapons in situations like the ones described above without training and practice can increase the likelihood of the perpetrator gaining control of that weapon and using it against you. Knives require you to be very close to the other person to inflict injury, increasing the chances that they will be able to grab you or that you will get cut in the process. Spraying pepper spray or Mace, especially depending on wind conditions, can cause your vision and breathing to be affected by the chemicals they contain.

Carrying a weapon can also give us a false sense of security, increasing the likelihood that we'll not pay as close attention to the other things mentioned above. And none of this speaks to the legalities of carrying these weapons in certain areas and what kinds of permits are required to do so. Deciding whether or not to carry a weapon while hiking is a very personal decision with lots to take into consideration; it's not a decision to make lightly. But whatever you do, don't let a weapon take the place of awareness and common sense.

4

Do Your Research

*Understanding Trail Information
and Weather Forecasts*

Some people want to be surprised when exploring something or somewhere new. I am the opposite of that. I'm known in my family as the researcher. My husband jokes that I missed my calling: working in national intelligence. Regardless of my personal preferences, leaving things to chance *can* add to the enjoyment in certain situations. With hiking, however, taking this attitude can turn an enjoyable hiking trip into a dangerous one. Doing your research can help you prepare and see how the trail might match up with the questions we discussed in the previous chapter.

Get Trail Information from More Than One Source

There are many sources of information to consider when researching trails. These range from official guidebooks, to online printable maps, to a multitude of apps. When talking about sources of trail information for day hiking, we can't go too far without discussing the AllTrails app. Its usefulness is frequently debated in the hiking community. Many people use AllTrails as their go-to source for trail information. It is quite user-friendly and offers lots of information, and even enables you to look at a map and see nearby hikes. I use AllTrails but I don't *only* use AllTrails, and here's why: AllTrails can be a great place to start but certain types of information shared should be taken with a grain of salt.

Most of the information on AllTrails has not been verified by an AllTrails staff member. No one is going out on all the hikes featured on the app to verify how long they are, how difficult they are, or what amenities or obstacles might be found on the trail. As of now, most of the information is user-submitted, from opensource maps, or based on analysis of user data that's done by their software. For example, most hikes on AllTrails give a difficulty rating that's determined by the mileage and the elevation gain of the hike. A 400-foot elevation gain over a mile might be quite easy for one hiker and really difficult for another, so be careful how you interpret the difficulty designations. AllTrails also frequently offers information on how long a particular trail should take. I rarely pay any attention to these suggested times as they are frequently off from how fast I hike. Sometimes I even laugh at them. For example, AllTrails said completing the 2.8-mile loop in Greensboro near Lake Brandt that consists of the Palmetto Trail, Atlantic and Yadkin Greenway and the Nat Greene Trail should take 52 minutes. That's an average of 3.2 miles per hour. So many things can impact how fast you hike on any given day, and many people don't hike at a speed over three miles per hour. I certainly didn't when I completed this hike. Also, these times don't take into consideration any breaks you take. On this hike I took a 20-minute break sitting beside the lake watching the fish

This beautiful spot was well worth a 20-minute stop on a hike near Lake Brandt (Greensboro) that traversed the Palmetto Trail, Atlantic and Yadkin Greenway and Nat Greene Trail.

jump and a blue heron hunt—time that was well worth it in my enjoyment of the experience. Also, at the end of this hike, after tracking myself on the app, AllTrails said I hiked 3.49 miles. I hiked the same route as the one listed on AllTrails as being 2.8 miles. Mileage discrepancies are not unusual either.

So what *is* AllTrails useful for, then, if all this information can be somewhat unreliable? It's a great place to start researching information and to find new trails. There are trails that are *not* on AllTrails, so be sure to look at other sources for ideas too, but in my experience, AllTrails has the most trails listed in one place of any app, website or book. Also, the elevation profiles given are helpful and pretty reliable. Above all, though, to me the most helpful parts of AllTrails are the trail reviews and the pictures. Even in the reviews, I still take any difficulty comments lightly, but I have learned lots of other valuable information about trails from these reviews: obstacles on the trail, dogs from nearby homes that run free, stretches of trail that tend to be muddy after rain, trails that are not well marked, and even trails that are closed but still show up on the AllTrails map. As you read reviews and look at pictures be sure to check the dates they were posted and the activity listed as you can post reviews for everything from hiking to mountain biking to rock climbing.

AllTrails probably shouldn't be the only place you look for trail information, however. If you have found a trail that interests you on AllTrails, also look it up on other apps or do some looking online at other sources. Trail guidebooks can also be found depending on your area. By combining information from AllTrails with other sources, you'll have a much more accurate picture of what to expect. We'll talk more specifically about some sources for trail ideas in Part III of this book.

Know How to Read Basic Trail Guide and Map Information

Most hiking trails don't just spring up by themselves. While they might have started as game trails or historic roads, many established trails today are carefully designed, planned and constructed—often by volunteers working alongside government agencies and conservation organizations. Professional trail-building organizations get involved as well. Trail guides and maps are based on the plans that go into building and maintaining trails and these resources can be helpful if you understand how to use the information shared. Terminology is a good place to start. First, let's talk about the anatomy of a hiking trail. All trails have a beginning and an end. The beginning of the trail is referred to as the trailhead and it is usually found at a roadside or in a parking area. The end is referred to as the destination. This could be the top of a mountain, a waterfall, some other point of interest or even back at the trailhead.

Trail Tread, Slope and Cross Slope

The trail tread is the surface upon which you travel as a hiker and it's important to know. Some trails are natural surface, meaning rocks, roots, dirt, sand, pine needles or grass. Some trails are gravel, either larger rocks, as you might find on a gravel driveway, or crushed, smaller gravel. Some trails contain wooden boardwalks or bridges, and some trails are paved with asphalt or concrete. Many have some combination of these. Trail tread surface can impact accessibility. A wheelchair, a walker, or even an adaptive hiking chair will likely have a hard time on a heavily rooted natural surface trail but a much easier time on a paved trail, one with crushed gravel, a grass trail or even one with smaller and fewer roots. We'll talk more about trail accessibility in the next chapter.

Trail tread can also impact the type of gear you use. For example, a good pair of general athletic shoes might be okay for a paved or gravel trail, but you might opt for trail runners or hiking boots with some good grip or ankle support for a natural surface trail with lots of roots and rocks. You might also decide to take along some trekking poles for this type of trail but feel okay leaving them at home for a paved trail. Improvements made to trail treads are designed to conserve soil and protect surrounding plants, habitats, and water sources. These often help stabilize the soil or other trail surface to prevent erosion and drain water away, so the trail does not become or stay muddy or flooded. The added benefit is that most of these improvements make hiking on the trail easier and more enjoyable. Despite these improvements, some trails, especially popular ones, can still receive damage. You will occasionally notice sections of trail that have been rerouted and the original trail closed off. Please respect these boundaries and stay on the currently designated trail, even if it differs slightly from your map. These closures help restore areas that have received a lot of use.

The slope of a trail speaks to how steep it is, and this is generally expressed as a grade percent. For example, a trail with a 1 percent grade would be essentially flat while a trail with a 30 percent grade would feel quite steep. Occasionally trail guides will share an overall or general slope or grade

This section of the Uwharrie National Trail north of the Jumpingoff Rocks trailhead shows significant cross slope. A hiker on this stretch definitely feels the impacts of walking with one foot higher up the mountainside than the other. This type of cross slope would also be inaccessible to those using adaptive hiking equipment.

as well as the maximum grade found on a particular trail. Many trail apps show an elevation profile, which we'll discuss below. Often placing your finger or cursor on a point of the elevation profile in a hiking app will give you the percent grade for that section of the trail.

Trails also have a cross slope. This is the amount the trail tread tips left or right from horizontal. A trail that has a large cross slope will have one side of the trail tread much higher than the other. Unfortunately, this type of information isn't always included in trail descriptions, but you can often get some idea of the cross slope by reading reviews and looking at pictures of the trail.

Trail Types

You might also see different trail types listed in a trail description:

Access Trail: an access trail usually leads to a parking area, road, visitor's center, campground, or town. Also sometimes called a connector trail.
Backcountry Trail: these trails are normally unmaintained or minimally maintained and exist in areas without roads or other amenities.
Connector Trail: a trail that links two or more trails or trail systems.
Fire Road: a dirt road designed to provide rangers and firefighters access to backcountry areas.
Horseshoe Trail: a trail that has different start and end points at different parking or road access areas. It essentially has two trailheads. This can also be referred to as a point-to-point trail. For most hikers, these are also out-and-back trails as they must hike down the same trail to return to their car.
Interpretive Trail: typically a shorter trail designed to give hikers information about the flora and fauna of an area or to highlight geological features or historical locations. These are also sometimes referred to as nature trails.
Loop: sometimes also called a ring trail. On this trail you will start and end at the same spot without crossing over the same stretch of trail twice.
Multi-Use Trail: a trail that is not only for hikers. In most places this indicates a trail that is for both mountain biking and hiking. In my experience, these trails tend to be constructed more with mountain biking in mind and with hiking as an afterthought. You may find tight switchbacks and banked turns and occasional built-up hill jumps. These features can impact the enjoyment of hiking on multi-use trails. Multi-use can also mean that the trail allows horses or off-road vehicles.
Out-and-Back Trail: a trail on which you will cross over the same trail twice as you go from and back to your car. Often these are trails that lead to a specific destination such as a mountain summit or waterfall.
Rail Trail: trails that are rights-of-way from railways converted after tracks are no longer in use. They tend to be flat and wide with a variety of surface types.
Single-Track: trails that are very narrow and only wide enough for one hiker to pass through at a time.
Trail System: a group of interconnected trails with multiple access points and often multiple destinations.

Some multi-use trails allow for horses and hikers. On this day in March of 2024, I met a very friendly (and funny) group of women riders enjoying the trail to Nifty Rocks in the Badin Lake area of Uwharrie National Forest.

Topographical Lines

Even if you aren't interested in taking an orienteering course or learning how to fully read topographical lines, it's good to know some basics in order to take advantage of the information being shared on trail maps. On a map, the topographical lines represent different elevations. Often certain lines will be labeled with these elevation numbers to give you points of reference. Changes in elevation levels represent where you will find inclines on your hike. The tighter together the lines are, the steeper the incline. You can get a sense of how the trail navigates an incline by looking at the trail map compared to the topographical lines. For example, if the trail goes straight up an area of incline, it will be a lot more strenuous than if it zig-zags

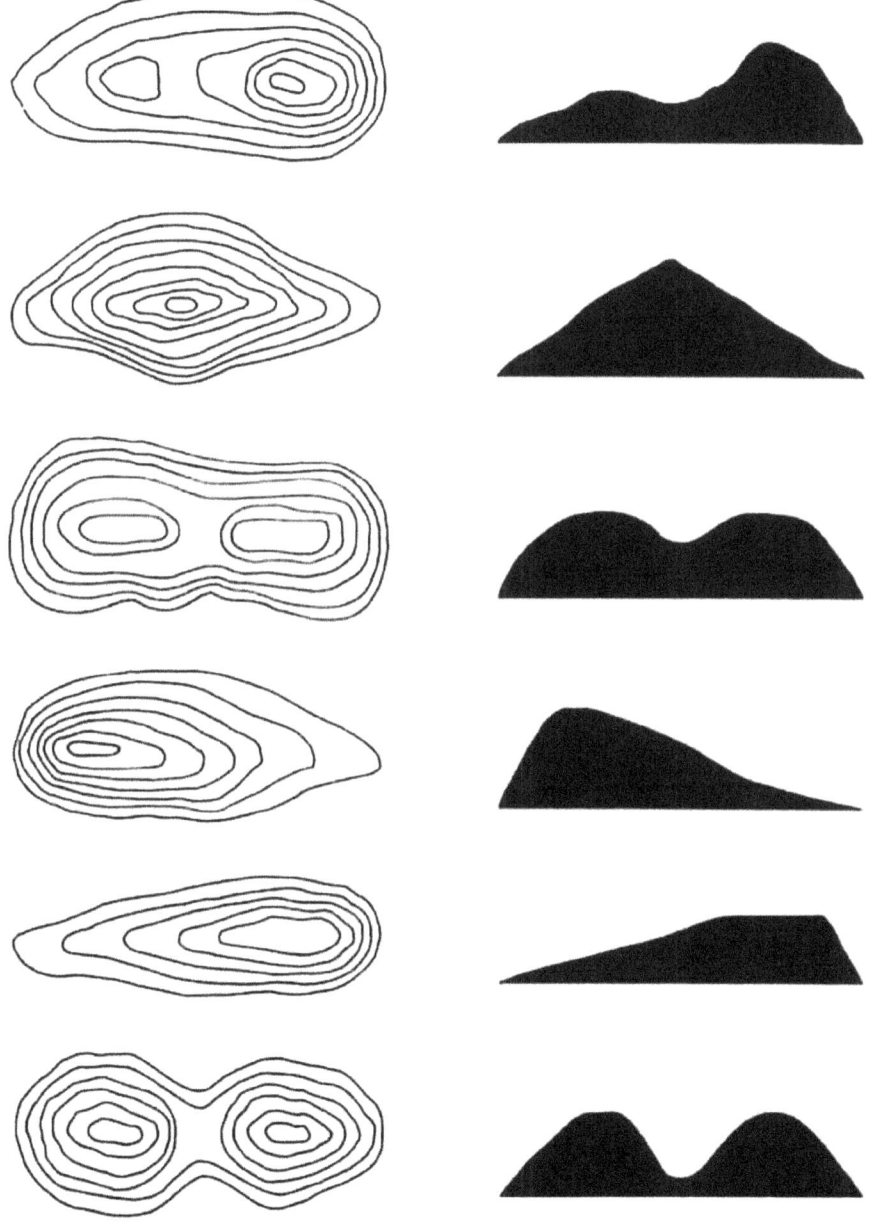

These diagrams show how different topographical maps would translate to an elevation profile. The closer the lines are together, the steeper the slope.

back and forth up the incline—also called switchbacks. A completed round figure on a topographical map indicates the top of an incline. The smaller that figure, the steeper the top of that ridge.

Mileage

Understanding how the mileage is indicated on your particular trail map is also important, especially for out-and-back trails. Most maps give out-and-back distance as a total amount for the entire trip. For example, if from the trailhead to the destination was 1.5 miles, the guide would list the entire hike as three miles. This is worth paying attention to, however, especially if you are hiking a point-to-point trail as an out-and-back. The map might say the trail is only as long as the distance to walk from point A to point B, but you'll need to double that if you're coming back on the same trail.

Elevation Profile

Lastly, if the information is available, be sure to look at the elevation profile of your trail and not just the overall elevation gain for the entire hike. For example, let's say your trail guide says that the elevation gain over a two-mile hike is 400 feet, from a low of 800 feet above sea level to a high point of 1,200 feet. That doesn't seem too bad. If we do a little math, that shows us that the average percent grade of the trail is about 4 percent *if that incline is spread out across all two miles of the hike.* But then let's say we look at the elevation profile for the trail and realize that the first half mile of the trail is basically flat and then all our elevation gain happens between a distance of .50 and 1.0 mile down the trail. Suddenly, the incline of this trail jumps from a pretty manageable 4 percent grade to a much steeper 15 percent grade for that half a mile of trail.

Since we're talking about inclines, one concluding point here: It's easy to assume that hiking downhill—or down stairs—will be much easier than hiking uphill—or up stairs. This is not necessarily the case. They work your body differently and both can be plenty challenging. I have found that hiking uphill is harder on my upper legs, hips and lungs (cardiovascular), but hiking downhill is much harder on my knees, toes, and brain. Hiking down a steep incline often takes more concentration and you're much more likely to fall going downhill.

I thoroughly research every hike I complete in advance, and yes, research does take some of the surprise out of the trail. On the other hand, feeling prepared before I head out helps me to be more confident and relaxed and helps me not miss exciting and unique features of the hikes I complete.

One of the hikes I researched the most involved three waterfalls and a trail that crossed in and out of North Carolina and Tennessee several times. The hike started at Elk River Falls near Banner Elk, which is well known. But in doing some research I discovered that there were two other falls nearby—Jones Falls and Splash Dam Falls. I had to do a lot of research to find the loop of trails that would take me to all three as at the time the complete route was not yet on AllTrails. My research showed that this three-waterfall hike would involve a decent amount of elevation gain, including a

I have seen evidence of beaver activity on plenty of trails, but this hike at Clarks Creek Preserve near Charlotte was the first time I'd seen an actual dam. I would have missed it if I hadn't done my research and read reviews about the side trail that led to the dam.

couple of quite steep sections. I also discovered that the trail was easy to lose in a couple of locations and I was prepared so I didn't get lost. I knew the hike would be longer than my typical hike, so I came prepared with enough water and food and ideas on how to pace myself. All of this combined help me to have a very enjoyable and, most of all, safe hike.

This three-waterfall hike took lots of research to plan and was a challenge—and joy—to complete. From left (June 2021): Elk River Falls, Jones Falls and Splash Dam Falls.

Check Reliable Weather Forecasts and Know Typical Weather Patterns

When our family lived in the northwest mountains of North Carolina we knew certain locations tended to be foggy. I knew limited visibility was possible if I hiked in those areas. We also knew about the almost constant winds in the winters. When I'd head out to hike in the winter, I knew to take the windchill into account when planning what clothes to wear and even what impacts the direction of the wind could have on how cold I felt. Knowing these kinds of things often comes from living in an area over time. Interestingly, the more you hike, the more you'll become aware of typical weather patterns and recognize them—and when they change—even when you aren't out on the trail.

Having this overall weather knowledge does not mean you shouldn't carefully check the specific weather forecast for a day you plan to hike, and this is not the time to rely on the built-in weather app on your phone. They are notoriously inaccurate. Checking the local weather forecast for your area with the National Weather Service (*www.weather.gov*) is probably the best place to start and might be all you need. The hourly forecast (found under Additional Resources toward the bottom of the website) is especially helpful as it shows the following information: temperature, heat index/windchill, dewpoint, surface level sustained wind speeds and direction, wind gust speeds and direction, relative humidity, precipitation potential, percentage of sky cover, and the specific possibilities of rain, thunder, and different types of winter precipitation. This information is given for six days into the future. The amount of rain and winter precipitation anticipated is also given for three of those days. This information is given in a graphic format that makes trends in the upcoming weather easy to spot.

Most people will understand the information presented about temperature, heat index/windchill, wind speeds, and percentage of sky cover. Dewpoint, relative humidity and precipitation percentages can cause some confusion, so let's have a short meteorology lesson. First, the precipitation potential percentage simply gives the probability that the forecast location will receive *at least* .01 (one hundredth) of an inch of rain.

What does that mean for real life? Let's say the forecast for rain in my county is 50 percent for this afternoon. That means that there is a 50 percent chance of at least one hundredth of an inch of rain falling at *any* location in the county between noon and 6:00 p.m. local time. It does not mean that I will see rain for three hours—50 percent of that timeframe—nor does it mean that 50 percent of the forecast area will receive rain.

Next, dewpoint and relative humidity both give us information on how humid, or muggy, it feels outside and there is an important reason to know this if you are going to be spending time outdoors. A relative humidity of 100 percent means that the air is saturated with moisture in its water vapor (gas) form. It means that no more moisture can be absorbed by the air around you. When you sweat, if the relative humidity is 100 percent, that moisture cannot evaporate off your skin. Sweat evaporation is a primary means by which our bodies cool, and if that can't happen, we aren't going to cool down very well. So, in some ways, it really *isn't* the heat ... it's the humidity!

The dewpoint is the temperature to which the air needs to be cooled in order to achieve a relative humidity of 100 percent. The higher the dewpoint temperature, the more humid it will feel. In the summer months, a dewpoint of equal to or greater than 65 degrees means lots of moisture is in the air and the air is likely to feel oppressive.

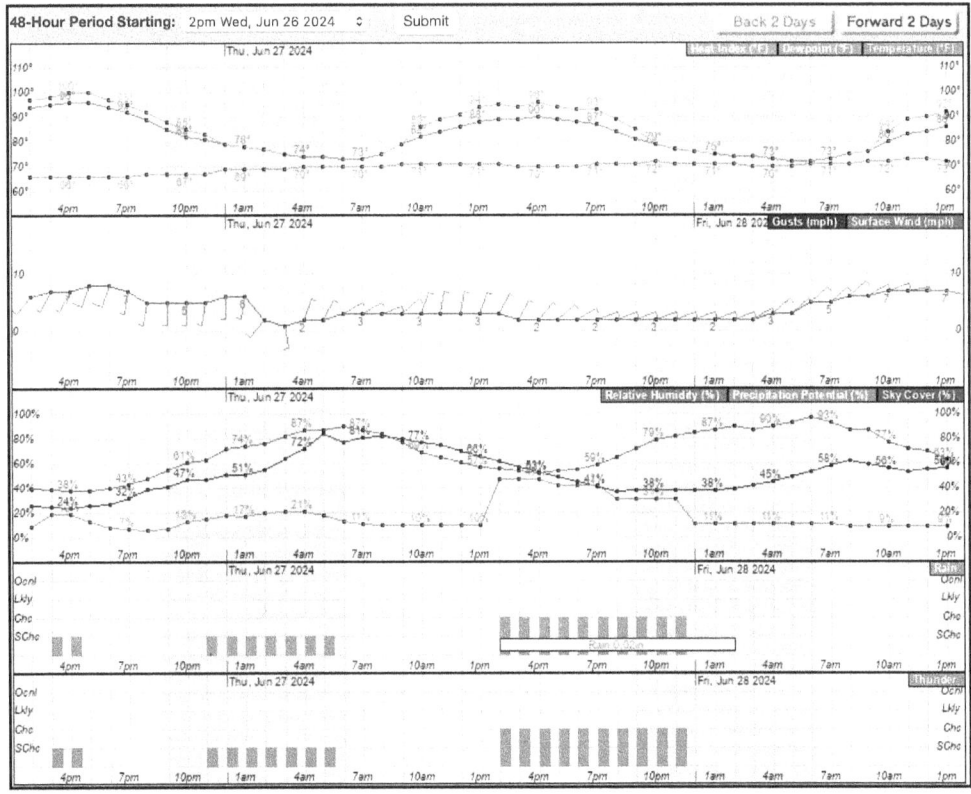

This hourly National Weather Service forecast graph for Lexington on Thursday, June 27, 2024, shows that Thursday afternoon would probably not be my favorite time to hike. A heat index in the mid to upper 90s, virtually no breeze, a dewpoint of a muggy 70 degrees and a good chance of thunderstorms ... sounds like a day to stay in the air conditioning and plan for cooler-weather hiking (National Weather Service).

As Brad Panovich, a favorite local meteorologist in Charlotte, likes to say, "Air you can wear." A dewpoint less than or equal to 55 degrees will feel dry and comfortable. Looking at the complete picture of the weather this information presents—how hot or cold it might be, the humidity levels, the chances of thunderstorms or other severe weather, how cloudy or breezy it might be—helps me to decide when and where to hike, what clothes to wear and even how much water to carry.

Knowing what weather to expect before you hike is important, but we all know that weather often does what it wants, despite even the best predictions. Parts of North Carolina definitely follow the saying, "If you don't like the weather, wait five minutes or drive five miles." Knowing how to read some weather signs in the moment can prove helpful in keeping you safe on the trail.

Clouds

Different sizes, shapes, colors and heights of clouds can give you some clues as to what types of weather might be developing.[1] Some types of clouds, specifically mid- and high-level clouds, predict weather that is further away in time, likely not an immediate concern if you are out on a shorter day hike. Any low-level clouds can give you clues to

Different types of clouds often mean that different types of weather can be expected. Learning the basics of reading the clouds can help you be prepared for bad weather while hiking. These cumulus clouds, seen along the Blue Ridge Parkway on a hot summer day in August 2021, gave warning of potential afternoon thunderstorms. Thankfully I was off the trail before that weather hit. Being out in the open along this section of the Bluff Mountain Trail in the Doughton Recreation Area would not have been safe with lightning in the area.

more immediately troubling weather, however. Lower-level clouds often contain water in some form. What kind and how much of a problem it could present depends on the temperature and the uniformity and height of the clouds. Flat, uniform but thin gray or white clouds may produce drizzle or flurries that could last for hours. Thicker layers of clouds indicate more steady rain or snow.[2] Do the clouds seem to be growing or building, especially up into higher altitudes in the sky? These are likely storm clouds that could produce rain, thunder, lightning and potentially severe weather.[3]

Cloud and sky color can also give clues about the weather. The darker the clouds, especially the base of the clouds, the more likely precipitation is to occur and the worse it might be. A greenish or deep blue/gray color is indicative of severe precipitation such as very heavy rain or hail.

Lightning

Lightning can be deadly and should be taken seriously. Hikers can and do get struck by lightning. For example, in August 2021 seven hikers were struck by lightning on Grandfather Mountain's MacRae. Thankfully, all survived their injuries.[4] Lightning is the second most deadly weather phenomena, falling only behind flash flooding,[5] and North Carolina ranks in the top five states for the highest number of lightning-related fatalities each year.[6] If you are ever outdoors and feel your hair start to stand on end, hear a crackling in the air, or feel your skin begin to tingle, even if you have not heard thunder, seek a safe location immediately. In most cases, however, this doesn't occur, and thunder is your best warning sign of lightning, as thunder is created when the rapid, extreme heating of the air caused by lightning creates a shock wave we can hear. If you can hear thunder, you are at risk of being struck by lightning, even if the thunder sounds far away. Lightning can strike ahead of or behind a storm—up to eight to 10 miles away from the storm causing it[7]—and it is unpredictable and not well understood. You can count the number of seconds between seeing a lightning flash and hearing thunder to determine a rough distance to the strike with this formula: count the number of seconds between the flash of lightning and the sound of thunder; divide this number by five to get the distance in miles to the lightning. Five seconds = one mile. Fifteen seconds = three miles. Thirty seconds = six miles. While this can be a helpful tool, remember this: Thunder can usually only be heard within 10 miles of a lightning strike. If you can hear thunder, you are likely within striking distance of the storm.[8]

No outdoor locations are truly safe when lightning is in the area. The only completely safe place during lightning is inside an enclosed building with electrical wiring and plumbing. The wiring and plumbing conduct electricity better than a human and will direct lightning into the ground. Picnic shelters, trail shelters, tents, caves and other such enclosures are *not* safe. If no safe buildings are available, an enclosed metal vehicle with rubber tires is your next best option; convertibles or other open cab vehicles are not a safe alternative.

If you cannot reach safe shelter, seek the lowest point possible. This could be in a valley, gulley, ditch or even just a depression in the landscape. Get below the tree line and away from open fields, ridges, exposed slopes, or balds. Do not stand near any tall, isolated objects, and if you are around trees, stand among a clump of smaller trees or brush. Lightning is attracted to objects that are isolated, tall, and pointed, regardless of the material that makes up the object, so try to make sure you don't meet one of these

This 2012 image, taken by the Look Rock webcam on the western side of Great Smoky Mountains National Park, shows a lightning strike during a spring storm (National Park Service).

criteria. If you are hiking with a group, make sure everyone stands at least 100 feet from each other, as lightning strikes can travel between people. Do not lie flat on the ground as most lightning strikes occur when a nearby strike travels through the ground.[9] You may have also heard of the "lightning position," a specific crouched position that's supposed to keep you safe from lightning. Breaking news: it doesn't offer protection, and the National Weather Service and National Lightning Safety Council stopped recommending it in 2008.[10] If you find yourself out in the open in a lightning storm, run and try to reach a more protected location; don't waste time assuming the "lightning position."[11]

Wind

A warm breeze on a chilly day or a cool one on a hot day can feel nice when hiking, but winds that are too strong can prove dangerous. Some state and national parks will even close when winds are supposed to be too high, even in the absence of other kinds of severe weather. Hiking in wind at some point is inevitable but knowing when it's *too* windy to hike safely is important.

The Beaufort Wind Scale[12] gives some indications of how strong the wind is by observable conditions as well as some idea of the damage that can be caused by high winds.

Description	Speed (mph)	Observable Conditions
Calm	0–1	no observable wind; smoke rises vertically
Light Air	1–3	direction of wind shown by smoke drift
Light Breeze	4–7	wind felt on face; leaves rustle
Gentle Breeze	8–12	leaves and small twigs in constant motion; winds would extend a light flag

Description	Speed (mph)	Observable Conditions
Moderate Breeze	13–18	raises dust and loose papers; small branches are moved
Fresh Breeze	19–24	small trees in leaf begin to sway; crested wavelets begin to form on inland waters
Strong Breeze	25–31	large branches in motion; whistling can be heard in wires
Near Gale	32–38	whole trees in motion; inconvenience felt when walking against the wind
Gale	39–46	breaks twigs off trees; impedes movement progress
Severe Gale	47–54	slight structural damage begins to occur
Storm	55–63	trees uprooted; considerable structural damage; seldom experienced inland except during severe storms

As this scale makes clear, hiking becomes more difficult in the 30-mph range and can be downright dangerous not much above that. Taking the wind forecast into account when planning a hike is important, but also watch for changes in wind speed as you hike, especially if the wind seems to be consistently picking up. It might be time to get off the trail if you start noticing some of those 30–40 mph signs. Hearing trees creaking in the wind can be nerve-wracking as you hike, but keeping in mind the Beaufort Wind Scale will help you to know when it's just an eerie sound versus when you might be in danger.

The wind direction also impacts the weather, especially the temperature, in North Carolina. Winds coming from the south and southwest generally mean warmer, more humid air, while winds from the north and northeast typically bring cooler, drier air.[13]

Plants and Animals

A long history of folklore exists in North Carolina centered on the weather.[14] Many of these tales and sayings are said to predict long-term weather, often related to the harshness of an upcoming winter. Perhaps you've heard some of them. Probably the most well-known saying involves the woolly worm: the more black a woolly worm has on its body and/or the wider the black stripes compared to the brown ones, the worse the coming winter will be. If you've ever attended the Woolly Worm Festival in Banner Elk, you've helped celebrate this enduring bit of folklore! These sayings are often shared in the *Farmer's Almanac* and the historic *Foxfire* series of books and many originated in the beliefs of Indigenous peoples.

Scientific evidence has shown that many of these folklore signs do contain some elements of truth, even though most don't predict the weather exactly as indicated. So can you rely on any of these to help you predict upcoming weather when you're out on the trail? Maybe. Studies of certain species of birds have shown they leave an area before storms that produce tornadoes hit. Frog calls often change when it's about to rain, possibly triggered by a rise in humidity in the air. There is also truth in the belief that crickets can tell you the temperature. Count the number of chirps in 15 seconds and then add 40 to this number. It will give a rough estimate of the temperature in Fahrenheit.[15] On the other side of the temperature scale, rhododendron leaf curling can tell low temperatures. Below 20°F they will be curled up tight, but when temperatures are near or above freezing, they will typically maintain their normal flat appearance. So the answer is yes—some plant and animal signs can point to certain kinds of incoming weather, but they should never replace careful research on the forecast for the day of your hike. And our favorite woolly worms? In reality, they hold little weather prediction ability. In fact, their coloration is based on how long they have been feeding and their age and species. Feel free to still enjoy the Woolly Worm Festival, though!

Other Things to Consider

When you are hiking in the mountains, remember that the temperature will change with elevation. If you are climbing in elevation, the temperature will generally decrease by 5.4°F for every 1,000 feet you climb if no rain or snow is falling. If precipitation is falling, the temperature will still fall as you climb but only by about 3.3°F per 1,000 feet. Of course, how the temperature feels has to do with the winds, how much sun or shade is present on the trail and other factors, but this gives you a good rule of thumb to follow.

Now that you've done some thinking about what kind of hiker you are and some research on possible trails and the weather, let's talk a bit about trail accessibility.

5

Trail Accessibility and Adaptive Hiking

Nature—the outdoors—is for everyone. Regardless of gender, sexual orientation, race, ethnicity, nationality, size, shape, age, ability, or disability. Developing accessible trails and facilities and creating adaptive hiking experiences are important goals, and I'm thankful for the organizations across North Carolina that are doing this work.

The term "accessible trails" often leads to images of trails that a wheelchair or other mobility aid user could hike. Some might assume that all paved trails are accessible (not true) or that natural surface trails never are (also not true). In reality, trail accessibility involves way more than just the trail tread surface, and lots of other things are at play that should be considered when picking a trail from an accessibility standpoint. There is not a one-size-fits-all description of an accessible trail as every disabled hiker, and the adaptive devices they might use, has unique needs.

Features of an Accessible Trail

Federal guidelines have been developed for trail accessibility by the U.S. Access Board,[1] an "independent federal agency that promotes equality for people with disabilities through leadership in accessible design and the development of accessibility guidelines and standards."[2] The U.S. Forest Service also worked with the Access Board to develop the Forest Service Trail Accessibility Guidelines (FSTAG).[3] According to these entities, accessible trail tread surfaces, including passing spaces and resting intervals, must be firm and stable. What does this mean? A firm trail surface resists indentations. For example, a cane would sink into (or cause an indentation in) a sand or deep, loose gravel trail but would not on a paved or hard-packed natural surface trail. Other trail surfaces such as boardwalks and wood chips can feature varying degrees of accessibility. For example, a softer trail surface like wood chips might feel better for someone with knee issues but likely would be much more challenging for certain kinds of walkers or wheelchairs. The guidelines also state that the trail must feature a clear width of 36 inches or a minimum of 32 inches under certain exceptions. If the trail is narrower than this, passing spaces must be provided.

Accessible trails are allowed to have a slope (grade) of up to 5 percent for any distance, but those with grades above 5 percent must adhere to maximum segment lengths before a resting "interval" of 5 percent grade or less is provided. For example, if the grade of a segment of trail falls between 8.33 percent and 10 percent, there must be a resting interval at least every 30 feet. Accessible trails should not exceed a 12 percent grade at any point and similar guidelines are provided for passing areas and trail intersections. An excessive cross slope can present significant challenges for those in wheelchairs as well as pedestrians and the guidelines state that cross slope cannot exceed 2 percent, except on unpaved trails where drainage is required.

Obstacles on unpaved trail tread, such as rocks or roots, should not be taller than two inches at the highest point. On paved paths, offset sections should not be more than half an inch higher than the surrounding pavement, and openings in the trail surface, such as between boards on a boardwalk or between sections of concrete paving, should be a maximum of half an inch wide.[4]

Trailhead facilities and signage guidelines are also provided. For example, these guidelines state that signs should include, at a minimum, the length of the trail or trail segment; the trail tread surface type; the typical and minimum trail width; the typical and maximum trail slope; and the typical and maximum cross slope.[5] I have rarely seen trail signs that contain all this information, but some of it is occasionally available online. Other guidelines cover parking, gates and barriers, and restroom facilities.

Bear in mind, not all trails are required to adhere to these guidelines, as land management organizations can apply for exemptions for a variety of reasons, so always do your research on actual trail conditions before heading out.

The High Point Greenway near University Park (left) and the riverfront section of the River Run Trail at New River State Park (right) would likely both be accessible to almost any hiker, even though they are quite different. Both are at least 36 inches wide with a firm trail tread, slopes of less than 5 percent, minimal cross slope, and obstacles less than two inches tall.

Adaptive Hiking Equipment and Programs

Thankfully, more adaptive hiking equipment is becoming available. One example is the GRIT Freedom Chair, an all-terrain wheelchair developed by MIT engineers that involves using levers to propel the chair rather than grabbing onto the wheels directly.

These wheelchairs are ready and waiting for hikers at Reed Gold Mine Historic Site. They are especially designed to travel the trail that visits the underground mine.

Another example is the Joëlette Adventure chair that allows a disabled person to go hiking with two guides who help support the chair. Yet another example is the FreeWheel Wheelchair Attachment that can attach to the footrest of a typical wheelchair and turn it into a three-wheeled, all-terrain vehicle.

More adaptive hiking programs are also being started within the state. For example, Catalyst Sports utilizes these types of equipment (and others) alongside trained volunteer support to offer a variety of adaptive outdoor activities, including hiking. We'll discuss their partnership with Great Smoky Mountains National Park later in Part III. Waypoint Adventure NC, based in Black Mountain, offers adaptive hiking programs as well as adaptive hiking equipment rental. The North Carolina Wildlife Resources Commission offers eight Action Trackchairs (another type of all-terrain wheelchair) for use at locations across the state, free of charge,[6] and Mecklenburg County Parks and Recreation has five all-terrain wheelchairs available at various locations across the county.[7]

How Else Might a Trail Be Accessible ... or Not?

In addition to the elements discussed above related to physical accessibility, what other aspects of a trail might make it more or less accessible for someone with cognitive, emotional, or sensory accessibility needs? Again, this all depends on the specific needs of each hiker. If a hiker is particularly sun or light sensitive, a trail with lots of open spaces and little tree cover might not be accessible for them. A trail that stays close to roadways might not be enjoyable for someone with autism or other sound sensitivities if the road noise is loud. Someone with significant anxiety may wish to hike on a trail that is shorter and stays relatively close to their car. Someone with a cognitive disability might benefit from especially clear signage.

These types of accessibility features are often not covered by published guidelines or included in hiking guidebooks, unfortunately. Doing your research is especially important if you or someone you know has these types of accessibility needs. Read as many trail reviews as you can, from multiple sources; look at lots of pictures, including those that go beyond the typical view, waterfall, or wildflower field that most people highlight online; and if you plan to participate in a group hike, ask lots of questions of the leader until you get the information you need.

Sometimes, even doing the kind of research and planning needed to go on a safe hike can create an accessibility barrier. For some people, the work required to plan a hike, gather the needed gear, get out the door and drive to the trailhead might require so much of their energy reserves that they have nothing left for the hike itself. If you know someone who fits this category but might like to go on a hike, offer to do some of the planning with them or to give them a ride. If you are planning to hike with someone who has different accessibility needs than your own, don't assume what their needs might be. Ask them. They are the experts in their own body, brain and experience.

Transportation to Trails

Reaching the trailhead can present accessibility challenges, especially if you don't drive. Riding with friends or carpooling with other members of a hiking group might be an option. I have also known hikers that have used Uber and Lyft to get to and from a hiking location. Thankfully, more communities and transportation providers are starting to recognize the importance of access to green spaces, and public transportation options are popping up in some places as well. For example, in the Piedmont region, Ride the Triad has provided a Transit to Trails map that gives information on public transportation routes that lead to various hiking locations across the region.[8] A company in Asheville, Loyal Lifts, offers transportation to local accessible hiking locations (and other points of interest) alongside their offerings of transportation to medical appointments and other needs.[9]

Finding Information About Accessible Trail Options

As with other terms used when describing trails, don't assume a description of "accessible" to be accurate, especially when given as a part of user-generated trail data. Always do your research to verify trail conditions and determine the suitability of a specific hike for your needs. Carefully consider any trail recommended as "accessible" or (especially) "wheelchair friendly" or "mobility aid friendly" before heading out. For example, AllTrails recommends the Dry Falls Trail as one of its "Best Wheelchair Friendly Trails in Nantahala National Forest." Sure, this trail is short and paved and has accessible parking. But the only truly "wheelchair friendly" portion of the trail is the first 250 feet to the viewing platform. While this provides a lovely view of the falls, it is far from the majority of the trail. The remainder of the trail that travels behind the falls—the views shown in almost every image online of this trail—involves quite a few stairs and slopes up to 17 percent grade, not to mention quite slippery pavement due to spray from the falls. A beautiful location, but certainly not very wheelchair friendly beyond the first five-hundredths of a mile, or even very friendly for any hiker with stability challenges of any variety, even if they don't use a wheelchair.

AllTrails is starting to list some accessibility information for well-known trails, but this is far from being offered for every trail in the app. The TrailLink app also features some accessibility information for some trails. North Carolina State Parks makes available downloadable information that highlights some of the accessibility features of each state park, including trails.[10] A list of accessible trails near the Blue Ridge Parkway can also be found online,[11] and the North Carolina Department of Natural and Cultural Resources provides accessibility information for attractions across the state, including those locations that host trails.[12] Catalyst Sports will soon be launching their accessible trails assessment project, the focus of which is to collect trail information and make it available to the public. The Trail Access Project maintains a list of accessible hiking trails by state.[13] They only have one North Carolina trail currently listed but are looking for volunteers to evaluate and submit trails for inclusion in their list. They offer training on their website on how to evaluate a trail.[14] Even just Googling your location and "accessible trails" can lead to some good suggestions from organizations and individual hiking bloggers.

As mentioned before, most accessibility information resources focus on physical accessibility. Very, very few offer any information related to hiking trails and developmental disabilities such as autism, mental health considerations or sense-based disabilities such as visual impairment or hearing difficulties. Hopefully all kinds of trail accessibility information will start becoming more available and more accessible trails will be developed. If hikers let trail-building organizations and local and state governments know that we value these types of trails, we can help make North Carolina's natural spaces welcoming for all.

6

The 10 Essentials

The list of potential hiking gear to purchase is a long one, and while checking it all out can be fun and exciting, you may find it intimidating when you're trying to decide how to spend your money. What do you really need? What products are worth spending extra money to buy the best available? First and foremost, know that you *do not* have to go out and buy a bunch of new stuff to start day hiking. You likely already have many of the things you need, and some gear can be purchased second-hand. As you spend more time hiking, you'll discover what gear you might like to upgrade and what you're happy with as-is.

The 10 Essentials

When considering hiking gear, the 10 Essentials is a great place to start. Most people would agree that you should carry these 10 items, or categories of items, whenever you hit the trail. The 10 Essentials are typically given as a version of the following (in no particular order):

1. A way to navigate
2. A headlamp
3. Sun protection
4. First aid kit
5. A knife and a repair kit
6. A way to start a fire
7. A form of shelter
8. Extra food
9. Extra water
10. Extra clothes

This list assumes the possibility that you might end up needing to spend a night (or more) in the wilderness. You may think you don't really need to worry about this happening when completing hikes like the ones we're discussing in this book. Truth be told, this is a possibility on *any* hike and hikers have gotten lost or injured on short, popular trails. We often assume that someone will just be a phone call away to rescue us if we get in trouble. The availability of search and rescue personnel depends on everything from staffing levels to the number of other calls that have come in. And the amount of time someone may need to get to you can change based on the weather, the length of the trail you're on and the ruggedness of the terrain. As hikers we need to, as much as possible, take responsibility for ourselves and be as prepared as possible.

In this chapter we'll discuss items that fall under the 10 Essentials and in the next we'll cover some other items that go beyond these—items that might enhance your safety and enjoyment while hiking and that might feel essential to you depending on your hiking needs.

You may feel like I'm suggesting you carry lots of stuff, way more than you usually see people carrying while they hike. When it comes to hiking, a certain amount of "be ready for anything" is important. Doing so can help keep you safe in most situations, at least until someone with more resources and training is able to reach you. Surprisingly, carrying all this doesn't have to weigh much. Everything I mention in this chapter and the next, I carry in my pack, seen here, on all my hikes. The amount and types of food I carry and the extra clothing I pack changes based on the season and hike location, but everything else is in my pack every single time. And my pack usually weighs seven pounds or so.

Is it necessary to carry all we're going to discuss if you are hiking on a trail in a smaller county park surrounded by neighborhoods, frequented by other people and with strong cell service? Probably not all of it. But you should at least run through the list every time you hike to make sure you're prepared for conditions expected and unexpected. Also, you should practice using your gear before you carry it on a hike. You don't want to get out on the trail and suddenly realize you don't know how something works.

Water

Staying hydrated while hiking is very important, regardless of the time of year. Dehydration can not only make you feel miserable but can also become dangerous quickly; dehydration and exposure to the elements are the two things that most frequently get hikers in trouble, especially when a hike doesn't go as planned.

Dehydration

The level of dehydration you experience will depend on how much fluid you've lost compared to how much you're taking in. Mild dehydration can present as thirst, headache, muscle cramps, dry and cool skin, dry mouth, a decrease in urination or a darker yellow color to the urine. There isn't one particular type of headache that can signal dehydration, but as you hike more, you'll probably learn your body better and what your particular "dehydration headache" feels like. Signs of severe dehydration can include irritability and confusion, rapid breathing or a rapid heart rate, listlessness or lethargy, dizziness or lightheadedness and a lack of urine or very dark or amber-colored urine. Severe dehydration is a life-threatening emergency, and you should seek medical help as quickly as possible.[1]

Carrying Water

The trick to not getting dehydrated is to start off your hike well hydrated and to stay that way by carrying plenty of water with you and making sure you drink it. Reusable water bottles are preferable, but if you must carry single-use water bottles, be sure to properly dispose of your used ones. I prefer the 14-ounce Nalgene bottles that are available at REI, and I carry several with me rather than one large water bottle. That way, one bottle stays in an outside pocket on my pack, but the others are carried in my pack which can help them stay cooler on a hot day rather than all my water heating up as it's exposed to the sun.

While certainly not required to hike safely—water bottles will do that just fine—using a hydration bladder that fits into your pack can be an ideal way to carry water. I do find that I drink more water when I use my hydration bladder. The mouthpiece for it attaches to the chest strap of my backpack, so taking sips as I hike is super easy. Using the bladder means that I don't have to stop and take off my pack to retrieve and put away water bottles every time I want a drink. If I'm going on a longer hike or the weather is particularly hot, I will use both my hydration bladder and my water bottles. However you carry it, the most important thing is that you actually drink the water. So do whatever you need to do to make sure this happens. Some people dislike the taste of plain water. If that's you, feel free to mix some flavored drink mix in. You're still drinking water! If having a warm drink available during the winter would make you more likely to drink it, make some hot tea and carry it in a thermos. For a longer hike make sure to include some electrolyte drinks or packets like Propel or Liquid IV to add to your water, especially if you'll be sweating. You lose minerals, not just water, when you sweat, and you need to replace those as well.

Drinking Water Safety

As a day hiker sticking to lower mileage trails, you can probably carry enough water if you plan well. But if you will be hiking for longer mileage, especially on a hot day, know if there are potable water sources along the way for refills. If there are not any, then know about water sources you'll have to treat and know how to treat that water, a skill that is beyond the scope of this book. Unless you have no other option and you know you're getting dangerously dehydrated, do not drink untreated water. All sorts of unpleasant consequence can occur if you do. If you have no other choice but to drink untreated water rather than becoming severely dehydrated, drink from fast-flowing, cold sources rather than still or stagnant water, and pour the water through a bandana or shirt to help filter out larger debris. One last little trick: Leave a small cooler with some extra waters or electrolyte drinks in your car. There's nothing better than knowing you have a nice cold drink waiting for you when you finish your hike!

Food Appropriate for the Length and Difficulty of the Hike

You don't have to talk to too many hikers before the subject of their favorite hiking snack or meal comes up. Appropriate fuel, i.e., food, is an important consideration even for short day hikes. You shouldn't be thinking about cutting back on your food consumption when you're hiking, even if you're hitting the trail for a shorter period. Your body needs energy for the physical and mental work of hiking, and you want to avoid the dreaded "bonk."

Bonking can also be referred to as "hitting the wall" or when your "wheels fall off." How do you know if you're bonking? Your pace slows down considerably, or you feel the need to stop altogether, and this is often a sudden and significant change. You might feel ravenous or nauseous, get a headache or feel shaky. You might suddenly not care at all about a hike that you were really excited about just moments before, or you might get irritable—"hangry," if you will.

There is an actual physiological cause for bonking. When we start a hike, we usually have a certain amount of fuel in our bodies. For most people, this stored fuel will last you about two hours—your mileage may vary on this timeframe depending on *many* factors. If you don't replenish this fuel as it gets used up on your hike, it will run out and you will start to feel terrible. When this happens, you have officially bonked.

Preventing this is better than trying to treat it. If you start a hike in the morning, eat a good meal the night before and eat something an hour or two before you start your hike. Then plan on eating something of *at least* 200 calories for every hour that you hike.

Again, the amount you need can vary depending on your body and the difficulty of your hike. Remember, "difficulty" means how difficult it feels to *you*. Ideally the calories you consume should be a mixture of carbs, fats and protein, as this combination will help sustain steady blood sugar and glycogen levels rather than creating a "spike and crash" situation.[2]

Another thing to consider is what you'll actually like to eat while you're hiking. This can take a bit of trial and error. You might find that some of your favorite snacks are not appealing while you hike. For some reason things just taste different. Try packing a few bites of several different things to try out along the trail to figure out your favorites. You might even find that there are foods that you only like when you're hiking! Of course, stay away from anything that you know you are sensitive or allergic to. A hike is not a good time to try a new food.

Lastly, think about ease of transport. For example, beware of things that might melt; yes, unfortunately, chocolate is usually included. Soft cheeses sometimes don't fare well, but harder cheeses can. Many people prefer to make wraps rather than sandwiches as tortillas generally hold up better than most sandwich breads when stuffed into a backpack. Nuts and many types of bars pack well. Fruits that don't easily bruise or squish are a good pick. Many people prefer Pringles-type chips over bagged chips because they are less likely to get crushed. Again, try out a few things over some hikes and see what you like and what holds up best.

What should you do if, despite everything, you start to bonk? First, stop and rest for a few minutes. Immediately eat and drink something. If the full bonk feeling comes on suddenly, try to consume at least 300 calories in an easily digestible form as quickly as possible without upsetting your stomach. A full-sugar (not "zero" or "diet") sport drink like Gatorade or Powerade can be good for this, and some hikers carry energy gels, gummies or "jellybeans" in their first aid kits for this very situation. Once you've been able to stop the bonk, concentrate on eating at least 200 calories for every hour you hike to prevent it from returning.[3] If you find that the feeling keeps returning despite your efforts, it's probably time to head back to your car. If you have any medical conditions that impact your body's ability to regulate your blood sugar levels, such as diabetes or hypoglycemia, you will want to be especially careful about this. Pack more snacks and drinks than you think you'll need for the length of the hike and do whatever you need to remember to eat them. If you live with either of these, even if you don't check your blood sugar levels regularly, carrying a glucose monitor when you hike and checking if you start feeling any symptoms at all is a good idea. "Eating food in cooler places" is not only one of the fun parts about hiking but it is also important for safety and health. So don't forget to pack those snacks!

Taking Care of Your Feet

The feet are the primary point of contact with the trail for most hikers, so what you put on your feet when you hike is important and not only impacts your comfort but your safety as well. Inappropriate footwear is a leading cause of hiker injuries that require search and rescue extraction each year. While you do not have to run out and buy new, hiking-specific clothes, especially as you get started you do want to pay some special attention to what you wear on your feet.

Hiking Shoes

When I first started hiking regularly, I was wearing the athletic shoes I wore to Zumba class. Bad idea, as these shoes had essentially no tread. I went on one hike not long after a rain and came to a point in the trail that involved walking down some tall, rock steps. These smooth-bottomed shoes made me feel like I was standing on ice. After slipping a couple of times, I headed back to my car and decided, "I'm going to have to get some better shoes for this."

Not long after, I was the proud owner of my first pair of trail runners for hiking. And my wallet was a good bit lighter. Good hiking shoes bought new are not inexpensive, but if you are going to invest in any gear, I would suggest making it good shoes and good quality hiking socks. They will be worth what you pay for them. My first pair of hiking-specific shoes lasted hundreds of miles before I finally replaced them. Most hiking footwear companies have recommended distances after which you should replace your shoes, and you can readily find this information on Google. I've seen anything from 300 to 1,000 miles.

Where you buy your shoes can matter as well. If possible, buy your shoes in person, rather than online, especially when buying your first pair. Also, getting your shoes from a store where staff can help you find the right fit can be beneficial. For example, I have had good luck buying shoes from knowledgeable staff at more than one REI store and I bought my first pair of shoes at Footsloggers in Boone. (They also have stores in Blowing Rock, West Jefferson, and Banner Elk.) Shop for hiking shoes at the end of the day, as your feet will be a little swollen. This will better mimic your feet as you hike, as they *will* swell, especially in warmer weather. Also wear a thicker pair of socks when trying on hiking footwear, all the better if it's a pair of hiking socks that you plan to wear with the shoes. Many people buy hiking shoes that are a half to a full size above their street shoes to leave plenty of toe room.

Take time to try on different kinds of hiking shoes. Some people swear by hiking boots. Lots of people prefer trail runners instead. Hiking boots tend to have more ankle support and foot protection. They also tend to be sturdier and more durable. Hiking boots are also warmer for colder weather hiking and handle water, mud, and snow better. But hiking boots are heavier. Trail runners are lighter and tend to not need to be broken in like hiking boots do. They also are more breathable which helps to keep your feet cooler in hot-weather hiking. There are pros and cons to all kinds of hiking footwear, and a good outdoor outfitter can help you think through all the options and how they match you as a hiker.[4]

Even the lacing of your hiking shoes can make a difference in how your feet feel as you hike. Some hiking shoes have easily adjustable, elastic no-tie shoelaces rather than traditional laces. These can be helpful because they prevent your shoes from coming untied and allow you to easily tighten and loosen the no-tie laces as you hike. For traditional laces, different lacing patterns can support your feet in different ways or address foot movement within your shoes. Don't be afraid to try something different if you feel like you need to dial in the fit of your shoes.

In certain situations, a pair of athletic shoes with a good tread can work well, especially while you're learning what kind of hiker you are and what your shoe needs might be. Even athletic sandals can be okay; some styles of these might not be ideal for hiking, however, as their open-toe design leaves your toes vulnerable to injury from stubbing them against roots and rocks. Also, do not wear anything with a slick bottom and Crocs (yes, even in sport mode) and flip flops are a definite no-go. Appropriate shoes definitely contribute to your safety; I have seen more than one hiker slip and fall while wearing shoes that did not match the conditions.

Hiking Socks

Shoes tend to get the most attention, but socks can have just as much impact on how comfortably you hike. You can spend well over $100 on amazing hiking shoes, but your feet will still be miserable if you wear bad socks. The right socks can help cushion your footfall, keep your feet warm or cool and dry, and help prevent blisters.

When it comes to hiking socks, you should avoid cotton, instead choosing wool—typically Merino wool—or a synthetic fabric. Next, consider cushioning levels, which can range from none to heavy cushioning. The cushioning can also come in different patterns ranging from extra cushioning just under the heel and ball of the foot to all-over cushioning. The type of cushioning you prefer will likely change based on the weather, as extra cushioning also provides extra insulation for your feet. Sock length is another important consideration. Knee-high socks are available for hiking, but generally these won't be needed for the kind of hiking we're talking about in this book or for the types of trails or typical weather in most of North Carolina. Crew length is what's often pictured when talking about hiking socks. They can be worn with boots or trail runners and help protect your ankles from friction from your shoes. Generally no-show and ankle-length socks are best only for wearing with trail runners, not hiking boots. They don't offer as much protection, but they are cooler in warm weather. Lastly, make sure you pick the right size sock. Yes, it does matter! You want the socks to be snug but not too tight and you want the heel to fit well. Also consider purchasing no-seam socks, as then you don't have to worry about the seams creating fiction against your foot.[5]

Footcare

While appropriate footwear is important, the best hiking shoes and socks in the world won't make up for poor footcare. First, it may seem like a little thing, but take the time to cut your toenails before you hike. Long toenails can push up against your shoes, especially on downhill stretches of trail, causing discomfort and damage to the nail. Repeated damage to a nail can even cause it to fall off. Long nails can also cut into neighboring toes and damage socks. Do not cut your nails too short, however. Nails that are the appropriate length can help protect the ends of your toes and nails that are too short can become ingrown.

Good footcare continues while you're on the trail too. First, be on the lookout for hot spots—red, tender areas on the skin that appear just before a blister forms. If you begin to feel a hot spot, stop as soon as possible and treat the spot by covering it with Leukotape P. Leukotape P is a rigid, sticky medical tape that is breathable and stays put even when wet. The tape's cloth exterior absorbs the friction between your skin and nearby surfaces while also keeping the skin from stretching and moving as this movement and friction combined can lead to blisters. One note: Leukotape P does contain natural rubber, so if you're allergic to rubber or latex you'll want to avoid this product.

You can help prevent hot spots from forming by keeping your feet dry, as blisters form most easily in moist conditions. If you stop for a break, take off your shoes and socks and let your feet dry out. Also try to elevate your legs during breaks to reduce foot swelling. If your feet get wet, say, during a creek crossing or from sweat, change your socks as soon as possible. Remove any debris from your shoes as soon as you feel it. Even a tiny pebble can create friction that can lead to a blister.

Appropriate Clothing

The biggest consideration for clothes as you're getting started is dressing for the weather, rather than having a specific kind of clothes. Appropriate clothing not only helps you have a more comfortable hike but is also a safety consideration.

Picking Your Clothes

The trick to dressing for the weather, especially colder weather, is layering. In cold weather (or even warmer weather that is cloudy, rainy and windy) your goal is to stay warm *without* overheating and sweating through your layers. I have hiked in short sleeves in February in the mountains because it was a nice, sunny day on a trail without many trees and with lots of hills; I knew I would quickly get warm, even if I started out a little cold. In fact, when hiking in winter, starting out a bit cold to allow for the natural warming up that will occur as you move can be a good strategy. Often in conditions like this, however, as soon as you stop hiking even for a short break, or the sun goes behind the clouds, you will cool off, so be prepared with a warmer layer to put on when this happens.

Clothing layers typically, especially in colder weather, include a base layer, a mid-layer and an outer layer. The base layer wicks moisture away from your body to keep you warm and dry, and it often fits snuggly. The mid-layer provides insulation to help you retain body heat. This is where you often see puffy jackets or fleece. Ideally these items are quick-drying and lightweight. Your outer layer protects you from the elements and is usually waterproof, windproof and durable.

You'll want to avoid cotton clothing, if possible, especially in the winter and especially for longer hikes; you'll notice that a lot of outdoor and hiking-specific clothing does not contain it. Cotton does not wick moisture away from your skin the way wool or some synthetic fibers can. This keeps you cold and does not provide enough insulation. Cotton can work in the summer—although many don't even wear it then— to help you stay cool, but if you are in a location that will cool off late in the day even in the summer, you'll likely still want to avoid it so you don't cool off too quickly. We'll talk later about how clothing choice can help with sun protection and bugs but remember that long pants and long sleeves, even in the summer, can also help protect you from poison ivy and scratches from branches and thorns if you're hiking on a trail that is overgrown.

Lastly, don't forget that clothing includes things like gloves, hats, scarves, buffs, and balaclavas. Warm headwear and gloves are essential in the winter but may be needed other times of the year as well. Keeping your head and hands warm are keys to keeping everything else warm.

Hypothermia

Poison ivy leaflets are always arranged in groups of three, with the middle leaflet having a longer stalk than the other two. The edges of the leaflets can be smooth or have a few big "teeth," as opposed to the multiple smaller "teeth" that are seen on plants that can look similar. The plant can be shiny from the oil it produces, and the vine is typically hairy and can grow up to four inches in diameter. The oil produced from the plant causes skin irritation in humans; if it is washed off with water and oil-degrading soap within a few hours of exposure the reaction can often be minimized. While the plant can cause lots of problems for people and should be avoided, a variety of insects and animals can eat or live among all parts of poison ivy.

The core body temperature for most of us hovers somewhere around 98.6 degrees Fahrenheit. When our temperature drops below this level, especially as it approaches 95 degrees or lower, we are at risk of hypothermia. Hypothermia can be deadly, and it doesn't just occur in frigid temperatures. Hypothermia can occur even if the temperature is well above freezing and in any season. For example, getting wet from a rainstorm or a fall in cold water, especially when it's windy, can quickly lead to becoming too cold. Symptoms of early hypothermia include shivering, clumsiness and slurred speech and can then progress to drowsiness, very low energy, and confusion. If the hypothermia isn't treated, symptoms such as shallow breathing, a weak pulse and loss of consciousness develop that can lead to death.[6] A drop in our core temperature decreases our brain's metabolic rate, so many symptoms of hypothermia are behavioral in nature. For example, if a person's temperature drops to 85 degrees—severe hypothermia—they can experience a perceived "hot flash" and begin to undress.[7]

Some people are more susceptible to hypothermia than others, but everyone can fall victim to it. In order to prevent hypothermia, dress in layers as we discussed before. Finding the right mix of layers for yourself will probably require a bit of trial and error and you should be prepared for multiple stops as you hike to put on and remove clothing. Be sure to remove extra layers *before* you start sweating; if you sweat through those warmest layers they will then be wet, greatly decreasing their ability to keep you warm when you need them again. Be careful when wearing waterproof layers as these can cause you to sweat more, even in cold weather. If there is any chance you could get wet while hiking, pack an extra set of clothes. Also be sure you hike well hydrated and nourished as these help with body temperature regulation.

A Way to Navigate (and Another Way to Navigate)

In the "Do Your Research" chapter, we discussed the importance of getting trail information from a number of sources. The same advice holds true when navigating while on the trail: don't rely on just one source for navigation. When it comes to essential hiking gear, redundancy is often a good idea, so consider carrying at least two ways to navigate when hiking, especially when hiking in a new area.

Electronic Navigation Tools

Most hikers now use some kind of electronic navigation, typically in the form of an app. Some hiking apps include:

- AllTrails
- Avenza Maps
- FarOut Guides
- Footpath Route Planner
- Gaia GPS
- HiiKER (double i is not a mistake!)
- Hiking Project
- TrailLink
- Wikiloc Outdoor Navigation GPS

Many are available and new ones are being developed all the time. If you try out multiple hiking apps, you'll find that many of them contain the same basic information but with slightly different areas of focus or ways of presenting the data. Many also offer free and upgraded (paid) levels of information and navigation abilities.

For example, as was discussed earlier, AllTrails is the go-to app for many day hikers. AllTrails has both free and paid "premium" versions. The paid version allows for downloading of maps for offline use, which can be nice when you don't have a good cell phone signal. You must download their maps when you have cell signal or WIFI, but your phone's internal GPS will work for tracking you on those maps even when you don't have signal or are in airplane mode. Gaia GPS is another navigation app that has a free version but has much more information in the paid version. Gaia GPS has some of the most detailed maps available in an app, but it's also geared more toward backpacking and long-distance hiking, and the amount of information can be a bit overwhelming, especially in the paid version. Hiking Project also offers a place to find potential hikes and a way to navigate while on the trail. It allows for downloading of maps for offline use without a paid subscription—in fact, they don't even offer a paid version. Some might find it a little less user-friendly than AllTrails, however. TrailLink is powered by the Rails-to-Trails Conservancy and focuses mostly on greenways and rail trails, rather than single-track, natural surface hiking trails. I would encourage you to try out many different tracking and navigation apps and then decide which, if any, you wish to upgrade. (Look for sales, too! Many apps will run sales on their premium subscriptions around holidays.)

Some people also rely on their smart watches, hiking-specific smart watches, or GPS devices like certain versions of the Garmin InReach for navigation support. Almost all have some level of payment required to use their services, not to mention the cost of the device itself. You might decide to invest in one of these options if you find yourself doing a lot of hiking and you want to track your hikes more precisely (distance, elevation, time, etc.), if you routinely hike in very remote locations, or if you get into multi-day backpacking.

Paper Maps and a Compass

All of the above are good tools that can help you navigate safely on the trail, but they have their downfalls as well. They have batteries that can run down. Some of their functions might not be available if you don't have cell signal, especially if you don't upgrade to the paid version. And some rely on user-submitted data which can be faulty. So that's why I always recommend having another way to navigate that does not depend on a device. In addition to using an app, consider carrying a paper map as well.

While it is true that a paper map will not track your movements in real-time the way an app can, even a basic paper map can help you know where you are on the trail if you're paying attention to the bends and curves of the path and trail intersections as you hike. If you hike in a particular area frequently, investing in a guidebook with maps for that region might be a good idea. (You'll find some of my favorites listed in the additional resources list at the end of this book.) If you're doing longer distance hiking in more remote locations, say, for example, in parts of Great Smoky Mountains National Park, purchasing a complete map for the trails in the area would be a smart move. National Geographic Trails Illustrated Topographic Maps are generally excellent.

You can also often find free maps online that are suitable for printing and carrying along with you. Most state park maps are available, and many cities and counties have maps for trails they maintain available on their Parks and Rec department websites. Googling the trail name and location can often lead you to a map within a couple of pages of results. Visitors' centers of all kinds will often carry brochures that contain some trail maps. You can even sometimes find copies of printed maps available for the taking at trailheads, although I wouldn't count on this as your map source—come prepared with your own copy if at all possible. When I get a new copy of a map, I slide it into a sheet protector and keep it in a three-ring binder. That way I can use it the next time I hike at a location rather than having to print out or track down another copy.

To really get the most out of your paper map, you'll also want to know how to use a compass. If you decide that you want to make hiking a more regular part of your life and especially if you hope to visit some remote locations, it is worth the time and effort to purchase a basic navigation book and learn how to use a map and compass. Some places have local orienteering clubs you can learn from and some outdoors stores, like REI, offer navigation classes. There are even videos to be found on YouTube that can help you learn. Adding this skill to your hiking tools can offer an extra layer of confidence and safety to your outdoor adventures. We'll talk about some basic compass work and the "30–60–90 Walk" a little later in Chapter 8, but this should not replace a full orienteering course.

Sun Protection and Heat Exposure

The results of too much sun and heat exposure can range from unpleasant, such as an uncomfortable sunburn, to dangerous, such as heat-related illnesses (hyperthermia). Long-term inappropriate sun exposure can even lead to skin cancer. Sun protection should be on our minds any time we're outside, in every season, and in every kind of weather.

UV Rays

Some sunlight is good for most of us. Our bodies need sunlight to make Vitamin D, but you can definitely have too much of a good thing when it comes to the sun. Sunlight is made up of three major components. One is the visible light we can see. The second is ultraviolet (UV) light, and the third is infrared radiation, which is what creates the sense of warmth on our skin.[8] The UV rays are what we are protecting ourselves from with sunscreen and other measures. There are three types of ultraviolet rays—UVA, UVB and UVC. The Earth's atmosphere absorbs UVC rays. UVA rays are what can cause aging and wrinkling of our skin over time. UVB rays are what can lead to sunburn and skin cancer, although UVA can also increase the effects of UVB, including those harmful effects that can lead to skin cancer and cataracts.[9] Some factors make you more susceptible to the damaging effects of UV rays and knowing these can help you plan your sun protection accordingly. These risks include having light-colored hair, skin, or eyes; having had multiple sunburns; being over the age of 55 (although skin cancer can occur in anyone of any age); having lots of moles; having previously had skin cancer; and having a weakened immune system, certain inherited conditions, or exposure to certain chemicals.[10]

Three Approaches:
Behaviors, Clothing, and Sunscreen

Sunscreen is what often comes to mind when we think about sun protection, but effective sun protection doesn't only include sunscreen. Sun protective clothing and modifying our outdoor behaviors are also important. First, try to stay in the shade and avoid being out in direct sunlight during the parts of the day when the UV rays are the strongest, generally between 10:00 a.m. and 4:00 p.m. in the United States. A middle-of-the-day hike, in the summer, on a trail that doesn't provide much shade is probably not the best idea. This is where looking at trail reviews and pictures can come in very handy. A shady hike would be a better plan but shouldn't be your only method of sun protection. Your clothing choices also play a big role. Loose-fitting pants and long-sleeved shirts can help you stay cool while also reducing your skin's exposure to harmful UV rays. Your head and ears also need protection, so don't forget a hat. A wide-brimmed hat that protects your face, ears and neck is the best, as is one made of tightly woven material. Our eyes and lips also need protection, so don't forget UV-blocking sunglasses and lip balm with built in UV protection.

Even with these other measures in place, wearing a good sunscreen is still important and understanding SPF is key to picking the right one. "The SPF number tells you how long the sun's UV radiation would take to redden your skin when using the [sunscreen] product *exactly as directed* versus the amount of time without any sunscreen."[11]

For example, if you tend to sunburn quickly, say, within 15 minutes, without any sunscreen, wearing a sunscreen with SPF 30 means it would take 30 times longer for you to burn, or seven and half hours, *under ideal conditions* (such as in a laboratory setting).

But real life doesn't happen in a lab and many factors can impact the effectiveness of your sunscreen. Did you apply it adequately on all exposed skin? Is it water- and sweat-proof? Did you use a broad-spectrum sunscreen that protects against both UVA and UVB rays?[12] In reality, most sunscreens do not maintain their full effectiveness longer than about two hours, and higher SPF numbers can give us a false sense of security about how well our protection is working.

Adequate sun protection includes a broad-spectrum sunscreen of at least SPF 15. This should be applied at least every two hours to all exposed skin as well as to some skin covered by clothing. As a rule of thumb, if you can see light through the fabric of the clothes or hat you're wearing, then some UV rays can reach the skin under that clothing, and you should apply sunscreen in those locations.

These guidelines should be followed even if it's cloudy, even during the winter, and especially if you're going to be hiking on snow or light-colored sand, at a higher elevation or around a lot of water. The myth also exists that people with dark skin tones don't need to worry about sun exposure as much or wear sunscreen. This is simply not true. Melanin, the substance in our bodies that gives our eyes and hair their color and skin its pigmentation, is thought to be about SPF 4, definitely not enough to protect you from sun damage.[13]

Hyperthermia

Damage to our skin isn't the only reason we need to think about sun exposure. In hotter weather we also need to consider our risks for hyperthermia. "Hyperthermia is an abnormally high body temperature caused by a failure of the heat-regulating mechanisms of the body to deal with the heat coming from the environment."[14] Hyperthermia can come in a variety of progressively more serious forms starting with heat fatigue and progressing through heat dizziness, heat cramps, and heat exhaustion to heat stroke. Heat stroke, indicated by symptoms such as strong, rapid pulse, a lack of sweating, combativeness or confusion, and staggering, can be fatal and occurs when a person's body temperature increases substantially, typically higher than 104°F. Some risks factors for heat illness include being dehydrated; overdressing; older age; certain heart, lung and kidney conditions; taking certain medications; being significantly over- or under-weight; and being intoxicated.

If you suspect that you or someone you are hiking with is suffering from heat illness, try to get to a cool location, such as an air-conditioned car or building, as soon as possible. At the very least move into the shade. If possible, apply a cloth dipped in cold water to the neck, wrists, armpits and/or groin. Offer fluids but avoid caffeine, alcohol, or hot liquids. If you suspect heat stroke, call 911 or otherwise contact emergency services.

A Source of Light

When heading out for a hike at 10:00 a.m. on a bright, sunny day, you may not be thinking about making sure you have a source of light with you. Surely the weather will stay perfect, and you'll be back to your car well before dark, right? Hopefully so, but things happen and part of the reason you carry essential gear is for the "just in case" scenarios. According to a November 21, 2024, Facebook post by Great Smoky Mountains National Park, being out after dark without adequate lighting is the number one cause of missing or overdue hikers in the Smokies.

Many situations on a hike can make us reach for a flashlight or other light source. Perhaps the trail takes a bit longer than anticipated. The forest can be much darker, even well before the sun sets, than a more open landscape. If you are hiking in the mountains, dark comes earlier than anticipated if the sun drops behind a surrounding ridge line. Even an especially cloudy day or a bad storm rolling through can make it dark enough in the woods that you'll wish you had a light. Serious unforeseen circumstances such as an injury or getting lost can leave you out on the trail overnight even if help is on the way. If this happens, you'll be thankful for that light source.

Flashlights and Headlamps

Hiking is not the time to rely on your phone's flashlight as your only light source; it is typically not bright enough in these situations. Plan to carry at least one good flashlight or, even better, a headlamp. Having a headlamp as a light source allows your hands to stay free, which can be important if you need to complete other tasks such as build a fire, tend to an injured fellow hiker, use trekking poles, or hike on a more technical trail. If you are using a flashlight or headlamp that requires replaceable batteries, be sure to carry spares. Many hikers today prefer rechargeable headlamps, however, as they tend to be brighter, longer-lasting, lighter, more reliable, and more convenient. I will readily admit that this is one area where I probably overpack for a hike. There is just something about the thought of being stuck out in the woods, for whatever reason, in complete darkness by myself that is really not appealing, so I pack multiple light sources: a small flashlight, two clip-on lights, a headlamp, and a beanie hat with a built-in headlamp. I check each of these before I hike to make sure they are in working order and carry extra batteries for those that use them. If you ever meet me on a trail and are in need of a light, just ask.... I probably have at least three extra! Ha!

Fire

Another source of light is a fire, but of course a fire is so much more than just light. A fire offers heat and comfort as well and can be a lifesaver if you're stuck out in the woods overnight in cooler weather. Being able to warm a beverage over a fire (or with a light-weight camp stove) is a critical way of addressing early-stage hypothermia. (You'll also need to have a metal container such as a cup or a single-wall water bottle to warm up a liquid.) In an emergency you don't have to know how to build the perfect fire for it to be beneficial, but getting one going will be a lot easier if you carry something with which to start a fire. Carrying a simple lighter or waterproof matches can help. If you want to take preparation a step further, pack a fire starter in addition to your lighter or matches. These can be homemade[15] or you can buy premade ones from most stores that sell outdoor or camping gear. Whatever fire-making materials you decide to carry, make sure you practice with them beforehand, multiple times.

Chances are you will never have to use your fire-starting materials, but you'll be very glad to have them if you ever need them.

A Basic First Aid Kit

Even for a shorter hike, carrying at least a basic first aid kit or making sure one person in your group has one is a good idea. Bumps, bruises and scrapes are often just part of the experience of hiking and likely won't need any treatment except perhaps rinsing off with some water from your water bottle. But carrying a small selection of bandages and wraps along with a few other items for more significant cuts, scrapes and other injuries can be very handy.

You can purchase pre-assembled first aid kits in many stores and online. You will want to check the specific supplies included in these to make sure they meet your individual needs and supplement them if necessary. You can also easily assemble a first aid kit yourself. You might find that you already have a lot of the needed items at home. Consider including the following items in your first aid kit[16]:

- Bandages: assorted sizes
- 4x4 sterile dressing pads
- Gauze roll
- Small roll of adhesive medical tape
- Tweezers
- Small scissors
- Safety pins
- Cotton swabs
- Resealable plastic bags
- ACE or other similar bandage
- Topical antibiotic ointment
- Moleskin and Leukotape P
- Small packets or bottle of aloe vera gel
- OTC medications: pain relievers (aspirin, acetaminophen and ibuprofen); antihistamines; Imodium; antacid tablets
- Hydrocortisone cream
- Nitrile gloves (better than latex as some are allergic to latex)
- Electrolyte drink powder that can be mixed with water

Some people are sensitive to antibiotic ointments, and honey can serve the same purpose, so consider throwing some single-serve packets in your kit as well. (They can also be good for delivering energy very quickly.) Lastly, don't forget to check the supplies in your first aid kit frequently to see if anything needs to be replenished. I've only had to break out my first aid kit on a couple of occasions in all my hiking excursions, but I still carry an extensive kit (what's listed above and more) every time I hike alone or with a group. These are the kinds of things that, when you need them, you *really* need them, and you'll regret not having them. And remember, you shouldn't carry anything in this kit that you aren't comfortable with and willing to use on yourself or on another hiker.

Over-the-counter medications are mentioned above, but don't forget any prescription medications you might need too. Do you have conditions for which you have

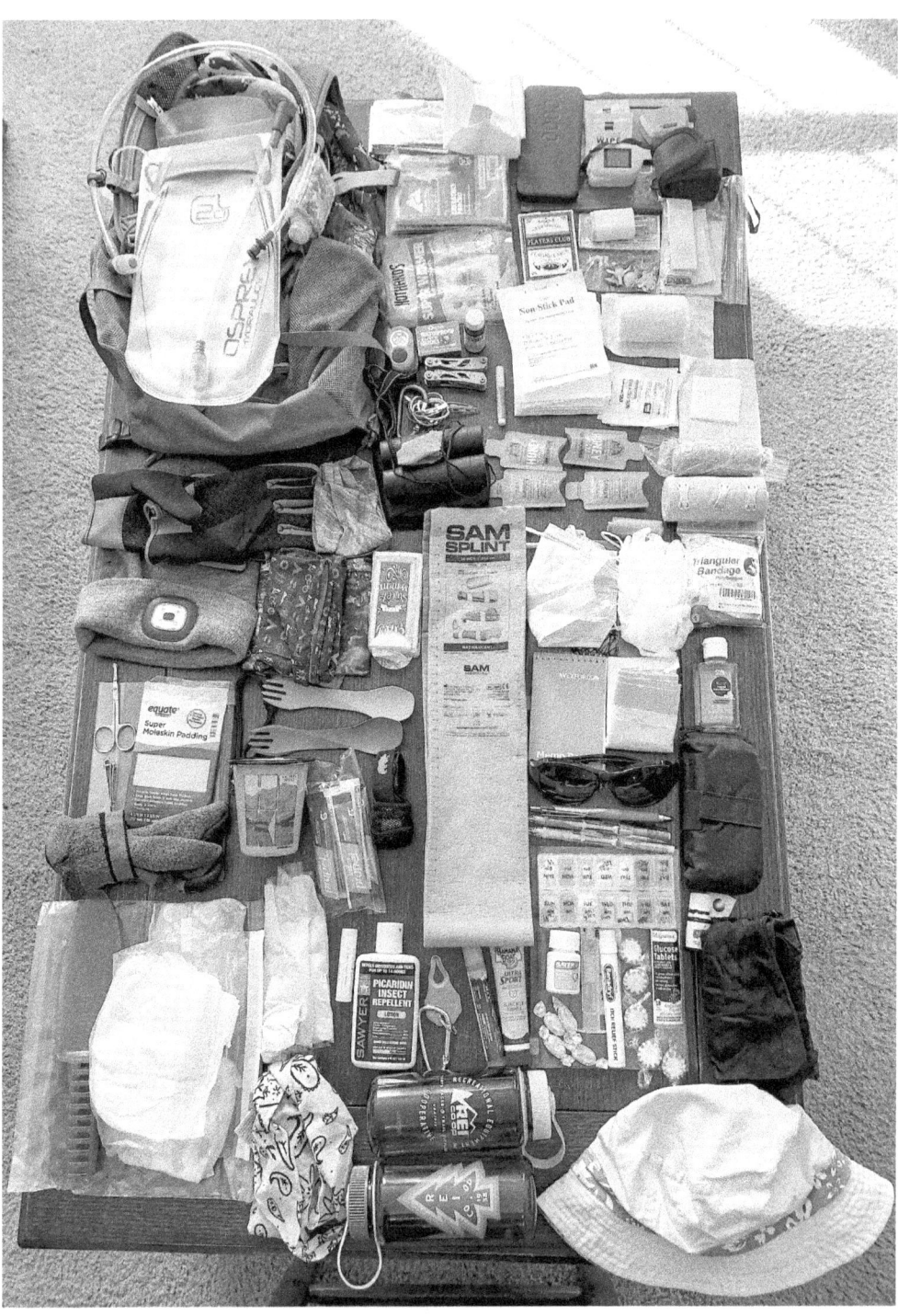

Here you see the gear I typically carry on hikes. Some items are switched out based on the weather (for example, the beanie and gloves for the summer hat) and some of the first aid items I carry are based on the wilderness first responder training I've received, so you might not need or want to carry all these items. You should be able to spot the 10 essentials here, however.

"rescue" medications? If so, carrying these with you is always a good idea, even if you use them infrequently. Hiking puts your body into situations and under stress that it's not used to which might trigger reactions you wouldn't normally experience even with other kinds of physical activity. Carry migraine medications and rescue inhalers. If you have any kind of allergy that requires an EpiPen, carry it and some Benadryl. If you have diabetes and take insulin, talk to your healthcare provider about if you should carry it while hiking and within what temperature range it should be kept. Also, carry your glucose meter and some glucose tablets. Do you have medications for panic attacks? Carrying those with you would be good as well. For day hikes you generally wouldn't need to carry any daily medications *unless* you have medications you have to take at a certain time of day and there is a chance you might get delayed and miss your dosage time.

Consider wearing a medical alert bracelet if you have ongoing health concerns, especially if you hike alone. If you were found unresponsive, how would someone know what could be wrong with you? First responders are taught to search through your gear for potential answers in these situations, so make finding those answers easy for them. Consider carrying a medical card and emergency contact information in an easy to locate section of your backpack or in your wallet. I would recommend something like what is offered by the company ROAD iD.[17] They offer bracelets of various kinds, ID tags, watch bands and even something that you can wear on your shoelaces that can include your name, emergency contact information and health information. They also offer a service for a yearly fee that will link your bracelet to a portal that can be accessed online and via telephone where you can list much more information about any health or developmental conditions.

The above list would be a great start for shorter day hiking. You would likely want to add to it for a longer trip, one in a very remote location or, especially, any kind of overnight trip.

Other Essential Items

Tarp and Emergency Blanket

Carrying a tent is probably not necessary for the kind of hiking we're discussing here, but carrying *something* that could keep you dry and off the ground if things go wrong is important. A tarp or Tyvek sheeting and some rope can help in this situation[18] and an inexpensive folding foam camping pad could work too. An emergency blanket can also help with staying warm, although it won't really help you in staying off the ground. Quite different from your favorite cozy throw, these blankets, sometimes referred to as "space blankets," are shiny, thin sheets of plastic that you can often find packaged in tightly folded bundles in stores that sell outdoor gear. They are often made of mylar. Yep, the same stuff that's used for balloons!

Emergency blankets are wind- and water-proof so they can help protect you from outside elements. They also keep your sweat from evaporating and their reflective material traps body heat, keeping you from losing the warmth you do have. An emergency blanket and something to keep you off the ground can help prevent hypothermia.

Duct Tape

Duct tape is renowned for its variety of uses (duct tape prom dresses, anyone?) and the same holds true for its many uses on the trail. Duct tape can prove an effective temporary repair in a number of situations ranging from a sole coming away from a shoe to a broken pack strap to damaged glasses. If you don't have moleskin or Leukotape P in your first aid kit, duct tape can even be used to cover hot spots before they turn into blisters. You probably don't want to lug around an entire roll of duct tape, so consider making your own small roll to carry easily in a pack. You can wind some around a small piece of cardboard or a chopstick, or even just a stick you find outside. You can also wrap it around anything plastic and smooth, like your water bottle, a hiking pole or a lighter.

Multi-Tool or Knife

A small multi-tool or a proper knife can help in a number of situations on the trail, but remember, you want to know how to use it safely *before* you carry it on a hike. These are items that can range greatly in price. Take some time to do research before buying one to make sure you're getting what you really need and are comfortable using.

In the next chapter we'll move beyond the 10 Essentials to other items you might wish to carry to make your hiking experience even more enjoyable and safe.

7

Beyond the 10 Essentials

In the last chapter we covered items that would fall under the 10 Essentials list of basic gear for hiking, but you may already have in mind other items that could be needed while out on the trail. Let's discuss a few of them.

Insect and Tick Repellents

Later, in the chapter about wildlife, we'll talk specifically about the arachnids and insects you might encounter while hiking, but trust me, you *will* encounter them. The interactions with some of these, especially ticks, mosquitoes, and other types of biting insects, can not only be annoying during your hike but also leave you itching for days after or worse. There are several things that attract these critters to us including our body heat; carbon dioxide in our breath; chemicals in our sweat; odors from soaps, lotions, and hair care products; and even certain colors and textures of clothing. In fact, a 2022 study found that certain species of mosquitoes were attracted specifically to reds and oranges.[1] Utilizing appropriate topical insect and tick repellents and taking other actions might not completely prevent bugs from bothering us but can help prevent bites and the aftereffects.[2]

The purpose of a good insect or tick repellent is to make you less attractive or less "visible" to these species. There are six kinds of EPA-registered repellents that can be applied to the skin.[3] When used appropriately, these are proven to be safe and effective. It often gets a bad rap, but DEET is the most effective repellent and is truly considered the gold standard when you are going to be in areas with high concentrations of ticks, mosquitoes, and other biting insects or in areas where these are known to transmit disease. Picaridin is another effective repellent ingredient that has been used in other parts of the world for some time and is now available in the United States. Other potential ingredients include oil of lemon eucalyptus (OLE), IR3535, para–Methane-3,8-diol (PMD), and 2-undecanone. You should read the instructions on all of these carefully before using them but in general you want to apply these to exposed skin and clothing but not under clothing. You should not spray them directly on your face but rather into your hands first and then apply to your face. You should not spray repellents on irritated skin or open wounds, in enclosed areas, or near food.[4]

Another type of repellent called Permethrin is intended to be put on clothing and other gear but not on your skin. It works by disrupting the nervous system of insects, which ultimately leads to death. You should consult the application instructions, but typically you can apply Permethrin as a spray or by soaking clothing in a diluted Permethrin bath. You should avoid direct skin contact with treated clothing until the product has dried. You can even treat your socks with Permethrin, but underwear should not be treated. Permethrin lasts much longer than repellents intended for skin application. One application on clothes or gear can last for up to six weeks or six washes, whichever comes first.[5] You can even purchase some clothing items that are pretreated with Permethrin.

In addition to using these products, there are other ways to prevent bites. Wear loose-fitting, long clothing. Some biting insects can bite through tight-fitting clothing, but loose, long-sleeved shirts and pants keep insects from reaching your skin. Consider tucking pant legs into your socks to prevent ticks from being able to crawl up the inside of your pants from the ankles. Avoiding areas with long grasses can help prevent tick bites, and staying away from standing water helps you avoid mosquitoes.

After coming inside, check closely for ticks all over your body, especially in areas that are harder to see, such as under your arms, in and around your hair and ears, behind your knees, and around your waistband.[6] Taking a shower soon after coming in—within two hours—can also be helpful as it's a good time to do a thorough tick check and may help wash off any unattached ticks. Lastly, place any dry clothing you were wearing outdoors in a dryer on high for 10 minutes to kill any tick hitchhikers. If clothing requires washing, wash in hot water and then dry on hot.

Trekking Poles

Trekking poles can be helpful tools for all kinds of hikers. I got a set of trekking poles within my first five hikes and now I rarely hike without them. They have helped me in so many ways that I would recommend them to anyone who is going to hike with any regularity. I use them on all different kinds of trails—flat trails, gravel trails, trails with lots of roots and without, muddy trails, trails with steep hills, trails with creek crossings. And they have helped me in all those situations in different ways. My trekking poles live in the back of my car, so I have them at the ready even for impromptu hiking adventures.

Benefits of Using Trekking Poles

Trekking poles help take some of the load off your knees, ankles and lower body muscles, especially when walking downhill or on level ground. Their use helps distribute the physical work of the hike across the whole body.[7] Using poles on uphill sections of trail has also been shown to reduce forces on the legs and feet by shifting some of the effort to your underworked arms.[8]

Trekking poles also help with balance. When crossing streams, stepping up and over objects, walking on loose rocks or slick mud or ice, trekking poles give you extra points of contact with the ground, providing a more stable foundation.[9] I've also found trekking poles to be great tools for knocking down spiderwebs across trails in early mornings and for moving brambles and other thorny plants out of the way on overgrown trails.

Purchasing Trekking Poles

Trekking poles are a piece of equipment that you can spend lots of money on if you decide you want to. Top-of-the-line varieties can go for almost $300. But you don't

7. Beyond the 10 Essentials

have to spend this kind of money to get a good pair that will serve you well. Good sets can be found for $50–$100 or even less. Truth be told, I bought my trekking poles from Walmart for $20, and I have used them on at least 200 hikes with no issues.

There are some important considerations when purchasing and using trekking poles. First, get poles that are right for your height. When you hold the handles, your elbows should be at 90-degree angles. Some trekking poles are adjustable. This feature can help you get the height just right. You can also shorten the poles by a couple of inches on long uphill sections of trail or lengthen them by the same amount on downhill stretches. Making these changes can help with balance and help keep your body in a more natural, upright position. Having adjustable poles also allows you to collapse them down and easily strap them to a backpack if you don't want to use them all the time but still want them handy. Next, check what tip options come with the poles that might be helpful for your typical hiking locations. For example, some poles come with mud or snow "baskets" that prevent your poles from sinking too far into soggy or snowy conditions. Poles come in different weights as well, and while none are very heavy, there are some that are ultralight if you are concerned about that.

Once you have the right trekking poles selected, make sure you hold them correctly. The image here shows the proper method. Holding poles in this manner means that you don't have to grip them as tightly; a tight grip can tire out your hands and forearms. The proper grip also means that if you let go of your trekking poles, they will dangle from your wrists rather than falling to the ground.[10]

The correct grip for trekking poles. Notice how the hands go up through the straps (left) and then back down to grab the handles and the point where the straps attach to the poles, leaving the strap to cross the heal of the hand and the wrist (right).

Chafing Prevention and Treatment

Chafing can be an unpleasant side effect of hiking and can occur anywhere skin rubs against skin or clothing. The friction created between skin and another surface can create uncomfortable itching or even a painful rash or blistering. Prevention of and treatment for chafing is just as important as preventing and treating blisters on your feet. The key to reducing chafing is to reduce the friction. Where your particular chafing trouble spots are and how you address them is going to be as individual as your body and you might need to use a few different strategies to stay comfortable during your hike.[11]

Pick Your Clothes Wisely

Choosing your hiking clothing wisely is the first way to reduce the chances of chafing. First, pick clothes that fit well. Clothing that is too loose can bunch up and cause friction. On the other hand, seams on clothing that is too tight can dig into your skin and contribute to chafing. You're looking for a Goldilocks fit here—clothing that is snug but not too tight. If you prefer to wear looser fitting pants or shorts, try wearing spandex leggings or shorts or compression underwear under them to help reduce friction. Also don't forget that your underwear is next to your skin and can cause chafing. Consider what style and size of underwear you're wearing too.

Also consider the fabric of your clothing. Natural fibers such as cottons and linens tend to be rougher in texture but, more importantly, they soak up sweat and other moisture and don't dry out easily. This leaves rough, damp material next to your skin which can lead to friction. Choose synthetic fibers such as nylon, polyester or other "technical" fabrics, or blends of these, for your clothing whenever possible, including for your underwear.

Lastly, even if you aren't a person who is usually bothered by tags and seams in clothing, they can irritate your skin and lead to friction when hiking. Consider cutting out tags or finding clothing without tags or rough seams. It's a good idea to try out any hiking clothes you plan to wear on a shorter walk first to see if anything rubs, especially if it's new clothing you've just bought. You can't always feel these potential chafing spots standing in a dressing room or at home. You need to move in your clothes.

Use Anti-Chafing Lubricants

Anti-chafing products can help by adding lubrication to your skin, thus reducing friction. They are best used in areas such as the thighs, groin, armpits, waist, bra line and feet. Apply these products to clean, dry skin and reapply them as needed during your hike as they soak in and wear off. There are many different kinds of anti-chafing lubricants, and you may have to try a few before you find the one that works best for you. Gold Bond sticks and Body Glide generally come highly recommended, but there are other options as well. You're looking for products that are going to help create a barrier between your skin and the skin or fabric with which it's coming into contact. Also, although it may seem counterintuitive, hair can act as a barrier and some hikers don't shave for a while before a longer hike to take advantage of this natural buffer.

Check Your Backpack

If you are going to carry a backpack, adjust it to fit as well as possible. The shoulders and waist are prime spots where a backpack can cause chafing. Much like with your clothes, you're looking for a fit that's neither too tight nor too loose. Extra weight in your pack can also contribute to chafing by causing the straps to dig into your shoulders more.

Take a Break to Address Chafing

Just as you would stop and address blister hot spots on your feet as you hike, you should also stop and address chafing spots when you feel them starting to tingle, itch or hurt. As chafing can be exacerbated by dirt, sand and sweat on the skin, use some skin wipes, or even just water to wash off any areas possible and then take the time to let these areas dry. Reapply anti-chafing lubricants as needed.

Extra Phone Battery

Almost everyone hikes with a cell phone. Some people turn it off completely and only use it in an emergency. But if you're like me, you'll have your phone on and use it as one of your navigational aids and as your camera. Also, not everyone can completely "unplug" when hiking and some people need to be reachable due to their job or even because they serve as a primary caregiver. Not everyone can (or wants to) shut off their phones while they hike and having enough battery life can become very important.

Using an app like AllTrails to track your hike can use up lots of battery, especially if you are in an area with limited cell coverage. This battery loss is magnified if you are using multiple apps that track you at the same time. Temperature can also impact your battery life with both very cold and very hot weather causing a battery to drain faster. If you are hiking in cold weather, make sure to keep your phone in an insulated pocket close to your body. Don't store it in an outside pocket on the back of your pack. Some people will carry a child's mitten and tuck their phone inside to keep it warm. If you are hiking in hot weather, keep your phone out of direct sunlight and away from warm surfaces. Lastly, if you are using your phone as GPS to get to the trailhead, don't forget to plug your phone in as you drive and aim for starting out the hike with 100 percent battery.

Having an extra external battery, also called a power bank, can be helpful in making sure you have enough battery to use your phone in the ways you want and need. First, make sure you get a good one. Lots of different kinds are available, so check out the details before deciding which one to buy. Will it work with your particular phone? Does it come with attached cables for plugging your phone into it, will you have to get a separate cable, or is it wireless? How can you charge the power bank? Can it only be charged by plugging it in, or does it have solar charging capability? How many devices can it charge at once? How many full charges of your device can it handle before it needs to be recharged itself? Read user reviews. Some look great in the description and then you see in the reviews that people found a particular model to be unreliable or found that it charged especially slowly. This is one product where spending a few extra dollars to get a better model is a good idea.

If you see your phone beginning to die and you either (a) don't have an extra battery or (b) you have used up your extra battery too, there are a few things you can do to draw out your battery life at least a little. First, quit using as many apps as possible. If you are using more than one tracking or navigation app, quit all but one. This is also the time to turn off music and quit taking lots of pictures or videos. Next, turn the brightness on your phone way down. You can also go into Location Services/Location Requests on your phone and turn everything off so apps on your phone aren't continuously trying to ping your location. If you have a subscription to any of the navigation apps and have been able to download maps in advance, switch your phone into airplane mode. Lastly, *always* have a charger cable in your car. A dead phone battery could become an issue in trying to get home if you don't already know how to get back from the trailhead location.[12]

A Hiking Journal

A hiking journal can be a fun way to record your memories and a gentle reminder to stop and spend some time noticing what's around you. Some hiking challenges have a journal or record as a part of the experience and those can be great places to start. A simple, small notebook could work just fine. Don't forget something to write with! But how else could you journal? Do you like to draw? Maybe take a small sketchbook and some colored pencils. What about painting? There are lots of travel painting materials available for all kinds of painting. Do you like to write poetry? Great! Maybe carry a book of nature poetry to read and inspire you along with your surroundings. Mary Oliver is a favorite poet of mine that writes a lot about the natural world. Do you like photography? Taking pictures is a great way to journal about a hike. Consider carrying a small notebook or use the notes function in your phone to document the locations of your pictures or even what caught your eye and made you decide to stop. Maybe consider keeping a scrapbook of all your hikes. I've seen hikers carrying ukuleles and small guitars sit down and make up a little tune as they hike. Some people enjoy videography. Really, your creativity is the only limit when it comes to documenting and journaling about your hiking. Whatever works for you is the way to go.

I have enjoyed taking pictures and making "review" posts about each hike on Instagram. In addition to these posts, I have a simple notebook where I keep a written record of all my hikes along with some charts and graphs that show how long my hikes have been, the different places I've hiked, different waterfalls and lakes I've seen, etc. I have also *really* enjoyed using the "Hike Passport" journal available through Letterfolk. Each journal has space for information about 20 hikes and asks prompt questions such as your favorite moment, who you hiked with, and even what snacks you took on the hike. There's also a place to tape or draw a picture.

I would encourage you to do two types of journaling when it comes to hiking. First, I would encourage you to do some kind of journaling *while* you are hiking. Sometimes while hiking an insight strikes us, or a particular experience impacts us in a way that we think we'll never forget. Occasionally that's true, but often, even just a few hours later, remembering that thing that seemed so important and worth remembering in the moment is hard. When those moments of inspiration come, take a few minutes of rest to record them. There is something about recording an observation in the moment that gives it power when read later.

On the other hand, I would also encourage you to journal about your hiking experiences after the fact. Sometimes our brains "chew" on an experience for a while and we suddenly see something more clearly or see trends in our experiences over time. Your hiking journal can be as simple or as elaborate as you wish, but I would encourage you to keep one. When I journal it helps my hiking feel more transformational and relational rather than transactional and just something to check off my list.

Extra Health and Safety Items

Bandana

A good ol' bandana can serve a variety of purposes on a hike, and it takes up next to no space in your pack. You can easily find bandanas at Walmart or Target or even sometimes at dollar stores. North Carolina State Parks releases a new bandana every year to match the year's theme, and you can even buy bandanas treated with Permethrin to help repel insects when they are tied around your neck or head. You can use a bandana to blow your nose; clean your glasses; wipe sweat from your neck or forehead; tie up your hair; or tie things to your pack. You can dunk a bandana in a cool creek and wrap it around your neck or head to keep cool. You could also use a bandana as a mask (such as in a smoky area) or as a sling or bandage. A bandana can also come in handy as emergency toilet paper.

Blaze Orange Clothing

If you are hiking in an area that allows hunting, you'll want to invest in some hunter orange/blaze orange clothing. This includes hats and vests, and you can find these at any store that carries hunting gear. The law does not require that hikers wear blaze orange but doing so anyway is a good idea.[13] Check the hunting regulations and season dates for the areas where you'll be hiking and wear your orange to be safe.

Microspikes

If you are going to be hiking on ice or snow regularly, invest in a set of microspikes to add to your shoes for additional traction. You may have also heard of crampons. These are most suitable for technical mountaineering and likely not what you'll need. Microspikes attach to your shoes and have short metal spikes that help your shoes grip the trail surface better. They have helped me feel much more stable and secure when hiking in winter weather.

Reusable Splint

If a sprained or broken wrist or arm, or even ankle, needs to be immobilized to make your way safely back to the trailhead, a splint can be fashioned out of trekking poles, a rolled-up jacket, or even sticks you find in the woods. The process of temporarily splinting an injury can be made much easier, however, by using a multi-purpose, reusable splint. Often called a SAM Splint after the company that manufactures them,[14] these splints are made of a thin core of aluminum alloy encased in two layers of a waterproof, closed-cell foam. They are lightweight and easy to throw in a pack, come in a range of sizes, and are relatively inexpensive. When bent into a simple curve, these splints become very supportive to an injured limb. They are also easy to clean and radiolucent, meaning they can be left on for X-rays and CT scans. As with all first aid equipment, you should practice using these types of splints at home before including them in your first aid kit. Never carry something on a hike that you don't know how to use.

Small Hand Shovel

In the chapter on being a good trail citizen, we'll talk about how to properly dispose of human bodily waste while hiking. This process is made much easier if you have a small hand shovel to use. Some people might list this under "must have" gear, but you *could* get by without one; that would leave you digging a cat hole with a rock, a stick or your hands, however.

Trash Bag

Whether you have a trash bag or not, you should always carry out your own trash. Carrying a small trash bag gives you a place to put not just your own trash but also any other you might come across while hiking. A trash bag prevents you from having to put trash directly in your pack with your other gear. At the end of your hike, a trash bag comes in handy for transporting home any particularly muddy shoes or wet clothing. A large enough bag, say, 13 gallons or more, can be used as a makeshift rain poncho or pack rain cover, and a larger black trash bag could serve as an emergency blanket, although it wouldn't be nearly as effective as ones made with reflective material. Lastly, if you needed to help provide first aid to someone, a trash bag worn like a poncho can provide some measure of personal protection and help prevent exposure to blood or other bodily fluids.

Whistle

A whistle can be an important piece of hiking safety gear. It can be a simple coach's whistle on a string or a more official emergency whistle. (Fox 40 whistles are the gold standard here as they don't have any moving parts which makes them resistant to breaking or freezing.[15]) Some backpacks even have whistles built into their straps, although these are not nearly as good as other types and shouldn't be your first choice. The most important element is the volume of the whistle—the louder, the better! Whistles are good noisemakers for a variety of situations on the trail, say, for example, trying to make a lot of noise to alert an animal to your presence or even for creating a scene if a person is making you uncomfortable and you want to draw attention to the situation. Believe it or not, a whistle can also be a lifesaver if you get lost. We'll talk more about this in the "How Not to Get Lost" chapter, so stay tuned!

Don't Lose Your Stuff

A Backpack

I would argue that having *something* to carry your 10 Essentials is a necessary piece of gear. Depending on the trail you are hiking, you might need to have your hands free to hold on to trees for balance, climb ladders, use your trekking poles or check your map. Plus, trust me, you're going to get tired of carrying all that gear by hand.

What I'm talking about here is a specific hiking daypack. You can use a school backpack, or even a crossbody bag to carry gear, but a specific hiking daypack will likely have some features that can make hiking more fun and comfortable and help you keep your gear better organized and easier to access. Also, a daypack can have a place to carry a hydration bladder for water.

Daypacks are different from backpacking packs in that they are usually smaller, more lightweight and cheaper.[16] On the other hand, they typically don't have some of the comfort features that backpacking packs have, like more heavily padded shoulder straps and waist belts. As with hiking shoes, testing out a few packs before purchasing one is a good idea. Outdoor stores can often help you make sure you're getting a pack that fits you well and meets your needs as a hiker. After trying some out, you may decide that you'd prefer a smaller backpacking pack because of the additional features rather than a daypack. This is another piece of gear that can be expensive but is generally worth the cost if you're going to be hiking regularly. Also, keep an eye out for end-of-season sales. As manufacturers release new models of their packs, the older models can be found at a discount.[17]

Eyeglasses Cord

As you get sweaty, your glasses can start sliding around and, sometimes, they can just slide right off your nose. If you fall, your glasses can fly off. This happened to me once before I started using an eyeglasses cord. I was stepping over a downed tree and my back foot caught the log, sending me tumbling. Off flew my brown-rimmed glasses into the fall leaf litter about 18 inches ahead of me. My vision is about 20/800, so I really can't see without my glasses. Thankfully, after a few minutes of feeling around on my hands and knees, I found them, undamaged. If you were to fall on a stream crossing, your glasses might even float downstream.

Depending on how bad your vision is, losing your glasses could quickly become an emergency, hindering you from driving home once you return to your car, but also perhaps preventing you from finding your way safely back down the trail. You don't need a fancy or expensive glasses cord; just a simple one you can find at most big box or drug stores can do the job. If you have an extra pair of glasses, even ones with a slightly older prescription or a pair of prescription sunglasses, consider carrying them with you on the off chance you do lose your glasses. If you wear contacts, consider carrying an extra set or your backup glasses in case you lose a lens or get something in your eye and need to remove your contacts.

Phone Holder

The chances are much greater that you'll drop and damage your phone if you're trying to carry it by hand while hiking. And completely storing it away in your pack or some kind of waist belt can quickly become annoying if you want to frequently reference it as a navigation tool or take lots of pictures. A variety of phone holders are available on the market. Some are waterproof. Some attach to your belt, arm, or wrist. Some can be worn around your neck on a lanyard. Some, typically called a phone tether, can attach your phone to your pack.

I use one called the Koala that is made by Hangtime Gear.[18] I appreciate their tagline: "When adventure calls, or you're clumsy." Ha! Their phone harness wraps around your phone, keeping the screen easily readable and the camera uncovered, and the strap then attaches to your clothing with a strong clip or to your pack with a carabiner. I attach my phone to a loop on the left shoulder strap of my pack and, typically, just let it hang free. That way it's always available to reference or take pictures but I don't have to hold it in my hand. I have never had any issues with my phone falling out of the harness, even when one corner has come loose. Koala harnesses aren't the least expensive option available, and less expensive versions of similar products are available online, but I consider my phone an essential piece of gear and paying a little extra to make sure I have something that's going to keep my phone secure was worth it to me.

Where to Buy Gear

We've talked about a lot of gear in this chapter and the last and you may already have a list of things you need or want. There are lots of ways to obtain any gear you might need, and not all of them require a large outlay of funds. First, take a thorough inventory of what you already own. You might be surprised at what you have around the house that could be repurposed as hiking gear. Next ask around to friends and family or check out sites like Freecycle Network or "free to a good home" listings on places like Facebook Marketplace. Just like any other hobby, sometimes people get into hiking for only a season and end up with gear they are no longer using. Others decide to upgrade gear even though their old gear, while slightly used, is still perfectly good.

If you're looking to purchase gear but don't want to pay full price, check out second-hand and gear consignment stores. Play It Again Sports is a retail chain with locations in quite a few cities in North Carolina (and beyond) that occasionally carries hiking gear. There are also several non-chain stores across the state that carry second-hand gear. These include Regear Outdoors in Boone, Foothills Gear Garage in Morganton, and Gear Goat Xchg in Charlotte. Another great consignment store in Asheville, Second Gear, was destroyed by Hurricane Helene but thankfully quickly reopened at a new location. They always have a lot to offer. Many second-hand stores will carry some new items as well.

If you're looking to purchase new gear, lots of options are available. Walmart and Target typically have nice outdoor sections for some basic gear. To find more specific items, you'll likely need to purchase online or check out a sports or outdoor-specific store. Some of my favorites across the state include:

- Bass Pro Shops (Cary, Concord, Garner)
- Black Dome Mountain Sports (Asheville)
- Bluff Mountain Outfitters (Hot Springs)
- Bryson City Outdoors (Bryson City)
- Diamond Brand Outdoors (Asheville)
- Footsloggers (Boone, Blowing Rock, Banner Elk and West Jefferson)
- Great Outdoor Provision Co. (Chapel Hill, Charlotte, Greensboro, Greenville, Raleigh, Wilmington, Winston-Salem)
- Half-Moon Outfitters (Kannapolis, Southern Pines)

- Jesse Brown's Outdoors (Charlotte)
- Mast General Store (Asheville, Banner Elk, Boone, Hendersonville, Valle Crucis, Waynesville, Winston-Salem)
- Nantahala Outdoor Center Outfitter's Stores (near Bryson City and Asheville—inside the Grove Park Inn)
- Outdoor Supply Company (Hickory)
- REI (Asheville, Cary, Charlotte, Durham, Greensboro, Pineville, Raleigh)
- Roots Outdoor NC (Statesville)
- Take a Hike Mountain Outfitters (Black Mountain)
- Waypoint Outfitters (Boone)

Many outdoor stores, both North Carolina–based and national chains, are very involved in the hiking community and sponsor programs and events in their local regions. Several also offer loyalty discounts and other benefits. One example is REI's co-op membership.[19] To become a member of the REI co-op, you pay a one-time, lifetime fee ($30 at time of print) and you gain access to a variety of benefits and savings. First, you get 10 percent (typically) back on all eligible purchases. This comes as a member reward you receive once per year, and you can use it on any purchases online or in store. You also receive extended return deadlines on purchases, free standard shipping in the United States, special member offers and coupons sent throughout the year, early access to limited-edition gear, and a host of other discounts and extras. As a member you can also participate in their Re/Supply program, which allows you to trade in used gear as well as shop used gear. There are definitely some deals to be found! I found my favorite puffy vest for colder weather through this used gear program.

All hikers deserve to have clothing and gear they feel comfortable in, regardless of their particular body's needs, but I want to speak directly to my friends hiking in bigger bodies for a moment: You may not need specially-sized gear for some things—a water bottle is a water bottle, no matter the size of the hiker. But you will want to find clothes that fit well, and to say it can be a challenge to find good extended-size hiking clothing is an understatement. Thankfully, more outdoor companies are starting to offer extended sizes, slowly, so check brands like REI, Columbia, and Smart Wool. I have had some good luck with them. Some plus-size-specific outdoor clothing brands like Kinsa Active, SportivaPlus, Superfit Hero, 37 Minutes, and Thicket Adventure are becoming available. Gregory Packs offers the industry's first line of plus-size day and backpacking packs in a variety of sizes and shapes, and some hikers have had good luck with certain Osprey packs. If you decide you want to purchase new gear, take the time to research what's out there and ask the questions you need to find what works for you. You and your hiking journey are worth it!

8

How Not to Get Lost

And What to Do If You Do Anyway

Many of us have seen news stories about lost hikers and the search and rescue teams trying to locate them; we don't want to find ourselves in a similar situation if we can avoid it. Taking steps to avoid getting lost should be a consideration on *any* hike, and while some hiking locations might increase the likelihood of getting lost—backcountry trails that maybe aren't well marked or maintained or more remote trails without cell coverage—you absolutely can get lost on a well-traveled trail close to town. Some of my hiking group members have asked my thoughts about purchasing satellite tracking devices (like Garmin InReach) to aid in the case they were to get lost. For most day hikers on many trails, these fairly expensive tools with monthly subscription fees are not necessary. They can be invaluable for thru or other long-distance hikers or for people that always hike in areas with no cell signal for any distance, however. Even if you decide not to purchase one of these subscription services, you should still do what you can to prevent getting lost and know what steps to take if you do.

Have More Than One Way to Navigate

When hiking, you should have a means of navigating. Even if you've been on the trail before and even if you're hiking on a busy trail in a populated area. We covered ways of navigating in detail in "The 10 Essentials" chapter, but it's an important enough topic to reiterate some of that information as a part of this discussion. For most people, a means of navigating will likely be electronic in the form of an app. This should not be the only means of navigating that you carry, however. Lots of things can happen to a cell phone while hiking that make your electronic navigation tools unusable or unreliable. You might not have sufficient cell signal to use the app or your battery might run out. If a lack of cell signal is the only issue and you have a means of keeping your phone charged, you can download maps for offline use before you hit the trail when you do have signal or Wi-Fi. While it doesn't include the same level of information as downloaded maps, you can take screen shots of online maps on your phone. Taking a picture of any maps located on trailhead information boards for reference is also a good idea.

But running out of battery or spotty cell coverage aren't the only things that can happen to your phone while you hike. You might accidentally drown your phone in a creek or drop it down a cliff. A raccoon might steal your phone. (Just kidding about that last one … maybe. Raccoons are sneaky critters! Have you seen their little hands?)

Whenever possible, also carry a printed map of the hike you intend to do. As mentioned previously, you can look several places for printed or print-ready maps. Keep your printed map readily accessible in a pocket or in a spot easy to reach in your pack; you're more likely to reference it often if it's handy. And remember, to get the most out of your paper map, you'll want to learn some compass navigation skills. We'll talk about a basic way to use a compass if you were to get lost, the "30–60–90 Walk," a little later in this chapter.

Tell Someone Where You Are Going

Next, tell someone where you are going. Tell them where you are parking, what trail you plan to take and what direction you plan to go on the trail. Tell them when you are leaving, how long you will need to get to the trailhead, how long you plan to hike and how long you will need to get home. Even tell them what you are wearing or text them a selfie to show them. It is best to write down this information or text it to the person rather than just telling them verbally. If you go missing, they may be under so much stress that they could forget what you told them. Having all this information readily available can save precious time in finding you. Once you have shared this information, unless you must do so due to an emergency, *don't change plans unless you have a way to let the person know your plans have changed.* You may start hiking and find a side trail that looks interesting. If you can't let your contact person know and you're hiking alone, save that side trail for another day.

Learn How to Follow Trail Blazes

Trail blazes and trail signs are important on-the-ground navigational tools. They should not be relied upon as your only means of navigating, but they can certainly be valuable as you're hiking if you're not sure exactly where the trail goes. They can be especially important in the fall and winter when leaves or snow might obscure the trail tread or in the summer if trails

This trail blaze marker from Hammocks Beach State Park is one of the best I've seen for giving emergency location information. Most are not nearly this thorough.

are overgrown. Blazes show the direction of the trail. They are sometimes painted or carved directly on trees or rocks and are sometimes made of plastic and nailed to trees or posts. Blazes are typically at eye level so they can be spotted even in deep snow. When in doubt while hiking, look up and find the next trail blaze. Some trails are more well marked with blazes than others, and you'll often find this information contained in trail reviews, especially if a trail is *not* well marked. Some locations that have lots of trails in one place, such as in state parks, will have blazes of different colors or shapes to represent different trails. This information is often included on trail maps and can be especially helpful when two trails join up for a period of time or a new trail breaks off. For example, the Appalachian Trail is marked with a standard white, rectangular blaze that is two inches wide and six inches tall but a blue rectangular blaze along this trail indicates a spur trail that could lead to a shelter, a water source, a nice view or some unusual natural feature worth seeing.

There are some common ways blazes are arranged that indicate direction. These are not universal but can be of help. A single blaze means continue straight ahead. Double

Examples of different types of trail blazes including the iconic Appalachian Trail white blaze (top middle). The blaze at the top left is from the lower section of the Profile Trail at Grandfather Mountain State Park. It is bright orange and reflective, which allows it to be easily spotted in the woods, even at night.

blazes indicate a turn in the trail with the top blaze generally indicating the direction of the turn. Triple blazes indicate the start of the trail, the end of the trail or a spur trail leading to a different trail.

Blazes are not possible or allowed in some locations, such as in deserts or above the tree line on higher mountains. In these spots, unnatural looking piles of rocks called cairns are used. These are not often used in North Carolina, but they can be spotted from time to time. True cairns are large, often three feet or more in height and two feet or more wide. They serve the same purpose as blazes. In other places, smaller cairns, also referred to as trail ducks, might be built. These are much smaller, sometimes only a few rocks tall. They are obviously easier to construct than large cairns, but that also means that just about anyone can make one, even for fun, so they might be less trustworthy as directional aids than large cairns and blazes. Please do not build cairns for fun, large or small, especially where other types of blazes are available. Moving rocks, especially out of streams, can disrupt fragile wildlife habitats. And building extra cairns can confuse hikers that are using them as navigational aids.

Pay Attention

One of the best things you can do to avoid getting lost is to pay attention as you hike. Paying attention helps you spot the next trail blaze or realize when you've come to a trail intersection and need to make a turn. Paying attention helps you realize if you are covering the same ground and might be accidentally going in a loop. Paying attention also helps you notice if darkness is encroaching or if the weather is changing in a way that might impact your ability to navigate. A hike, especially in a more remote location or on a trail that is not as busy or well maintained, is not the time to pop in the earbuds with some tunes and disconnect from what's going on around you. It's also not the time to carry on a long phone conversation. You need to be actively engaged in the hiking process, for safety if for no other reason.

As an example, in November of 2022 I hiked the two-mile loop trail at Cascades Preserve north of Kernersville. Another hiker and I arrived at the same time and started hiking in the same direction. Not too long into the hike, the other hiker got on their phone and started a lengthy conversation. They were hiking at a faster pace than I was, and we were separated on the trail, but I came across them three additional times, lost in the loop. Each time they looked confused, I asked if I could help, and received the reply—with their phone temporarily put down—"I can't seem to find my way back to the parking area." They kept changing directions as they headed out from a break, so they never made it all the way back around in the loop. The first two times I pointed them in the right direction. The third time I asked, "Do you have a map?" and received a negative reply. I pulled up my map, showed them where they were on it and pointed them, again, in the right direction. Their car was gone from the parking lot when I got back, so I assume they aren't still hiking that loop!

What to Do If You Do Get Lost

If you follow the suggestions discussed here, you greatly reduce your likelihood of getting lost. But things do happen, and it's not impossible, so knowing what to do if you find yourself lost in the woods is very important. Some of the things you've done as you've prepared for your hike, like giving someone all your hike information and carrying appropriate gear, have already put you ahead of the game in being found quickly and safely. There are some other things to do if you do find yourself lost—especially without the ability to call for help—that can make an even bigger difference.

As soon as you realize you might be lost, stop immediately and take a few deep breaths. Now is the time to break out that yoga breathing or those box breaths you may have learned at some point. Doing this will help calm your sympathetic nervous system and short circuit a panic response. Trust me, you are going to want to panic. It's a very natural reaction to the situation. There is nothing quite like the lump in your throat that comes up when you realize you're deep in the woods and you don't know where you are. I have had a couple of instances, both in the fall when the leaves were obscuring the trail, when I missed a turn and suddenly realized I wasn't actually on the trail any longer. It sends a jolt of electricity through you. But panicking is the absolute worst thing you can do in this situation. Panicking can lead you to make decisions that are counterproductive to your safety and can lead to you getting even more lost. Your situation is probably not going to change drastically in the next five minutes. *Unless you are in an unsafe area and MUST move*, take a few moments to take off your pack, take a few sips of water, maybe eat a bite of a snack and take some deep breaths, and you'll be in a much better position to move on in a way that can help you.

Next, before you move at all, take a few minutes to look around. Odds are, if you've been paying attention as you hiked, you haven't veered too far from the trail before realizing you're not still on it. If you can clearly find your location on your map (phone-based or otherwise) and easily find your way back to the trail, or to a significant road, do so. But if you are unsure and you are carrying even a basic compass, conduct a "30–60–90 Walk."

30–60–90 Walk[1]

To conduct a 30–60–90 Walk and hopefully find your way back to the trail, you're going to need two things: a compass and a bright object that can be hung or tied at eye level in a tree. For example, a bright bandana tied high on a tree limb would work great for this. A hunter's orange hat could also work if it can be tucked into the crook of a tree and still seen. Most people know that a compass is marked with the cardinal directions—north, south, east and west—and often also with the intercardinal (or ordinal) directions—northeast, southeast, southwest, and northwest. Many compasses are also marked with degree marks, from 0 to 360 degrees, and that's what we need here—a compass with a degree dial. If your compass looks something like the diagram provided here, you should be fine. The compass on your phone will *not* work for this.

As soon as you realize you are lost, mark your position—your starting point—with your bright object. *You never want to lose your starting point as that is where you are "least lost."* (The numbers included here correspond to the 30–60–90 Walk diagram provided.)

Next, take a bearing in the direction you believe the trail to be. (See instructions in the caption of the compass diagram for how to take a bearing.) Pick an easily identifiable object (like a particularly tall tree) that is in the direction of your bearing and walk to it. Don't keep your head down looking at your compass as you walk. Your goal is to walk 30

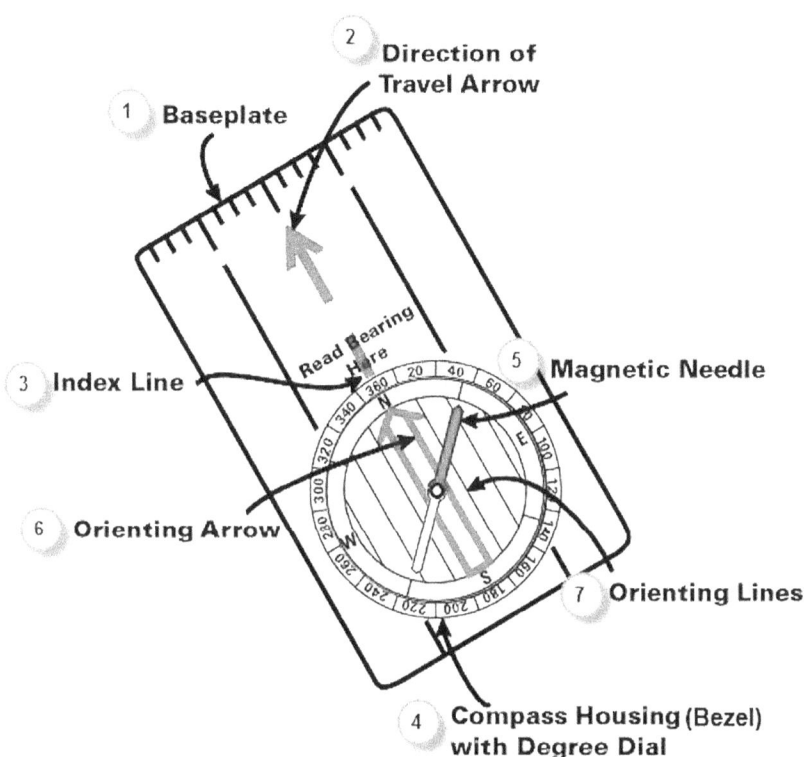

Taking a compass bearing: First, hold compass baseplate out and level, with the direction of travel arrow (2) pointing in the direction you want to go. Next, rotate the bezel (4) until the magnetic needle (5) is inside the orienting arrow (6). (The magnetic needle is often red; a saying to remember this step is "Put red in the shed.") Finally, read the number of degrees indicated by the index line (3). This is your bearing. Magnets, field-generating devices and ferrous metals can affect a magnetic compass. Do not use it near phones, pacemakers, overhead powerlines, knives, multitools or metal tables (courtesy Bill Sanderson and contained in "Land Navigation for CMC-SAR: Part 1—Pathfinding and Basic Compass Skills" training).

paces in the direction of your bearing. If the object you picked is less than 30 paces away, use the same bearing, pick another object and keep walking until you reach 30 paces (1).

If you don't hit the trail within the 30 paces, stop and determine your back bearing: If your original bearing was less than 180, then add 180. If your original bearing was more than 180, then subtract 180. This is your new bearing and the direction you want to walk back 30 paces to get back to your "least lost" spot and your bright object (2).

Once you return to your starting point, you're going to repeat this process, but at a 30- to 45-degree angle from the first bearing you used (3). If you don't locate the trail again, return to your starting point and repeat the process at a new 30- to 45-degree angle from where you just walked (4).

If you don't strike the trail using this process with 30 paces, repeat the process using 60 paces (5 and 6). If you still don't locate the trail, repeat the process using 90 paces. Remember, always return to your marker between movements.

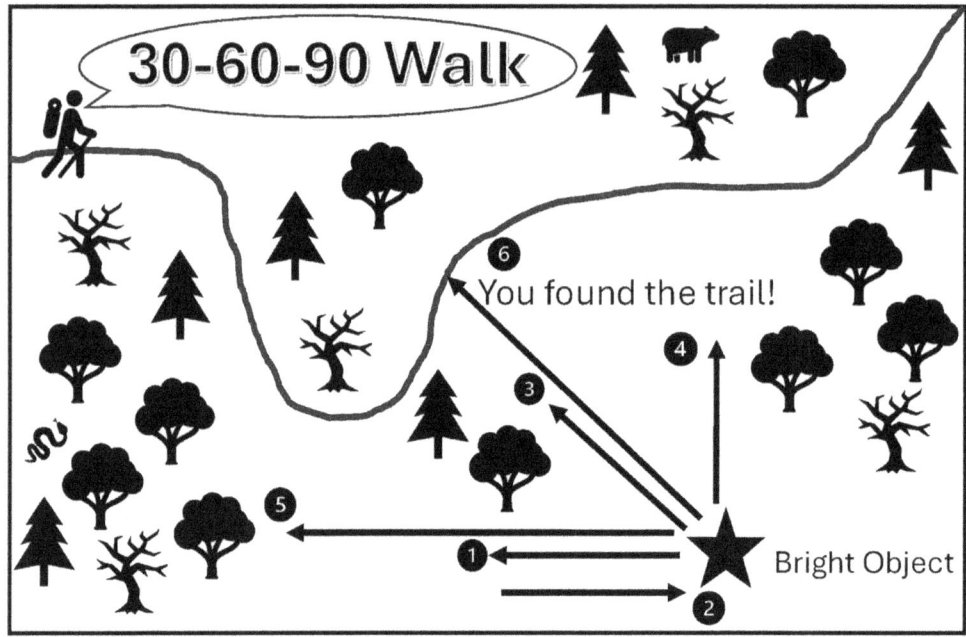

Diagram of how to conduct a 30–60–90 Walk. Numbers correspond to steps provided in the text (diagram created by author based on "Land Navigation for CMC-SAR: Part 1—Pathfinding and Basic Compass Skills" training).

Following this process will help make sure you don't wander in circles trying to find the trail. If you keep wandering, you run the risk of getting more lost and you make it harder for rescuers to find you. Searchers will look where they know you have been hiking, especially if you've left word with someone, and they have a much better chance of finding you if you are as close to the known path as possible.

Carry a Whistle

I included a whistle in the potential gear list discussed earlier and mentioned a few situations when it might be useful. It can also be essential if you were to get lost. If you are truly lost, start periodically blowing your whistle three times in a row. These whistle blasts should be loud and last about three seconds each. Why should you use a whistle instead of just yelling? You will be able to blow a whistle for a lot longer than you'll be able to yell. Your voice will give out a lot faster than a whistle will. Also, a whistle will stand out against the forest noises better and carry a lot farther than your voice.

Don't Believe the Internet

One last word of caution: Every now and then, a suggestion will make its way around social media that says, if you get lost, go on your phone and change your voicemail greeting to share where you are as best as you are able to tell. That way, even if your phone dies, if your loved ones call trying to find you, they will hear your voicemail greeting and know where to send people to look for you. Do not do this. First of all, you cannot change your voicemail greeting if you do not have a cell signal. If you do have signal but your battery is close to dying, you're better off using that little bit of battery to call 911 rather than changing your voicemail greeting or even calling a relative or friend.

While it is true that thousands of hikers across the United States require search and rescue assistance each year,[2] you can minimize your chances of getting lost and maximize your chances of being found if you follow some simple steps. If you'd like to learn more about search and rescue work and what to do if you get lost, I highly recommend the documentary film *Safe and Found* which features the Haywood County Search and Rescue Team.[3]

9

Wildlife Encounters

Sharing the Trail with Other Species

    I have had numerous wildlife encounters while hiking and they never cease to leave me amazed, inspired, and thankful. These can be exciting experiences! Unfortunately, however, there are news stories every year of people being hurt in wildlife encounters or of animals being injured or killed because of their encounters with humans. (Frankly, the wildlife often fare worse than the people.) Bear attacks, snake bites, issues with elk—even interactions with smaller wildlife can be dangerous for us *and* the wildlife. Many of these tragic events could be prevented if people followed some simple principles when encountering wildlife on the trail.

    A number of years ago there was a viral video where a woman, Veronica-Pooh Nash Poleate, was sitting in her car giving tips for how to have a safe summer and avoid shark attacks at the beach. At one point in this hilarious video, she tells her viewers to remember, "you in the shark's house now!" This is wise advice for anyone recreating in wild areas. You in the bear's house now! You in the copperhead's house now! You in the squirrel's house now! When out enjoying natural areas, you really are in the habitat of numerous wildlife—where they live, hunt, eat, and reproduce. Respecting wildlife keeps them wild and helps keep us safe.

    We're going to discuss encounters with specific types of wildlife for the remainder of this chapter, but there are numerous ways to respect wildlife that can apply in almost any situation. First, observe wildlife from a distance. Getting excited and wanting to get closer to the animal can be natural. We should never, however, chase or follow wildlife, and we should give animals plenty of space, even if they seem unbothered by our presence. If we get closer, they could get anxious and injure themselves or us trying to get away. Likewise, we should not disturb or try to stop natural behaviors in animals. Witnessing a predator hunt, kill and eat its prey can be difficult, especially if the prey animal is young, weak or already injured. Trying to intervene could get us injured, injure the animals involved and alter natural behavior in both the predator and prey. During one hike I came across a snake eating a frog. The frog was still alive, its head fully in the snake's mouth, but its hind legs were sticking out and thrashing about. I felt kind of bad for the frog, but I had to realize that I was watching the food web in action and trying to stop this likely wouldn't have saved the frog and could have injured the snake, who is also an important part of its local ecosystem. Wildlife may be especially sensitive to our presence and stressed by it during certain times of the year such as mating or nesting season, while they are nursing young or during times of diminished resources such as during droughts or winter months or after natural disasters. Be especially careful around wildlife during these times and give them extra space.

Also, never feed wildlife while hiking. First, you are introducing foods into the environment that are not normally a part of it. This can cause illness in wildlife or even death. At the very least the food likely does not provide the right nutrients that each animal needs to survive and thrive. Second, feeding wildlife teaches them to associate humans with food. *You* might not hurt the wildlife that you are feeding, but that might not be true for every human that animal approaches. Animals can become aggressive toward humans when they are looking for food and the people they have come to associate with it are not giving that food up. When this begins to happen, a situation can quickly become dangerous for both wildlife and humans.

Insects and Arachnids

It's easy to focus on the bigger wild things we might encounter while hiking as those tend to be the ones that, rightfully, make the news. But you are much more likely to encounter, and be annoyed by, the tiny wildlife. A run-in with some of them could even lead to long-term illness. So let's start with the bugs.

Approximately 80 percent of the species on Earth are insects or arachnids, so you are way more likely to come across some as you hike than you are any other kind of wildlife. Some we like to see. Tiger swallowtail butterflies in the spring or monarchs migrating in the fall. Awesome dragonflies darting around. Impressive stag beetles or fireflies blinking on a summer night. Some are just annoying. And some can harm us. Here we're going to concentrate on how to deal with or avoid the annoying or harmful ones.

Gnats and Flies

Gnats are the generic name we tend to use for a whole host of small, flying insects that we might encounter as we hike. In reality, what we call "gnats" can be any number of species of small flies—more than 600 species in North America. As someone who wears glasses, I think I've experienced all 600 of those species trying their best to get between my face and my lenses as I hike! They are mostly just annoying, but some species can bite, causing pain, itching, and even localized swelling, similar to a mosquito bite. Some larger species of flies can be even more annoying and capable of painful bites. These include horse flies and deer flies.

It's often not possible to entirely avoid these pests while hiking, but use of a good repellent applied to both the skin and clothing, as covered in the "Beyond the 10 Essentials" chapter, can help. No one knows exactly why but wearing a broad-brimmed hat can deter gnats and flies from gathering around your face. A bug net hood can be a lifesaver for situations where you have to hike through clouds of gnats. I carry one with me whenever I hike in the spring and summer. You might feel silly wearing one, but they are so much better than having a face, eyes, ears, or mouth full of gnats. Bug nets tend to work best when worn over a broad-brimmed hat that helps keep the netting away from your face.

Mosquitoes

Second only to gnats in annoyance potential, but definitely more able to transmit disease, are mosquitoes. There are more than 60 different species of mosquitoes in

North Carolina, and while they can be found anywhere a meal is available, they are most frequently found around standing water. Most of the time a mosquito bite only causes itching and a swollen bump, although people can have allergic reactions to mosquito bites. Unfortunately, mosquitoes can also transmit some serious illnesses, and not just in tropical, far-flung places. Several mosquito-borne illnesses are present right here in the Great North State—West Nile virus, eastern equine encephalitis and La Crosse encephalitis.[1] Cases of other mosquito-borne illnesses reported in the state, such as malaria, dengue fever, yellow fever, and Zika virus, are a result of international travel and are not contracted locally. This may not always be the case, however. For example, in recent years, locally acquired cases of malaria have been reported in Maryland, Texas, and Florida,[2] and as climates change, we could possibly one day see some of these more tropically associated diseases in parts of North Carolina. All the more reason to avoid mosquito bites as much as possible. As discussed in greater detail in the "Beyond the 10 Essentials" chapter, a good repellent, appropriate clothing, and smart timing of your hikes are your best defenses against mosquitoes.

Ticks

When reading trail reviews on AllTrails, you may see tick reports. "Watch out for ticks. Pulled 8 off my dog and 3 off me when I got home from this hike." Ticks aren't actually insects. Instead, they are related to spiders and mites and many different species live in North Carolina. The four most common are the American dog tick, the brown dog tick, the lone star tick, and the blacklegged tick. Ticks are most active in spring, summer and fall, although there are adults of some species that are active during the winter. Ticks do not fly or drop down from trees. They engage in a behavior called "questing" to find their next host. Usually ticks live in protected locations, but when they need their next meal, they climb to grasses or bushes and stick out their front legs until a suitable potential host happens to come by and they can grab on. Then they crawl on the host until they find a location to attach.

Ticks can carry numerous diseases that they can transfer to humans,[3] but the most well-known diseases (and present in North Carolina) are Rocky Mountain spotted fever and Lyme disease. The American dog tick carries Rocky Mountain spotted fever and is most active in the spring, summer, and fall. It is found throughout North Carolina but is most common in the Piedmont. The blacklegged tick (a.k.a. the deer tick) transmits the bacterium that causes Lyme disease. It is found most commonly in the Coastal Plain region but can also be found in the Piedmont. The adults of this species are most active in late fall and early spring but may also be active in the winter if the temperatures rise above freezing.[4] We now know, however, that all life stages of the deer tick, even the tiny larvae, can carry and transmit Lyme disease.

Another, less well-known, tick-borne disease is Alpha-gal syndrome. Alpha-gal syndrome is a food allergy to mammal meat products that can be triggered by the bite of a lone star tick when a particular sugar molecule, called alpha-galactose, is transferred into the body.[5] This may result in the person experiencing a severe allergic reaction to ingestion of or contact with most (if not all) meat products. For some people, this can even include contact with leather or ingestion of medications contained in gelatin capsules derived from mammal proteins. Alpha-gal syndrome comes with a long list of devastating side effects and there is scant evidence that the allergy fades with time. Also, unlike Rocky Mountain spotted fever and Lyme disease, this cannot be treated with antibiotics, even if caught early. The adults of the lone star tick are most active during the spring and summer and are most frequently found in the Coastal Plain region, less frequently in the Piedmont. Bites from these ticks can also cause Southern Tick Associated Rash Illness (STARI). This illness presents with a rash similar to that of Lyme disease, but it is not caused by the same organism and does not lead to the same neurological or chronic symptoms found with Lyme disease.[6]

If you start feeling any new or unusual symptoms—not only the tell-tale bullseye rash so frequently mentioned—after a known tick bite, be sure to see a doctor. If you aren't aware of being bitten by a tick but start experiencing new symptoms after spending time in areas where ticks can be found, be sure to let the doctor know that you've been spending time outdoors. As was mentioned in more detail earlier, use an appropriate chemical repellent, dress in long pants, and do frequent tick checks to reduce your chances of being bitten. Even adult ticks can be tiny, generally no larger than a sesame seed, so checking carefully is important. Unlike with mosquitoes where parasites and bacterium are transferred as soon as the mosquito bites you, a tick must be attached for a number of hours—two at a minimum—before either Rocky Mountain spotted fever or Lyme disease can be transferred to the host,[7] so the faster you can remove a tick that has attached, the less likely you are to develop either illness.

Spiders

More than 730 different species of spiders have been identified in North Carolina[8] and many of them are beautiful and engaging to watch. Thankfully there are only two kinds that we need to be truly concerned about while hiking. Sure, many people may be creeped out by spiders, but they are rarely dangerous and they play an important role in the ecosystem. So, if you find a spider while hiking, please leave it be. Spiders produce venom they can inject into prey or in defense and are therefore considered, well, venomous. (A quick vocabulary point: Venom is injected into you, whereas you ingest poison. So, a spider, scorpion, wasp or copperhead are venomous but that brightly colored mushroom or that tree frog you thought about licking is poisonous.) Despite the fact that spiders are venomous, their bites tend to not cause problems for *most* people. Just as bees can cause allergic reactions in some people but not others, the same can be true for spiders. The two species in North Carolina that are most likely to cause serious issues for people are brown recluse and black widow spiders.

Brown recluse spiders are found in North Carolina, but they are not very common. Many other species resemble them, and misidentification is frequent. Outdoors, these spiders can be found under debris or rocks or in wood piles. They are ¼- to ½-inch long and have a dark, violin-shaped mark on their bodies, although several other species can have similar markings. A brown recluse bite can take many hours, sometimes six to eight, to show. The wound will then start to blister, forming a necrotic lesion. If you develop this type of wound, be sure to see a doctor and mention that you've spent time outdoors.[9]

Most people are familiar with the shiny black body and red hourglass markings of the black widow spider. This coloration and marking pattern are only found on adult females, however. Young spiders are lighter in color and have orange and white markings. Black widow spiders are found in protected locations, like under wood or rocks or in dense vegetation. Hikers should be especially careful around any abandoned buildings or equipment they come across along the trail, as these spiders are frequently found in corners that are damp and dark. Unlike the brown recluse, whose bite primarily only affects the local tissue around which the bite occurred, black widow venom impacts the body systemically through the nervous system. The actual bite can be mild, so those bitten may not know they've been bitten. Pain in the lymph nodes is a primary symptom, but a more severe bite can cause elevated blood pressure, nausea, sweating and tremors. If you start experiencing any of these symptoms, especially after being in a habitat where black widows might live, be sure to see a doctor.[10]

Obviously, the best way to avoid serious complications from spider bites is to not get bitten in the first place. Carefully check and vigorously shake out any clothing or gear, such as jackets, hiking boots or backpacks, that have been left outside or stored in basements or garages for any amount of time before putting them on. Avoid sticking your hands into or sitting down in dark areas where you can't see, like inside downed trees, under rocks, or in shelters and privies. Also, wear thick gloves if you must move firewood that's sat undisturbed for a period of time.

Bees, Wasps and Hornets

There are several types of bees that call North Carolina home and thank goodness for it. The very existence of the beautiful places we like to explore while hiking is partly thanks to these busy pollinators. North Carolina has more than 500 species of native bees, and you might encounter any number of these while out hiking. Not all bees sting, but most definitely do, so you should be cautious around them. Repellents do not work for bees, and there are even stories of some kinds attracting them, so your best bet is to understand a little about bee behavior in order to not provoke them, as this is the most likely time that you could be stung. Of course, if you know you are highly allergic to bees you should always carry Benadryl and an EpiPen when you are going to be in areas where bees might be found.

Honey bees are one of the most well known of North Carolina's bees. They do not tend to be aggressive but will defend their hive if they feel it is threatened. (The more aggressive Africanized honey bee has not established a permanent population in North Carolina, although the possibility of that happening in the future exists.[11]) While on a hike you might come across honey bees in their large hives in hollow trees or in buildings. Steer clear of them and you should be okay. Several other kinds of bees commonly found in North Carolina, such as carpenter bees, bumble bees, mason bees, leafcutter bees and mining bees, are known to be fairly docile unless provoked or handled roughly. Again, being on the lookout for them and avoiding them if possible should help prevent you from being stung. (Despite some myths, cute, fuzzy bumble bees *can and will* sting if they feel threatened. Just ask my son who ran over a bumble bee ground nest with our lawnmower!)[12]

Oftentimes we refer to all stinging insects as "bees," but this is incorrect. Wasps, hornets and other stinging insects are different than the bees discussed above. Wasps tend to have more slender bodies than bees and they typically feed on other insects instead of nectar and pollen as bees do. Hornets are a subset of wasps—all hornets are wasps but not all wasps are hornets.

9. Wildlife Encounters 117

Yellowjackets are the most well-known wasp in North Carolina and have the reputation for being aggressive. They certainly can be and they will swarm if their nests are disturbed. But so will honey bees if disturbed in this way. One difference between the two that makes yellowjackets a bit more dangerous, especially in a swarm situation, is that individual yellowjackets can sting more than once, whereas honey bees (other than the queen) cannot. Yellowjackets typically build their nests in the ground—often on open ground, like the footbed of a trail—and they are disturbed by vibrations around the nest. This could happen even if a person simply walked over the nest, which is definitely possible while hiking.[13] Also, yellowjacket nests are often dug up by bears and walking anywhere nearby for a day or two afterward is a sure-fire way to get swarmed.

The only true hornet that can be found in North Carolina is the European hornet, which is not native to the United States. Another common insect, baldfaced hornets are not true hornets but actually a type of paper wasp, related to yellowjackets. These are the insects that build the stereotypical gray, football-shaped nests that hang from trees or roof overhangs. All these insects can sting and should be avoided. Unlike honey bees, wasp and hornet colonies die out each year. In spite of their bad reputations, wasps and hornets are beneficial as they eat many insects we consider pests. They also serve as food for many other insects, birds and small mammals.[14]

As said before, the best way to avoid issues with bees, wasps and hornets is to give them a wide berth and not attract them in the first place. Avoid using scented body care products before you hike, especially those with floral or banana scents. Keep any food

This paper wasp was found resting on the railing at the Neuse River overlook at Cliffs of the Neuse State Park.

you are carrying in closed containers. If you come upon a nest, stay clear of it as much as possible and do not attempt to handle the bees. If one or more lands on you, try your best to not react quickly or swipe at the insect. Watch out for lots of bees, wasps, or hornets coming and going in one place, as this can signal the location of a nest.

If you do get stung, rinse off the sting with plain, cool water. If the stinger is still in the skin, use a fingernail, ID or credit card, or even just a piece of gauze to scrape across the area and remove the stinger. Do not squeeze the stinger or use tweezers to remove it. Apply ice to reduce the swelling if you have some or place a bottle filled with cool water over the area. Even dunking the sting site in a cold stream would help. Try not to scratch the site. Be on the lookout for any signs of a possible reaction, take OTC painkillers if necessary, and consider taking a Benadryl if you have some, on the off chance you do have an allergic reaction

Reptiles and Amphibians

More than half of the different species of reptiles and amphibians found in the United States can be found in North Carolina and more than 100 of those NC species live nowhere else in the world.[15] The state even has a state reptile (the eastern box turtle), a state frog (the Pine Barrens treefrog) and a state salamander (the marbled salamander).

I've been lucky to see many amphibians and reptiles while I've been out hiking—a cute little green treefrog that hopped onto my green backpack, a bullfrog bigger than my hand at a nature preserve in the middle of Charlotte and several eastern box turtles, among others. I've even seen a few snakes along the way. While some people may not be huge fans of turtles, lizards, alligators, frogs, toads, and salamanders, most are not afraid of

This small eastern box turtle was spotted along the trail at Ridges Mountain Preserve near Asheboro. Aside from frogs and toads, turtles are the animal I've most frequently spotted while hiking.

them. The same cannot be said of snakes. Unfortunately, they tend to elicit a lot more fear, despite being fascinating creatures that are important members of the ecosystem.

Snakes

There are 38 different snake species in North Carolina and a bite from the vast majority of these would not be medically significant to humans.[16] As you hike you might see one basking in the sun on the trail or a rock or swimming along in a stream or lake or you might catch the swish of a tail moving through the leaf litter. Once when we were hiking at Lake Norman State Park, my sister and I looked over and saw a small, slender, bright green snake climbing up a small tree—a rough green snake. We were so excited to see it as the species can be hard to find because they blend in with their surroundings so well. It remains one of my favorite wildlife sightings.

I've heard more than once that "the only good snake is a dead snake." This is sad and simply not true. Snakes serve as both predator and prey in the food web, which helps to maintain biodiversity. They also provide a wonderful form of natural pest control by helping to keep rodent populations down. This, in turn, also helps control the numbers of ticks in an area. Snake venom is even being investigated as a potential source of new medications, including cancer treatments![17]

Again, the vast majority of the snakes found in North Carolina cannot harm humans, even if, for some reason, you were to be bitten by one. So if you come across a snake while hiking, please leave it be. Admire it, but don't touch it; let it go about its business. There is a set of snakes that call North Carolina home, however, that you should be especially cautious around—not be terrified of but be extra careful to keep an eye out for and take steps to avoid.

Six venomous snakes can be found in North Carolina. **Copperheads** are found throughout North Carolina, and they are the most common venomous snake in the state. "NC Poison Control receives 10 times the number of calls about copperhead bites than all other snakes combined. Copperhead bites can be severe but generally not as bad as other NC snakes."[18] **Cottonmouths** (a.k.a. water moccasins) are typically found in or near freshwater in the eastern counties of North Carolina. Their bites are on par with a copperhead bite but can be a bit more complex to manage and potentially severe.

Eastern diamondback rattlesnakes live in sandy coastal areas in the southeastern corner of the state. These snakes are physically very large, so they can deliver a massive dose of venom, making them more dangerous and their bites usually more severe than those of other snakes in the state. **Pigmy rattlesnakes** live in forested habitats in the southeastern corner of the state in a similar range to eastern diamondback rattlesnakes. There is also a population found in southern Gaston and Cleveland counties. As with all species of rattlesnakes, their bites tend to be more severe than copperheads. **Timber rattlesnakes** live in many areas of the state but are not found throughout the entire state as copperheads are. They live in the mountains, foothills, southern piedmont and coastal plain areas. While timber rattlesnakes rank as the most severe in the toxic complexity of their venom, they are smaller animals with a smaller venom capacity and the medical consequences of a bite are generally less dramatic.[19]

Eastern coral snakes are found in the very southeastern tip of North Carolina. They are highly venomous and much more likely to cause death than the other species mentioned here. On the other hand, bites from eastern coral snakes are extremely rare. The common saying to identify a coral snake by the pattern of its brightly colored stripes—"red on yellow kill a fellow, red on black friend of Jack"—is not entirely reliable, so to be on the safe side, you should avoid any snake that at all resembles the eastern coral snake.[20]

There are ways to distinguish venomous from nonvenomous snakes, including a diamond-shaped head, cat-like pupils (rather than round pupils), and long fangs. For rattlesnakes, listen for the tell-tale rattle. The trick is, you have to be fairly close to the snake to really see some of these features ... close enough that you could be within strike distance. And some nonvenomous snakes mimic venomous ones in looks and behavior as a defense mechanism. My son was once quite startled hearing a rattle in some leaves next to a trail while on a hike. Turns out it was a rat snake shaking his tail in some leaf litter to mimic a rattlesnake. The ruse certainly worked! Since distinguishing venomous from nonvenomous snakes from a safe distance (unless you are well educated on snake identification) can sometimes be difficult, just stay at least five feet from all snakes.

One way to distinguish a copperhead from other snakes is that their dark markings are often in a "Hershey's kiss" shape—wider at the bottom and narrowing at the top when looking at the snake from the side—that form an hourglass shape across the top of the snake's body. These two were spotted near Wilmington (courtesy Ken Hackney).

There are other ways to reduce your risk of being bitten. Snakes in North Carolina are most active between April and October, so be especially careful during these months. Wear sturdy boots or closed-toe shoes as well as long pants when hiking. Watch where you are walking and where you put your hands. Don't reach into places you can't see and be careful stepping over downed trees or big rocks when you can't easily see what's on the other side of them. Back away slowly if you see a snake and don't ever try to pick one up to move it.[21]

If you do get bitten by a venomous snake, first, don't panic. Staying as calm as possible will allow your heart rate to stay lower; a rapid heartbeat will only serve to spread any venom through your system faster. Several things can impact how a person reacts to a snake bite. These include the type and size of the snake and how much venom it releases as well as the size and overall health of the person bitten. Reactions can range from just mild swelling and pain (about half of all copperhead bites fall into this category) all the way to difficulty breathing and low blood pressure.

There are many myths about how to treat a snake bite. Cut the area to drain the venom. Wrong. Apply a tourniquet above the wound. Wrong. Suck out the venom. Most definitely wrong. You also shouldn't apply ice to the wound. All of these actions can do more harm than good. You should not try to capture or kill the snake to give to emergency medical professionals. Messing with an already-frightened snake is a good way to get bitten again or add new patients to the list, and even a dead snake can still envenomate you because its bite reflex remains active for up to an hour. (Yes, even a recently removed head can still bite.) And one last thing, because it makes its way around social media fairly regularly: taking Benadryl will not do anything for a snake bite, for you or your pet. It will just make you sleepy and you'll still have the bite to deal with! The definitive treatment for snake envenomation is antivenom. Period.

While remaining as calm as possible, wash the wound with warm soapy water, or at least rinse it well with clean water if warm water and soap aren't available. Next, remove any tight clothing or jewelry near the bite location. Try to keep the bite area still and, if possible, raise it to at least heart level. The higher the elevation, the better, really. Next, especially if the victim is having chest pain, facial swelling or difficulty breathing or has lost consciousness, call 911 immediately. In truth, all venomous snake bites should be considered a medical emergency until proven otherwise through a thorough evaluation, including bloodwork, so even if you transport yourself, you should head to your local emergency room. You can also call NC Poison Control at 1-800-222-1222 if you have a question about a snake bite. During peak season, the agency answers two to three calls *a day* related to snake bites![22]

In all my hiking I have only ever seen five snakes, and none of them were venomous. I know they are out there, but the fact that I haven't seen more in the hours upon hours I've spent wandering around in the woods tells you what you need to know about snakes and humans. They want nothing to do with us and are not out there looking to get us. Just give them their space and move along.

Alligators

Alligators are another reptile to be safe around if you'll be doing any hiking in the southeastern parts of North Carolina. They can be found in rivers, marshes, creeks, Carolina bays, lakes, ponds and swamps. Obviously, you're more likely to encounter an alligator if you are swimming or boating in these regions, but you can also come across them if hiking on trails that border these bodies of water.

Alligators are most active during their mating season in the spring. Being cold-blooded, they are least active during the winter, although on warm days they may be found basking in the sun. They also tend to be most active between dusk and dawn. Despite their size, alligators are shy and naturally fear people, trying to avoid us when possible. They will attack if provoked or harassed, however. It is illegal to touch, feed, harm, harass, or poach an alligator in North Carolina. Keep your distance if you see one—a recommended 50 feet at minimum—and make sure pets and children stay away from bodies of water where alligators are known to live.[23]

Mammals

One hundred and twenty-one mammal species are known to live in North Carolina. Twenty-one of these are state or federally listed as endangered, threatened, or of special concern.[24] North Carolina's mammal species show huge variety ranging from the star-nosed mole and the American mink to the nine-banded armadillo and gray wolf.[25] Some of these mammals are quite common and you're likely to see them as you hike, for example, squirrels, deer, chipmunks, rabbits and even beaver and otters. It's important to remember that all these wild animals are just that … wild. They can all bite or otherwise injure you if they feel threatened. Give *all* wild animals plenty of space. There are a handful of mammals, however, that are worth a specific mention here.

Bears

The black bear is the only bear found in North Carolina. They are abundant in the Mountains and Coastal Plain regions but are becoming increasingly common in the Piedmont as well. They are opportunistic omnivores and will eat just about anything, both naturally growing and human produced, and they are important members of the ecological community. Black bears rely on their strong senses of smell and hearing, as their eyesight is poor. They are good swimmers, climbers and diggers and they have been clocked running at speeds of 35 mph for short distances. Black bears can enter their hibernation dens as early as November or as late as January and typically emerge in March or early April. Male bears in the Coastal Plain can remain active throughout the winter months.

As bear habitat shrinks and human habitat increases, more frequent interactions between humans and bears occur, both on and off the trail. It's important to not view bears as either vicious animals *or* cuddly toys, because they are neither of these extremes. Typically bears want to avoid people, but they can become dangerous if they begin to associate people with food. You can help keep yourself as well as others safe if you take steps to mitigate this. When you are hiking, pay attention to your surroundings. Occasionally make noise, even if you are alone, to alert any bears in the area to your presence. Sing, whistle, or even just say, "Hey bears, hey bears." When hiking in known bear areas, double bag any food you are carrying and be sure to carry out any trash, including food scraps even if they are biodegradable. Also, keep your pets leashed and children within sight to better avoid unexpected bear encounters. If you plan to

9. Wildlife Encounters 123

camp overnight, be sure to learn how to safely store your food so as not to attract bears to your area.[26] Many areas in the western portions of the state require bear canisters for food when camping. While canisters are not currently required for day hikers, that time is fast approaching as too many people are careless with food and even day hiker behavior is leading to trouble between bears and humans.

If you do encounter a bear, first, don't panic. (Have I mentioned that before?) If the bear has not noticed you, enjoy the excitement of seeing it in the wild and then quietly move away. If the bear does notice you, back away slowly *without running*. Running could trigger a chase response, and you absolutely cannot outrun a bear. If the bear approaches you, stand your ground, wave your arms above your head (make yourself look as big as possible), and yell, "Hey, bear!" until the bear leaves.

If the bear continues toward you, use bear spray if you have it available. You should carry some if you routinely hike in areas known for high bear activity. It is proven to be the best, and easiest, way to deter a bear that is threatening you. It should only be sprayed toward an aggressive bear. It's not meant to be sprayed on your body or your clothing or gear—it's not like insect repellent. If the bear makes contact with you, fight back as aggressively as you can. Do not play dead, as this will not deter an attacking

I have never seen a bear while hiking in North Carolina. Where I have seen one, up close and personal, was when this yearling decided to investigate our front yard and came right up to our living room window in Jefferson. My son snapped this picture through the window while the bear sniffed around outside. I have also seen numerous bears at my sister's home in the Haw Creek area of Asheville. In some ways you are more likely to encounter a bear in certain developed areas, as these bears have often lost their fear of humans, but you should absolutely remain bear aware anytime you are in bear territory (courtesy Nathaniel Wallace).

black bear. (Note: This is different than what you should do if threatened by a grizzly bear. Since grizzlies don't live in North Carolina—or anywhere else east of the Mississippi River—we won't go into that here but be sure to read up on what to do if you plan to do any camping or hiking out west.[27])

Elk

While bears probably get the most press when it comes to animal encounters, others need to be considered. Elk are the largest mammals in North Carolina, even surpassing black bears in size. Elk, specifically the eastern elk species, used to be numerous in parts of the state. These animals were hunted or driven out of North Carolina by 1800, and the last eastern elk was killed in Pennsylvania in 1877. The elk that are found in North Carolina today are a transplanted subspecies that were first reintroduced in 2001 and 2002 by the National Park Service into the Cataloochee area of Great Smoky Mountains National Park. Fifty-two elk were reintroduced during this initial phase and the North Carolina Wildlife Resources Commission estimates that there are between 150 and 200 elk now living in a slightly expanded area in Western North Carolina.[28]

As the number of these majestic animals increases, so do the chances for elk/human interactions. Elk are herbivores so they don't view humans as a meal, but they can still be very aggressive, especially during the fall mating season, called the rut. Occasionally fields where elk gather during this time can be closed for use by people. Please respect these closings. You should always give elk at least 150 feet of clearance and failure to do so can result in fines or arrest. If you happen to come upon an elk in a more remote location, quietly back away and give the animal its space.

Coyotes

Coyotes are some of the most adaptable animals found in America. They can live in a wide range of habitats, including in suburban areas, which has led to an increase in sightings. Coyotes can be found in every county in North Carolina, so wherever you hike in the state, there is a chance you could see a coyote. Coyotes resemble red wolves but are smaller at about two feet tall and four feet long. They will feed on a variety of food sources, depending on what's easiest to obtain. Coyotes appear in U.S. history as far back as it is recorded, and they feature in many Indigenous stories.

Although they often have a negative reputation today, coyotes are naturally wary of people and will try to avoid us and places we frequent. On the other hand, they may become used to people where food sources such as pet food and garbage are available and threats are few. In other words, you're more likely to see a coyote around trash cans at a trailhead parking area or at well-used (and unkept) campgrounds than you are in the middle of the woods on a trail. If you do see a coyote, stand tall and be assertive. Until the animal leaves the area, wave your arms around, make loud noises and throw small objects in the coyote's direction. Do not run from the coyote as this can trigger the chase instinct. If a coyote does not respond to this or acts aggressively toward you, do what you need to do to get away from the animal and contact local animal control. Coyote attacks on people in North Carolina are rare, but they can happen. For example, in April 2024 two hikers received minor injuries in an encounter with a coyote on the Uwharrie National Trail near Big Island Creek.[29]

If you hear coyotes howling, be aware, but there is no reason to be fearful. The tone of a coyote's howl makes it seem closer than it is and can make just a few animals sound like a large group.[30]

A Word About Cougars
(a.k.a. Mountain Lions, Panthers, Pumas,
Painters, and Catamounts)

Cougars were once common in North Carolina, and you can see that reflected in many place names and school mascots across the state. I attended Asheville High School and cheered on the Cougars throughout my four years there, and my dad still cheers for his alma mater, the Western Carolina University Catamounts. Of all the cougar subspecies that have ever been documented in North America, only the eastern cougar and the Florida cougar (panther) were ever found east of the Mississippi River. Today, a small population of just over 200 Florida panthers lives in a small region of that state along the Gulf of Mexico, and most believe that the eastern cougar has been extinct—in North Carolina and elsewhere—for at least 100 years. The last confirmed sighting of an eastern cougar in North Carolina was in 1886.[31] But that doesn't stop people from *thinking* they are seeing cougars in the wild.

This beautiful feline is Logan, one of the resident cougars at Grandfather Mountain. He and his sister, Trinity, are western cougars who were found as orphans in Idaho. They were deemed un-releasable and came to live at the wildlife habitats at Grandfather Mountain in March 2016. Wild cougars no longer live in North Carolina, but the thought of coming across one on the trail is an exciting—and slightly frightening—prospect (courtesy Nathaniel Wallace).

Cougar sightings are occasionally reported in North Carolina, but investigations usually conclude that these are other animals. Some sightings have even turned out to be escaped captive animals or ones that were released illegally. Nevertheless, there are people across the state who swear they have seen the big cats roaming the woods, hunting, or crossing roads. And these stories are not just ones shared by someone's grandpa 60 years ago but include much more recent encounters too.[32] Who knows? *Officially*, there are no cougars in North Carolina, but we love ourselves some tall-tales in this state, so the cougar-sighting stories will likely continue. If you definitely want to see one of these apex predators, visit one in a zoo. Grandfather Mountain and the North Carolina Zoo both have cougar residents—transplants from Oregon and Idaho orphaned as kittens and now cared for by the amazing staff at these facilities. You could also always attend a football game in Charlotte and meet Sir Purr!

We may worry about wildlife encounters on hikes, and while we do need to be aware and careful, unfortunately humans are a way bigger threat to most wildlife than they are to us. Habitat destruction and roadway mortality are causing large declines in populations of all kinds of wildlife. For example, North Carolina's populations of eastern diamondback rattlesnakes and coral snakes have essentially disappeared due to these events.

Irresponsible outdoor recreation not only threatens wildlife and their habitat but can also lead to the destruction of and loss of public access to the very places we wish to visit when we hike. Next, we'll talk about what it means to be a good trail citizen and how you can do your part to help preserve these natural spaces for future generations.

A beautiful field of wildflowers greeted me during a sunset hike along the Bluff Mountain Trail in Doughton Park along the Blue Ridge Parkway.

The cork-like bark of a young common hackberry tree, like this one found on the Saxapahaw Island Trail in southern Alamance County, builds up layers that look like cliffs and canyons when viewed closely.

A painted trillium, found along the trail at E.B. Jeffress Park off the Blue Ridge Parkway. At least 13 different species of trillium grow natively in North Carolina.

These Venus flytraps were spotted along the trail in Green Swamp Preserve. Although they've been transplanted and grown in many places around the world, these plants only grow natively in a 75-miles radius around Wilmington.

This adorable green tree frog decided to hop on to my green daypack at Gibson Park near High Point before deciding not to come along for the ride.

This small mushroom was spotted along the trail at the Piedmont Environmental Center in High Point. I am not very good at identifying mushrooms, so I admire them without touching and definitely without tasting!

Winter hiking has a beauty all its own. The Summit Trail at Mount Jefferson State Natural Area was sparkling on this snowy, blue-sky day.

A small sampling of the variety of hues found among the shells of Shackleford Banks.

These ghost pipe plants were spotted on the Balsam Nature Trail at Mount Mitchell State Park. Interestingly, they do not contain chlorophyl and therefore do not get their nutrients from sunlight. Instead, they get their nutrients from tree roots through an intermediate fungus. Because of this, they can grow where there is little sunlight available. They are typically white but can range to pink like those pictured here.

This tree was cut because it had fallen and was blocking the trail near E.B. Jeffress Park off the Blue Ridge Parkway. What you see dripping here is not water but rather sticky sap from the freshly cut tree.

The pink-shell azalea is native only to North Carolina where it grows in three counties in the mountains. It is considered endangered globally and the largest native population in the world is on Grandfather Mountain (courtesy of Nathaniel Wallace).

Trout lilies, like the one pictured here from J. Douglass Williams Park in Sugar Mountain, bloom early in the spring. There are several theories on how they got this name, one of which compares the markings on the leaves to the look of a brook trout swimming through the water. Brook trout, often referred to as "speckled trout" or "brookies" by locals, are the only native North Carolina trout species. They are found in cold, clean waters in isolated spots in the mountains, so these beautiful wildflowers grow well outside the fish's territory.

I unfortunately disturbed this colorful marbled orb weaver when I ran into her web while hiking at Ward Nature Preserve near Asheboro. Thankfully she hung around long enough for me to take her picture.

This bumble bee was certainly enjoying the nectar of these wild-growing flame azaleas at Grandfather Mountain. One of the primary pollinators of these beautiful plants is the North Carolina state butterfly, the eastern tiger swallowtail (courtesy Nathaniel Wallace).

No filter needed for this picture. The forest was exactly this green on this Mountains-to-Sea Trail hike near the Devils Garden Overlook off the Blue Ridge Parkway. Just minutes after this picture was taken, the sky opened up and it started pouring.

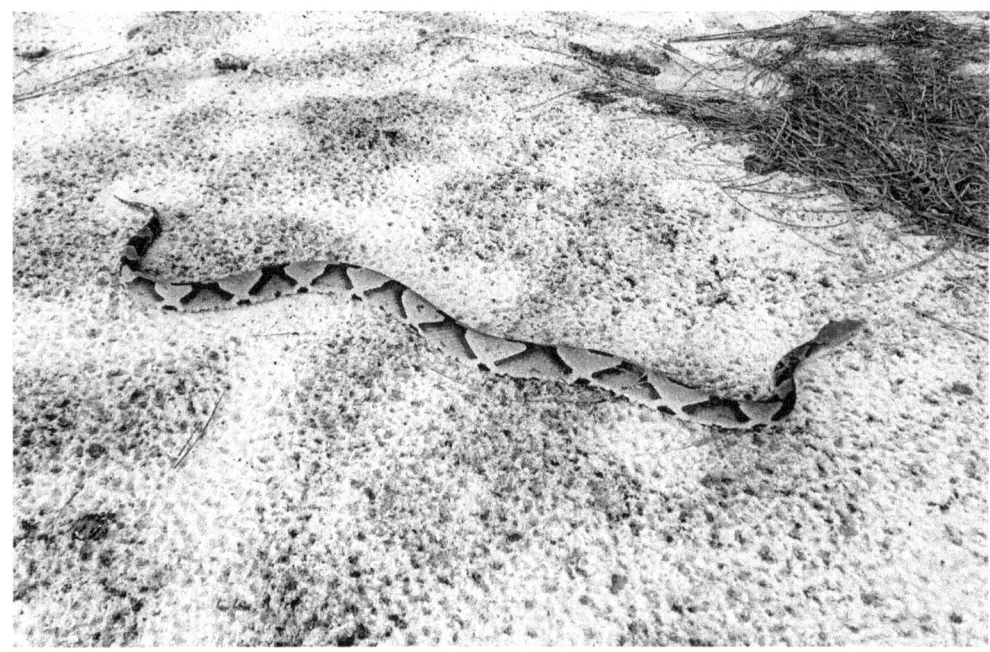

Copperheads can vary in their coloring, but it's not hard to guess where they get their name when looking at this individual, photographed near Wilmington (courtesy Ken Hackney).

While hiking I have seen two rough green snakes, like this one photographed at Duke Forest in Durham by Ken Hackney. They always make me smile. As they are excellent climbers, these graceful snakes with their gorgeous green color spend most of their time in trees and small brush. They are non-venomous and generally docile but still should not be handled when found in the wild (courtesy Ken Hackney).

10

Be a Good Trail Citizen

Sharing the Trail with Other Humans

It is rare to find yourself completely alone on a trail, especially if you are hiking on more popular trails or in more populated areas. Unfortunately, sometimes trails are closed for a time, often a couple of years or more, because they have received so much use that the ecosystem around the trail has been damaged. The Appalachian Trail on the North Carolina/Tennessee border in the Roan Highlands is well known for its beautiful views. I knew this was a popular hike, but I realized just how popular it was when I arrived to hike on a beautiful Saturday morning in May 2021. The parking lot at the trailhead was full and lots more people were parked along the sides of the road. Hikers were everywhere. While good portions of the trail were fairly wide, some sections were single track and tight. There are also delicate flora and fauna on those balds that could be damaged if people aren't conscientious. Thankfully, everyone was minding their manners that day, but it was easy to see how the experience could have become unenjoyable and even dangerous if they hadn't been. Following some simple, common trail etiquette and Leave No Trace principles shows respect for your fellow hikers and the land on which you are hiking.

Trail Etiquette

Thankfully, common trail etiquette principles are much easier to remember than which fork to use at a fancy dinner, and if you make hiking a regular part of your life, you'll have plenty of chances to practice them.

Know Right-of-Way and Passing Rules

Some trails are plenty wide for multiple people to use them at once. For example, the trail at Salem Lake in Winston-Salem is eight to ten feet wide and it's entirely possible for a group of people to hike while others are passing in the opposite direction and people on bikes are speeding past. Often this is not the case, however, especially in more remote locations in state parks, national forests or nature preserves. Single-track trails are often only wide enough for one hiker at a time. In cases like this, knowing the right-of-way and passing rules for the trail is important. They can become even more complex on multi-use trails where you're potentially sharing the path with mountain bikers, ATVs, or horses or on trails accessible to people using mobility aids or adaptive hiking equipment.

The wide trail tread on the Flat Top Mountain Trail at Moses H. Cone Memorial Park near Blowing Rock (left) offers plenty of space for hikers, even in groups. However, this section of the Bluff Mountain Trail in Doughton Park Recreation Area, between the Basin Cove and Alligator Back Overlooks (right), is only wide enough for one person, with inclines on either side. It would be especially important to follow "right of way" and passing rules here.

Let's start by concentrating on right-of-way etiquette when there are only other foot hikers involved. First, hikers coming uphill have the right-of-way. This might seem a bit counterintuitive. Wouldn't those coming uphill rather stop and have a short break while those heading downhill pass by? This rule has more to do with who has the better sightlines when both parties are moving than it does with who needs a break. When you are heading downhill, even if you are looking down to watch your footing, you still have a pretty good view further down the trail. You are more likely to see oncoming hikers in advance. People hiking uphill who are looking down have a much more limited view, sometimes just a few feet in front of them, and are less likely to see obstacles as far in advance as those coming down. Also, this rule takes into account that it's often harder to resume your pace after stopping if you're going uphill than if you're headed downhill. Of course, if you're coming uphill and want the break, you are more than welcome to step to the side and catch your breath while letting others pass, but this should always be the uphill hiker's call. Regardless of the terrain, if you are stopping during a hike, whether it's to consult your map, drink some water, or check out something cool you see, you should always step to the side of the trail and out of the main line of traffic.

Additional guidelines come into play when hiking groups are involved. First, solo hikers yield to large groups, letting them pass by so they can stay together. On the other hand, those hiking in a group should be careful not to take up the entire width of the trail. This could even mean hiking in a single-file line rather than in pairs or small groups depending on the trail. Yes, this might not make for the best conversation, but it's the safest and most courteous way to bring a group down a narrower trail.

When you're exploring a multi-use trail, there are some other rules to remember on who should yield to whom. Let's say you are on a trail that allows hikers, mountain bikers, and horseback riders. Mountain bikers must yield to both hikers and horses, and hikers must only yield to horses. ATVs allowed on a multi-use trail must yield to mountain bikers, hikers *and* horses, while everyone, including horses, must yield to those using mobility aids such as wheelchairs. Of course, much like driving, it's all well and good for you to know and follow the rules, but what if everyone else doesn't? Many multi-use trails will have signs reminding everyone of these guidelines, but practicing a little "defensive driving" and being aware of your surroundings is a good idea. I wouldn't assume that a mountain biker zooming down a hill is going to stop for you hiking up the hill if they show no indication of doing so.

When you come across another person on the trail, especially if you are coming up behind them, call out to make yourself known. A simple "Hello!" or "Just so you know, I'm behind you" will usually suffice. I am not necessarily a quiet hiker, but you'd be surprised how many times I have come upon another hiker who obviously had no idea I was there. Sometimes it was because they had on headphones, but often it was just because they were lost in thought or paying attention to something else. No one likes to be startled in the woods, especially if they are alone, so be courteous and give them a little warning to let them know you're sharing the trail with them. If you do need to pass someone, always pass on the left and let the other person know what you're doing with an "on your left" or something similar.

Cell Phones

As in so many other places in modern life, cell phone usage has become ubiquitous in the outdoors. There is no shortage of outdoor and hiking-related apps available to enhance your experience and many people use their smart phones for navigation and to take pictures. As cell network coverage improves, more places also have cell signal. This can be a lifesaver in emergencies. There's no quicker way to let someone know you need help. On the other hand, this increased availability of coverage also opens up the possibilities for hikers to multitask and spend time catching up with a best friend or Aunt Sally while they hike. Trail etiquette discourages having loud phone conversations or listening to loud music as you hike. Part of the draw of hiking for many people is to unplug and get away from it all. They enjoy the quiet of the trail and the space to think and enjoy the sights, sounds and smells of being in nature. Cell phone usage can hinder this. I know it's not possible for everyone to just turn off their phone while they hike, but if all possible, keep conversations to a minimum. If you must make or take a call, stop, step out of the main line of traffic, and keep it as brief as possible.

Be Friendly

I am very lucky; most people I have encountered on the trail have been nothing but pleasant and friendly. Generally people are happy to be out hiking and are enjoying their experience. You'll often hear lots of "Beautiful day for a hike!" or "The view is wonderful just ahead!" or even just a friendly "Hi, how ya doing?" as you pass others on the trail. One word of caution: "You're almost there!" should be taken with a grain of salt. These words offered in encouragement may have no relationship to how far "there" actually is! Your fellow hikers mean well. Don't be afraid to say hi and offer a smile. If you want to take "being friendly" to the next level, consider carrying something extra to share with someone who might need it. Maybe pack an extra bottle of water or some snacks. I often carry an extra emergency rain poncho in case of a sudden downpour or an extra HotHands on cold days. These items weigh next to nothing and don't take up much space in my pack, but they can mean the world to a fellow hiker caught without raingear or who forgot their gloves. If you are hiking as a day hiker on a long-distance trail such as the Appalachian Trail or the Mountains-to-Sea Trail, consider carrying an empty trash bag. Thru hikers on these trails would always appreciate an offer to take and dispose of some of the trash they are likely carrying. You could even share some extra snacks or drinks with these hikers. Offers like these are often referred to as "trail magic"—an unexpected gesture of generosity or kindness that long-distance hikers sometimes experience along the trail.

Leave No Trace

The Leave No Trace principles were designed to help all those spending time in the outdoors understand how they can have a minimum impact on those natural places. The seven principles can be applied to any natural setting, from the most remote and wild to local parks and preserves to your own yard. These principles are regularly studied to ensure they continue to reflect best practices and current research in land management, ecology, biology and outdoor education. The seven Leave No Trace principles[1] are:

1. Plan Ahead and Prepare
2. Travel and Camp on Durable Surfaces
3. Dispose of Waste Properly
4. Leave What You Find
5. Minimize Campfire Impacts
6. Respect Wildlife
7. Be Considerate of Others

We have already discussed a few of these principles in detail: Plan Ahead and Prepare, Respect Wildlife and Be Considerate of Others. Minimizing campfire impacts is a little beyond our purposes here since we're not covering camping in this book. But let's go ahead and talk about the other three principles that are left as these *are* involved in day hiking: Travel and Camp on Durable Surfaces; Dispose of Waste Properly; and Leave What You Find.

Travel and Camp on Durable Surfaces

The goal of this principle is to protect plants and animals, the land, and waterways as you travel through natural areas. Some especially popular trails can experience thousands of footfalls per day. By ensuring that you're traveling on durable surfaces, you're keeping the impaction to the soil caused by all those footfalls limited to a small area. Plants and other organisms often can't grow as well in impacted soil and by going off trail you also risk trampling vegetation and organisms directly. Sometimes these plants and animals can recover, but other times they are not able to. To practice this principle, stick to established trails with durable surfaces. Durable surfaces include established dirt trails, paved and gravel paths, wooden boardwalks and bridges, dry grasses and snow. Do not cut across switchbacks or create shortcuts between sections of trail. If you are hiking with a group, hike in a single file line unless the trail surface is wide enough to accommodate hiking side by side. If a trail is muddy, walk through the mud, unless there is space to walk around the mud without going off trail. When hikers consistently walk around muddy areas in trails, the trails widen slowly but surely over time; this is referred to as "trail creep."

Traveling on established trails with durable surfaces also benefits you as a hiker. User-created or undesignated trails often aren't as well designed or as accessible as official trails which means they may have poorer drainage (hence *more* mud), more roots, steeper inclines or less safe conditions overall, increasing chances of falls and injuries. When you go off trail it's also not always easy to see where the hazards are. For example, you might not see that copperhead hiding in the leaf litter or run into a patch of poison ivy.

Dispose of Waste Properly

Anything that you bring into an area where you are hiking is potential waste and learning how to dispose of it properly is an important part of being a good steward of the land on which you recreate. I'm sure we've all been to inspiring natural spots only to have the beauty diminished by trash that's been left behind. Everything from disposable water bottles to cigarette butts to pet waste disposal bags. Our waste impacts the natural world in big and small ways. It's up to us as individual hikers to make sure we're handling our waste properly so we don't contribute to the problem.

We may think that backpackers contribute the most waste on the trail, but we day hikers can create plenty of waste all on our own. The long and short of it is this: Whatever you bring with you on a hike should leave with you as well. Anticipate what kind of waste you might generate and have a plan for how to carry it back to a proper receptacle either at the trailhead or at your home. This includes leftover food or scraps—things like nut shells, orange peels and apple cores. We think of these things as biodegradable and assume it's okay for us to just throw them out into the woods. First, these things take longer to decompose back into the soil than you think they do. Second, you are introducing food items into an ecosystem that are not natural food sources for the animals that live there. Eating these things could make them sick. It could also attract these animals to areas of human recreation, creating the potential for dangerous interactions with wildlife.

Let's also not forget about the type of waste no one really wants to think about: human bodily waste. That's right, we're going to talk about how to pee and poop in the woods. You may think this is something only long-distance or thru hikers need to consider, but if you're going to spend any time in an area that does not provide restroom facilities, you need to know how to handle this issue correctly. Properly disposing of human waste helps it to decompose more quickly while protecting water sources and minimizing the spread of disease. In most places, especially in the eastern United States, burial is the proper way to handle solid human waste. Certain desert and alpine locations require that it be packed out and there are several sanitary methods of doing this. Be sure to check the regulations for your hiking location.

To properly bury your waste, you'll need to dig a cat hole. That's why carrying a small shovel in your pack is a good idea. Cat holes should be located at least 200 feet (about 70 or so adult pace lengths) from water, campsites and trails and located in a spot where other people likely won't walk or camp. Cat holes should be six to eight inches deep and four to six inches wide and should be covered and disguised with natural materials after use. You should also avoid digging cat holes in spots where obvious runoff toward a body of water will occur. Toilet paper should be completely buried in a cat hole or packed out and wipes should always be packed out.

Urine does not need to be buried, although urinating on rocks or pine needles is less likely to attract wildlife. You should also try to urinate at least 200 feet from water sources or trails when possible. Again, toilet paper should be buried in a cat hole or carried out. Instead of toilet paper, some hikers like to use anti-microbial, reusable cloths that can be used to wipe after urinating and then rinsed out with water and washed when you return home. (Kula is one brand of these.) Menstrual products and diapers should always be packed out as they do not readily decompose even when buried.

Leave What You Find

You've probably heard the phrase "Take only pictures, leave only footprints" to describe this principle. The rocks, plants and animals in an area make up the ecosystem and they each play a role and tell part of the story of the land. Certain locations, like state parks or nature preserves, can have strict rules about, and steep penalties for, removing any natural items from their locations. Many states have laws that prohibit the removal of human artifacts without the proper research-related permissions. On the other hand, some public lands allow limited gathering of plants or rocks for personal use and even allow hunting. Be sure to check into the rules of the area where you'll be hiking before removing anything from the land.

In general, you should leave things where and how you find them, even if you don't plan on taking items with you. For example, do not pick rocks up and move them around in streams. Sure, it's fine to pick up a pebble and skip it across a calm pool. But it's not a good idea to move bigger rocks for stacking into cairns or creating temporary dams or channels in a creek or stream. Certain aquatic wildlife use these bigger rocks in the streambed and moving them can disrupt their habitat or reproduction. For example, the eastern hellbender, also known as the mud devil, water dog, Allegheny alligator or (my personal favorite) snot otter, is especially sensitive to the movement of rocks. The hellbender is a large aquatic salamander that spends most of its life under large flat rocks that it uses for shelter. Moving these rocks can wash away the hellbenders' eggs or even crush the salamanders themselves. Be careful moving even small rocks and pebbles. Certain species of fish build pebble nests in which to lay their eggs and you wouldn't want to disturb them. So have a great time wading in a cool stream on a hot day and checking out all the wildlife, but leave things where you find them.

Another example of "leaving things how you found them" is carving on trees. Some historical tree carvings, technically called arborglyphs or dendroglyphs, have been studied and used to trace the movements of groups of people and some Indigenous peoples around the world have carved designs and symbols into trees that hold a cultural or spiritual significance for the group. Most tree carvings you see as you hike do not fit into either of these categories, however. They are the typical initials or even sometimes crude pictures—essentially graffiti on trees. American beech and aspen trees are often the victims of these carvings as they have quite smooth bark. Tree bark acts as a barrier for the tree, much like our skin does for us. Also, like our skin, tree bark can heal as the tree grows. But in the meantime, these cuts into the bark of the tree leave it open to diseases and pests. If the cuts are deep enough, they can impact the tissues within the tree that transport nutrients. There's no need today for most people to carve into trees to mark where we've been. We have plenty of other ways to document our travels. So, as tempting as it might be to leave your mark on a tree, especially when lots of other people have already done so, keep your pocketknife put away and memorialize your adventures in another way.

Hiking with Pets

Hiking with pets means you have a few other things you need to remember if you want to be a good trail citizen. First, and possibly most important: Follow leash laws and any park-, preserve-, or trail-specific leash requirements. The pet included most frequently on a hike is the family dog, and while we love our furry companions with all our hearts (me included), not everyone likes dogs. Some people are quite scared of them. Even as a dog mom, I can be somewhat uncomfortable around large dogs due to some negative experiences with them when I was young. I have had more than one experience with unleashed dogs coming around a bend on a trail, well ahead of their people, and starting to bark aggressively at me when they found me. It definitely got my heart rate up! I even once left a trail early because a dog from some nearby houses was running around alone through the woods and was obviously not happy about people being close to his home. It's not unusual to see remarks in AllTrails reviews about nearby dogs, both friendly and not.

But following leash requirements isn't just about the comfort and safety of your fellow hikers. It's about your dog's safety as well. Some people hike with their own dogs that might not react well to their fellow canines, and two unleashed dogs surprising each other on the trail could quickly become dangerous for both. Some people hike with service or guide dogs, and an unleashed dog could distract them, putting their handler at risk. Also, some people hike with animals other than dogs. I'll never forget hiking on a trail to see a beautiful waterfall near Valle Crucis, North Carolina, when I came across a group hiking with a tiny chihuahua … and a goat. The goat was on a leash and even carrying his own backpack. It was so funny! On the famous Mount LeConte in eastern Tennessee, weekly supplies such as fresh produce and linens for the hike-in only Leconte Lodge are brought up the mountain on llama-back. These llama transporters and their handlers utilize one of the same trails up the mountain as hikers. Some locations have multi-use trails that allow horses. How would your dog react to coming around a bend in the trail and finding a llama or horse? If a horse reacts badly to an unrestrained dog, the horse, its human rider, and dog could all be injured. Some people even hike with their cats!

In addition to domesticated animals, you also never know when you are going to come across wildlife that could injure your pet. Bears and snakes immediately come to

Our little dog Bella isn't into hiking on long trails, but she does enjoy short hikes, like this one at Yadkin River Park on the border of Davidson and Rowan counties, just off I-85. The one-mile trail at this park features Civil War–era earthworks and, specifically for the pooches, a nice dog park right by the trailhead. You'll also find access to the Yadkin River, the historic Wil-Cox Bridge, a pollinator garden, restrooms, a playground and more. Even on short hikes it's important to make sure that your four-legged hiking partners have access to water and food and that you follow leash laws and clean up after them appropriately.

mind, but, depending on where you're hiking, there are others to worry about as well. If your dog is off leash and out of sight they could get attacked by wildlife before you had any idea what was going on.

If you really want your dog to have some off-leash trail adventures, some locations do allow it or are even specifically designed for it. For example, the U.S. National Whitewater Center in Charlotte features Whitewater Off Leash, a 70-acre fenced area that includes a lake for pooches to play in, agility obstacles and the 1.5-mile Lake Loop trail.[2] Unlike on other trails at the Whitewater Center, mountain bikes are not allowed on this trail. There is a parking fee for the Whitewater Center, and a per-dog charge to use this area, but it's a great spot and a fun trail. It's even fun to hike if you don't have a dog but really like them, and you don't have to pay the activity fee if you want to hike without a dog. Sniffspot—a listing of private dog parks that are hosted by locals and available for rent—is also a good resource. (Think Airbnb for dog parks.) You can search for parks with hiking trails and find lots of fun places to explore off-leash with your canine companion.

Hiking with your pet is almost like hiking with a child. You have to plan for their health and safety just like you would your own, as they can't do it for themselves. Most of the things we have talked about with human hikers apply to our animal companions as well. Think about your pet's feet and the types of surfaces you'll be hiking on. Will the surface be very hot, cold, or sharp? You might need protective booties for your dog. Don't forget to pack plenty of food and water for your pet. Make sure they get breaks along the way too that allow them to really experience the joys of the trail … the smells!

Know your pet's limits. I have hiked a few times with our little dog, Bella. She's a RatCha, or half Rat Terrier and half Chihuahua. She's a spry, sturdy little dog, but she does not really enjoy hiking, especially for longer distances, whereas our former dog, a larger black and tan coonhound mix, could have out-hiked me any day of the week. She even had her own pack to carry her food and water! Do you know how long your dog can or likes to walk typically? Remember that a hike might be harder on them than a typical walk. Do they have any joint issues that might cause them pain on a hike? Are there tall steps or rock scrambles that might be harder for a smaller or an older dog? You'll need to consider these questions when picking a trail. Lastly, you need to properly dispose of your pet's waste as well. Pick up after your dog, and don't leave the bag by the trailside to pick up on the way back. Following some commonsense guidelines when hiking with your pet will help you and your pet have a safe and fun adventure out on the trails.

11

Mindful Hiking

There are as many different reasons to hike as there are hikers. Some people hike purely for the exercise or to challenge themselves physically. That's totally okay if that's your thing. Some people hike because they find the fresh air and sunshine to be calming and rejuvenating. Also, totally okay if that's your reason for hiking. Some people hike because they love to explore new places or they love learning about natural history—identifying plants, mushrooms, birds or other members of the local ecosystem. This also is a great reason to hike!

Whatever your reason for hitting the trail, taking some time to think intentionally about why you like being out there is part of what will keep you coming back. All of the above have been motivations for me at different times and they have influenced which trails I chose to hike. Taking some time to reflect on your "why" will go a long way toward making your hiking experience a positive one.

I am a certified forest therapy guide. Forest therapy is a mindfulness-based nature connection practice and forest therapy walks are not the same as hikes. (I would encourage you, if you ever have the opportunity, to try out a forest therapy walk with a trained guide.) You can, however, add some mindfulness practices to a hike, and I firmly believe doing so can enhance your hiking experience. There are varying definitions of mindfulness, but for our purposes here we're going to talk about mindfulness as noticing what's happening in the present moment, without judgement. Studies have shown that combining some mindfulness practices with time spent in nature only increases the stress-reduction and mood-lifting benefits of a hike, so let's talk about some ways to add mindfulness to your time on the trail.

Setting the Stage

Setting the stage for a mindful hike starts before you even reach the trailhead. There are several things you might try to help create an environment that will encourage space for mindfulness as you hike.

Start on the Drive There

I like to think that my hike truly starts the minute I leave home, and I try to create a driving experience that puts me in the right mood for the hike and for the nature connection I hope to find during it. As mentioned previously, research has shown we are spending less time in nature and—for many of us—our daily connection to nature is in decline. A 2017 study found that this growing disconnection is reflected in our culture as well. "Since [the 1950s] references to nature have been decreasing steadily in fiction books, song lyrics, and film storylines, whereas references to the human-made environment have not."[1] When I first heard of this study, I started to pay more attention to the lyrics of the music I listen to. Not many of them mentioned anything related to nature, so I went on a search for music I liked that *did* mention natural subjects. Now I have a whole playlist of these songs that I tend to listen to when I am driving to and from a hike. As soon as the music starts I can feel myself beginning to relax, almost like I do when I'm actually hiking.[2]

The route I take to the trailhead can also impact my experience. Sometimes I'm in a time crunch and I need to take the fastest route to the hike location, but occasionally I have all the time I want for a hike, and I'll choose driving directions that stick to the scenic route. This allows me to start taking in some natural scenes and beautiful views before I'm even on the trail and sets the mood for my time hiking.

Pause Before You Start

When you arrive at the trailhead it's tempting to jump right out, grab your gear and start hiking. Afterall, that's what you came for. But I would encourage you to pause for a moment before you start. Take a few deep breaths and perhaps do some simple stretches. Take a few minutes and try to shake off anything negative that might have happened on the drive or before you left for your hike. This might be a mental "shaking off" or even a physical one. Sometimes shaking out our hands or feet can help shake off stress and negative emotions.

Minimize Distractions

Many of us use our phones as navigational aids or to take pictures while we hike. Others have to be reachable for a variety of reasons. For whatever reason, you may not be able to completely turn your phone off and that's okay! I would encourage you, however, to look for ways to minimize the distractions from your phone while you hike. Maybe you temporarily silence notifications for certain apps or group chats. Maybe you turn off work emails. This doesn't have to be an "all or nothing" thing. Sometimes just silencing one or two things can make a big difference. Having a long phone conversation or listening to podcasts or music can also mentally take you away from the moment and the place where you are hiking.

Take Breaks

It is quite easy when you get started on a hike to just put your head down and keep walking. Before you know it, you may have covered a good distance, but several other things might have happened too. You may have forgotten to drink enough water. You may not have eaten anything. Your body might be working harder or differently than you're used to and you might need to take a few minutes to stretch. Setting the intention at the beginning of your hike to stop every so often, like at a certain distance or after a certain amount of time, to check in with yourself to see if you need water, a snack or just to sit and rest for a few minutes, is a good idea. A hike shouldn't feel like a forced march, and there's no better way to ensure you don't want to hike again than to skip breaks and arrive back at your car thirsty, hungry, and exhausted. Just taking a moment to stop and breathe has a way of bringing us into the present moment and can add mindfulness to your hike.

Mindful Moments

Once you have set the stage for a mindful hiking experience, you can continue to foster an attitude of mindfulness throughout your time on the trail. Sure, each of these takes some time, but I would argue that time spent focusing on mindfulness while hiking is never wasted, and you might decide it's even worth shortening the distance you try to cover in order to have time to incorporate some of these elements.

Practice Principles of Mindfulness

Depending on where you look, you'll see anywhere from seven to 11 mindfulness principles discussed. The list I like includes the following: acceptance, non-judging, non-striving, letting be/letting go, patience, trust, beginner's mind, gratitude, curiosity, humor, and kindness. Much has been written about these principles and how they can be applied in everyday life,[3] but how might they be practiced while hiking?

Every hike involves an element of acceptance, for example. No matter how much we research and plan, we do not have total control over what happens. We don't control the weather. We don't control that bear or those deer we come across. We don't control the trail conditions. Accepting this can help us have a peaceful and enjoyable hike that is not filled with excessive worry. Perhaps we also need to accept some things about ourselves along the way too.

Maybe we have hiked a particular trail many times. Approaching this trail with a beginner's mind attitude and a sense of curiosity might help us to appreciate it in a different way or help us to notice details we did not before. Trusting our bodies and having patience can not only help us be more mindful but can also help keep us safe while we hike.

100 Steps or Trail Blaze Moments

One way to include more mindfulness in your hikes is by practicing 100 Steps or Trail Blaze Moments. As you're hiking, make a decision to stop at every third or fourth trail blaze. Alternatively, when you think about it, count 100 steps and then stop. When you stop, take three intentional deep breaths and then spend a few moments looking around. If you're anything like me, you tend to look at your feet while you hike. I do this so I don't trip on roots or rocks or slip in mud. But if I'm not paying attention, I can spend my entire hike looking at the ground and not taking time to appreciate all the beauty around me. Using my steps or other elements already on the trail (like trail blazes) as reminders to stop and look around really helps me to be more present in the moment and not spend the entire hike lost in my thoughts as I stare at the ground.

Gratitude Hiking

Another way to increase mindfulness while hiking is to intentionally practice gratitude as you move down the trail. Look for things to be thankful for as you hike. Maybe

I am always grateful for the work that so many do to build and maintain trails across the state, but I'm especially grateful for the foot bridges that are built along the way. In many places they allow me to hike without getting my feet wet, but they also protect fragile ecosystems and in places like the Ocean Isle Nature Trail (pictured here) allow us as hikers to experience places we might not be able to otherwise. The bridges on this trail allow hikers to experience the marshlands on the Intracoastal Waterway up close.

it's having the time and resources to be out hiking in this moment. Maybe you're grateful for the beautiful variety of trees you see along the trail and the amazing diversity of nature they represent. Maybe, just maybe, you'll feel some gratitude toward your own body—your heart, your lungs, your feet, legs or arms—for carrying you down the trail safely and for bringing you to these places that you can only see by traveling in this way.

Mindful Walking

In mindful walking you draw your attention to the actual physical process of walking. You can notice the sensations of your legs moving and your weight shifting from foot to foot. You might notice how your arms swing or the natural rhythm you fall into over time. You might notice changes in your breathing or pulse as you traverse different parts of the trail. You might draw your attention to how the surface on which you're hiking feels under your feet. Is it soft, rough, squishy, or rocky? For example, it feels (and even sounds) very different to hike on hard-packed dirt than it does to hike on a trail covered in pine needles. If you're really daring, you might even take off your shoes for a short period of time and really feel the surface under your feet. I did this once on a moss-covered section of trail in the botanical gardens at the University of North Carolina at Charlotte and the feel of the moss under my feet was so soft ... like a plush carpet! A hike during the summer that includes creek crossings can be a great time to do this. Take off your shoes and feel the cold water and slick rocks as you walk across them. All of these can draw you out of your head and into your body and help you be more present in the moment.

Sensory Grounding

When you pause to drink some water or have a snack, or even if you use the 100 Steps or Trail Blaze Moments mentioned above, consider practicing some sensory grounding. Take a moment to notice one thing you can see, one thing you can touch, one thing you can hear, one thing you can smell and one thing you can taste. Sight is the dominant sense for most of us, but taking time to focus on the other senses can ground you in the moment and the place where you are. Maybe you notice the rough texture of the bark of a nearby tree. Maybe you notice a babbling creek, an owl calling in the distance, or a woodpecker hammering away. Maybe you smell the mustiness of the fallen leaves on the ground or the wildflowers blooming in the spring. Maybe you take a moment to really notice the taste of the water you're drinking or the snack you're eating. (It's not a good idea to taste wild plants along the trail unless you are experienced with foraging and know *for sure* what you're eating!)

Have Some Tea

One of my favorite ways to bring some mindfulness to a hike, especially in the winter, is to pack a thermos of hot tea. Somewhere along the hike I find a nice spot to sit, pour myself a cup and spend a few minutes savoring the warmth of the cup in my hands and the tea in my body, the taste of the tea, and the sights and sounds around me. To add to this experience, I often try to bring teas made from plants that I know grow naturally in the area where I'm hiking as this can help foster a connection to the place.

Enjoying a hot cup of tea in the shelter at Little Long Mountain on the Uwharrie National Trail.

Sit Spot

A "sit spot" practice is borrowed directly from forest therapy. To do this, find a place where you can sit and be still for at least 20 minutes. Doing this would be different from stopping for this long for a meal, for example. Here your plan is to observe and

This spot along the Chimney Run Trail at Southwest Park in southern Guilford County might be the perfect location for a sit spot. The trail is not busy, and the bench offers a comfortable place to sit for a time. Who knows what you might experience?

connect with your surroundings in an intentional and mindful way. When you do this, something kind of amazing happens. (It has never *not* happened to me.) The wildlife around you become accustomed to your presence and you "fade into the background" a bit. Suddenly you'll hear more birds singing. You might notice more squirrels or other small animals around. I've had birds and squirrels come right up to me during a sit spot before. Taking 20 minutes or more to just sit there may seem like a strange thing to do on a hike, but every time I have incorporated this practice in my hiking, I have left feeling more at peace, more rejuvenated, and more connected to the place than I do when I don't spend this quiet time.

Whatever your reason for hiking, approaching your time out on the trail with intentionality only creates a more meaningful experience and connection. Spend some time thinking about your "why" for hiking and incorporate whatever elements will bring you closer to that goal.

Part III

Finding Trails

My husband jokes that my hobby isn't only hiking but also finding new trails to hike. He's not wrong. I have so many lists of trails to try in the notes on my phone, on AllTrails, on pieces of paper tucked into trail guidebooks. (I might have a problem.) I could hike every day for a month and not clear out the lists I have at any given time. In fact, perhaps the hardest part of writing this book has been deciding when to call it "finished" because there are always more trails I want to explore that might fit well in this resource!

They say you never hike the same trail twice, even if you are covering the same ground. There is always something new to see and trails can be drastically different from season to season. But I also love visiting new places and I hike in new locations many times I head out. As a result, I've had the opportunity to see lots of trails across the state and many trails that don't necessarily hit the top five for a location on AllTrails.

In this section I'll share some sources for trail ideas. Of course, some locations like state and national parks are well known. Others might surprise you. I hope by the end of this section you'll have some great ideas for where to look for trails, possibly some right in your own backyard! At the end of each chapter, I'll highlight some of my favorite trails from across the state. I will focus on trails that could be hiked in an afternoon and would be accessible to many kinds of hikers. (You'll also find a list of 15 recommended hikes per region in Appendix I.)

I'll—primarily—stay away from the most well-known and popular trails to be found across the state, as information about these is readily available. Granted, these trails are popular for a reason. They often have beautiful views or other interesting or unique things to see. They can also have bigger crowds or issues with available parking or they can even run the risk of being closed due to overuse. I'm not saying you shouldn't try these popular trails, but I also want to encourage you to discover some less popular spots that might not be featured in other books. Let's find some new places to explore as you hike in North Carolina! Happy trails!

12

National Park Sites

> "When you drive to, say, ... the Great Smoky Mountains, you'll get some appreciation for the scale and beauty of the outdoors. When you walk into it, then you see it in a completely different way. You discover it in a much slower, more majestic sort of way."
>
> —Bill Bynum

When most people think of national parks in North Carolina, Great Smoky Mountains National Park is the first to come to mind and understandably so. Great Smoky Mountains National Park is the most visited national park in the country, more than Grand Canyon, Yosemite, and Yellowstone national parks combined.[1] We'll definitely spend time talking about hiking in Great Smoky Mountains National Park, but there are also nine other national park sites within North Carolina and they each have something to offer to hikers. As a note, the Appalachian Trail is considered a national scenic trail; it and the Blue Ridge Parkway come under National Park Service management in addition to the locations we'll discuss here. We'll explore those in other chapters, however.

National Seashores

Cape Lookout National Seashore

While the Harkers Island Visitor Center and Beaufort Visitor Information Center can be reached by car, the Cape Lookout National Seashore barrier islands are reachable only by ferry; passenger ferries run from Harkers Island and Beaufort and vehicle ferries run from Davis or Atlantic. There is much to do if you visit Cape Lookout, including birding, shelling, fishing, wild horse watching, camping and visiting the lighthouse or historic villages. There are only two official, marked trails within Cape Lookout National Seashore, and you'll find them both on Harkers Island.[2] These are short trails (less than a mile) that start from the Harkers Island Visitor Center (Soundside Loop Trail) and Core Sound Waterfowl and Heritage Museum (Willow Pond Trail); the two trails are also connected. There are also unofficial trails that people do hike on these barrier islands. Many of these trails are very sandy, so come prepared to walk on soft, often hot surfaces. There are no entrance fees to visit Cape Lookout National Seashore, but the ferries do charge a fee as do some activities such as guided tours.

There are many unofficial trails that crisscross the remote landscape of Shackleford Banks, part of Cape Lookout National Seashore. There are no facilities available here and very little shade so come prepared for lots of sun exposure and bring plenty of water. Also, be on the lookout for the wild horses that call this barrier island home. They are fascinating to see but should be given plenty of space.

Cape Hatteras National Seashore

Cape Hatteras National Seashore covers more than 70 miles of North Carolina's Outer Banks from Bodie Island to Ocracoke Island and it has many things for your enjoyment. Beach and water activities abound, and there's plenty of history to check out if that's your thing. Three designated trails explore parts of the island away from the beaches,[3] the Buxton Woods and the Hammock Hills trails—coming in at three-quarters of a mile each—and the longer Open Ponds Trail which is 4.5 miles (one direction) and part of the Mountains-to-Sea Trail. These trails consist of dirt, grass, boardwalk and sand and travel through maritime forests. They also travel near wetlands so you should be prepared for mosquitoes. Like Cape Lookout, there is no fee to enter this park, but there are fees for certain activities like climbing the lighthouses.

National Historic Sites

Fort Raleigh

Fort Raleigh is found on Roanoke Island, another barrier island, near Manteo. It preserves the location of the first English settlement in the present-day United States—the Roanoke Colony—as well as significant American Indian, African American and European American heritage in the area. There are two trails at the site, the Thomas Hariot Trail, a .9-mile dirt trail that begins at the reconstructed earthen fort, and the Freedom Trail, a 2.5-mile trail that leads to and from the Croatan Sound.[4] Both trails are flat and consist of dirt and grass surfaces with sections that are paved and sections that are sandy. You should come prepared for mosquitoes and be on the lookout for snakes—both venomous and not—always but especially on warmer fall and winter days. There is no fee to enter this park.

Carl Sandburg Home

Carl Sandburg was a famous American poet who lived from 1878 to 1967, and the home where he spent the last 22 years of his life is maintained by the National Park Service. Five miles of trails are found on the property, with hikes ranging in distance from .3 miles to 1.5 miles. Some of these trails climb to the tops of surrounding mountains with a fair amount of elevation gain.[5] Most of the trails are natural surface with trail treads typical of the mountains, but the trail from the hiker's parking lot to the goat barn and house is a wide, gravel, one-lane road. (The only vehicles that use this road are official park vehicles, such as the shuttle bus from the main parking lot—you'll definitely see more hikers than cars along this path!) There is no fee to access the visitor center (ground floor of the home), farm area, grounds or trails, but there can be a fee to tour the full home.

National Military Sites

Moores Creek National Battlefield

Moores Creek National Battlefield is located in Currie, northwest of Wilmington. The site commemorates the February 1776 battle at Moores Creek between the North Carolina Provincial Congress' militia forces and British Loyalists. The North Carolina

The trails at the Carl Sandburg home offer some lovely mountain hiking and the chance to see the Sandburg goats.

patriots won, and this important battle, one of the first of the American Revolution fought in the south, showed there was significant patriot support in the countryside of the state. The 1.25-miles of trails to explore at Moores Creek encompass their History Trail and Tarheel Trail, each with educational exhibits along the way. Both trails are essentially flat and trail tread surfaces include gravel, wooden boardwalk, paving and recycled rubber "mulch." There are no entrance fees for this park.[6]

Guilford Courthouse National Military Park

Guilford Courthouse National Military Park, located in the heart of Greensboro, is a national park site that preserves the site of the Battle of Guilford Courthouse during the Southern Campaign of the American Revolution. This battle, fought between the forces of Major General Nathanael Greene and British general Charles Cornwallis, "set the British Army on the path to ultimate surrender at the Siege of Yorktown."[7] The trails at this site are a combination of paved and gravel and there are loops of one to two miles. These can be combined for longer routes, however.[8] There are no fees to enter this park.

National Historic Trails

Overmountain Victory National Historic Trail

Signs like this one indicate sections of the Overmountain Victory Trail.

The Overmountain Victory National Historic Trail traces the route that was used by patriot militia as they assembled to fight at the Battle of Kings Mountain in 1780. This battle proved to be important as it demonstrated that the militiamen could coordinate, organize and execute a battle plan, and their success encouraged other patriots. In fact, General George Washington later said of these militiamen, "The crude, spirited, hardy, determined volunteers who crossed the mountains served as proof of the spirit and resources of the country."[9] If you've ever seen the summer outdoor drama *Horn in the West* in Boone, you'll remember the final battle scene which depicts the Battle of Kings Mountain.[10]

The entire trail extends 330 miles and passes through Virginia, Tennessee, North Carolina, and South Carolina. Parts of the trail can be followed through a motor route which uses existing state highways, but there are also 87 miles of walkable trails, although you couldn't hike all 87 miles from start to finish without having to drive between sections. Sections of the trail are managed by the individual property owners, so rules and access can vary from location to location. The hiking sections of the trail are located along or within half a mile of what is believed to be the probable route used by the patriots in 1780. These trails include paved greenway trails, such as the Yadkin River Greenway in Wilkes and Caldwell counties, and the Purple Martin Trail in Rutherfordton, as well as natural surface trails such as the Yellow Mountain Gap Trail in Pisgah National Forest and a section of the trail that passes through Lake James State Park.[11]

Trail of Tears National Historic Trail

Congress passed the Indian Removal Act in 1830 which required tribes in the southeastern United States to give up their lands in exchange for federal territory located west of the Mississippi River. The Cherokee people were a part of this, and their forced removal process began in May 1838. More than 16,000 Cherokee were removed from their homelands in Alabama, Georgia, Tennessee, and North Carolina. After initial travel west by water proved difficult, groups being moved between August and December 1838 traveled by existing roads. Thousands of Cherokee died during their trip west along this route which has come to be known as the Trail of Tears.[12] This is obviously a much-simplified account of this tragic event,

Junaluska was an important Cherokee leader during the 1800s. The stone monument pictured here is one of several that tell his story at the Junaluska Memorial in Robbinsville. This site is also considered to be the starting point of one branch of the Trail of Tears, as the nearby State Road 1110 (which becomes Tatham Gap Road) is believed to be built along a section of the original Old Army Road that connected present-day Robbinsville and Andrews. This road, which followed an older known Cherokee trail, was constructed in May 1838 to transport Cherokee out of the area.

and I would encourage you to learn more about it. If you visit the Cherokee area in the summer, in addition to visiting the sites mentioned below, you can attend the outdoor drama *Unto These Hills*, which was rewritten between 2006 and 2009 to tell a much more historically accurate account of the Cherokee people and the Trail of Tears.[13]

The Trail of Tears National Historic Trail passes through nine states and traces the routes of travel during this forced migration. Several locations in North Carolina are a part of this national historic trail and offer commemoration of and information about the Trail of Tears, including the Cherokee County Historical Museum, the Museum of the Cherokee People, Fontana Dam, Hiwassee Reservoir, the Cherokee Indian Reservation Welcome Center, the Oconaluftee Visitor Center for Great Smoky Mountains National Park, and the Junaluska Memorial in Robbinsville.[14] There are several hiking trails near these locations although none are considered to be hiking on the route of the Trail of Tears exactly. It is not possible at this time to follow the complete trail along its entire historic course.

At the Junaluska Memorial in Robbinsville you'll find Junaluska's burial location and a series of stone monuments telling his story. This site is also home to the short but very informative Medicine Wheel Trail. This wooded trail features examples of plants used in traditional Cherokee medicine and cooking along with educational signs about the plants. You'll also find resting benches named in honor of deceased members of the Cherokee Snowbird community. Unfortunately, when I visited, this trail and the memorial were showing some wear and tear, no doubt in part due to lack of resources and volunteers during the Covid-19 pandemic. I still enjoyed the trail and learned a lot, however.

National Memorial Site

The Wright Brothers National Memorial is located in Kill Devil Hills on the Outer Banks and preserves the location where Orville and Wilbur Wright, from Dayton, Ohio, spent 1900 to 1903 experimenting with flight. They achieved the first sustained flight of a manned, heavier-than-air, powered and controlled aircraft at the location on December 17, 1903. The paths at the site, totaling around 2.9 miles, are all paved, and mostly flat, except for the parts of the trails that climb about 100 feet up to the Wright Brothers Monument; these can be steep in sections.[15] There are plenty of interesting historical displays throughout the location to check out along the way. Note that there is an entrance fee of $10 for adults, 16 and older (as of the date of publication), unless you have a National Parks pass. Certain days of the year are free, but, of course, these are also likely to be some of the busiest days at the location.[16]

Great Smoky Mountains National Park

Great Smoky Mountains National Park is by far the most well-known national park site in North Carolina and one of the most well-known in the country. The park straddles the border of North Carolina and Tennessee and is divided almost evenly between the states. It is extremely popular and has averaged more than 13 million visits per year since 2020. Some other interesting statistics about Great Smoky Mountains National Park include:

- There are 11 picnic areas, totaling 1050 separate picnic sites.
- There are more than 100 backcountry campsites.
- There are 384 miles of road in the park; 238 of these are paved, and 146 are unpaved.
- There are 160 family cemeteries in the park and 4,847 gravestones.
- Approximately 200 permanent and 140 seasonal employees maintain the park and provide services to guests with the assistance of more than 2,700 volunteers per year.
- The park was designated an international Biosphere Reserve in October 1976 and a World Heritage Site in December 1983.
- Elevations within the park range from 875 feet to 6,643 feet and there are 16 peaks over 6,000 feet in elevation.
- There are 2,900 miles of streams in the park.
- There are more than 840 miles of trail in the park, including 74 miles of the Appalachian Trail and stretches of the Mountains-to-Sea Trail.[17]

This beautiful view from the porch of the Oconaluftee Visitor Center can be enjoyed by visitors without hiking at all. Elk are often seen in this field although I didn't spot any on the day I visited. The Oconaluftee River Trail departs from just beside this porch (National Park Service).

The Oconaluftee Visitor Center, located just north of Cherokee, is a great starting point for exploring the North Carolina section of the park. You'll find trail and other information in print and from knowledgeable park staff along with restrooms, educational displays, and a park store with maps, books, gifts, and snacks. You can also purchase the required parking tag at the visitor center. There is no entrance fee for the park, but the parking tags are required for all vehicles parking for longer than 15 minutes. Parking tags can be purchased for daily or weekly time frames, or you can purchase an annual tag. Vehicles with state-issued disabled placards or license plates do not need to purchase a parking tag.

Hiking trails in Great Smoky Mountains National Park[18] are frequently considered "backcountry." The park states, "Caution is advised in the backcountry. The park's backcountry is managed as a natural area where the forces of nature determine trail conditions. Please be prepared for swollen streams, bridge washouts, downed trees, and trail erosion—particularly between December and May due to the seasonal nature of the trail maintenance program."[19] Hiking in the mountains in these kinds of areas can certainly be strenuous. There are plenty of trails in the park that are 10 or more miles with impressive elevation gains. Even shorter trails can be more difficult because of elevation change and rough trail tread. There are trails to be found, however, that have lower mileage, less elevation gain, and some other accessibility features while still highlighting some interesting sights.

If you start your visit to the national park at the Oconaluftee Visitor Center, you're already near a great trail to check out—the Oconaluftee River Trail. I enjoyed this trail so much that it's my favorite national park hike. I'll share more about it at the end of this chapter.

Several other trails within the North Carolina section of the park would also be appropriate for many hikers. The Deep Creek area, just north of Bryson City, is a very popular spot for hikers and bikers as well as for tubers along the creek. Beware that parking can become an issue during peak season, especially on weekends. The Deep Creek Waterfall loop visits three falls (Tom Branch Falls, Indian Creek Falls, and Juney Whank Falls) over almost 2.5 miles with just under 500 feet of elevation gain. If you'd like a slightly shorter hike, you can take a section of this loop as an out-and-back hike of around two miles with much less elevation gain and see Tom Branch Falls and Indian Creek Falls.[20] An even shorter out-and-back around a mile will take you to Tom Branch Falls. You can also see Juney Whank Falls on its own short loop of under a mile, with between 150 and 200 feet of elevation gain.[21] Expect steeper trails and stairs on the Juney Whank Falls route.

Other spots for shorter hikes in the park are less well known. If you find yourself traveling along 441 (Newfound Gap Road) through the park watch for "Quiet Walkway" signs indicating a short trail or walkway into a less-visited natural spot in the park. The signs are simple and easy to miss, so keep an eye out for them for some off-the-beaten-path hikes. Just remember, these are still mountain trails and can include rugged conditions and steep inclines. You can also search for Quiet Walkway trails on AllTrails and find some listed along 441.

Great Smoky Mountains National Park is actively working to make the park accessible to visitors of all abilities and, beginning in 2023, started offering adaptive hiking, biking, kayaking and camping programs during the summer and early fall through a partnership with Catalyst Sports. Visitors who wish to explore on their own with a partner, rather than as a part of a program, can check out a GRIT Freedom Chair which gives access to approximately 12 miles of trails in the park. Park volunteers will even join in the hike if the hiker does not have a partner with them.[22]

No matter what kind of trail you decide to visit in the national park, you should do your research first. Cell phone coverage is likely to be spotty at best, and you should allow yourself plenty of time to complete your hike before dark. Sunset can occur as early as 5:00 p.m. in December but as late as almost 9:00 p.m. in June. Water sources that do not require treatment are often not available on trails and you should be on the lookout for wildlife of all kinds, including bears, elk and snakes. In fact, all the safety information we've covered in this book is likely to come into play while hiking in Great Smoky Mountains National Park!

Top Recommended National Park Hike

Great Smoky Mountains National Park: Oconaluftee River Trail

Trail Location: Oconaluftee Visitor Center in Great Smoky Mountains National Park, 1194 Newfound Gap Road, Cherokee, NC 28719
Trail Type: Out-and-back
Trail Length: Approximately 3 miles
Trail Elevation Change Description: An overall elevation change of less than 100 feet with a gentle descent on the way out and climb on the way back. One very

The Oconaluftee River Trail is a wide, mostly level trail that offers beautiful views of the river like this one (right) where the trail passes under the southern end of the Blue Ridge Parkway. The day I hiked this trail in May of 2024 there were hundreds of swallowtail butterflies around this area.

short, slightly steeper section as the trail passes under the southern terminus of the Blue Ridge Parkway.

Trail Tread: Natural surface and crushed gravel. Few roots or rocks to navigate, and some small wooden bridges.

Finding the Trail: The trail starts just behind the Oconaluftee Visitor Center and first passes by the adjacent Mountain Farm Museum. After the farm, the trail enters the wood line along the river and makes a right to follow the river.

Facilities: Restrooms, information, snacks, and places to sit at the visitor's center; a few benches to rest along the trail.

Favorite Feature: The views of the river along the way are beautiful. Also, be on the lookout for elk that frequent this area.

13

National and State Forests

"For more than 100 years, the Forest Service has brought people and communities together to answer the call of conservation. Grounded in world-class science and technology—and rooted in communities—the U.S. Department of Agriculture (USDA) Forest Service connects people to nature and to each other. As a federal agency in service to the American people, the Forest Service cares for shared natural resources in ways that promote lasting economic, ecological, and social vitality. In doing this, the agency supports nature in sustaining life."

—U.S. Forest Service[1]

North Carolina is home to four national forests managed by the U.S. Forest Service—Pisgah and Nantahala in the Mountain region, Uwharrie in the Piedmont, and Croatan in the Coastal Plain. Together they cover more than 1.25 million acres.[2] Each national forest offers a variety of outdoor recreation options, ranging from off-road vehicle trails to water sports, camping to climbing, hunting to fishing. And, of course, lots of opportunities for hiking. There are more than 1,700 miles of trails across the four national forests ranging from shorter day hikes to longer distance backpacking trails.[3]

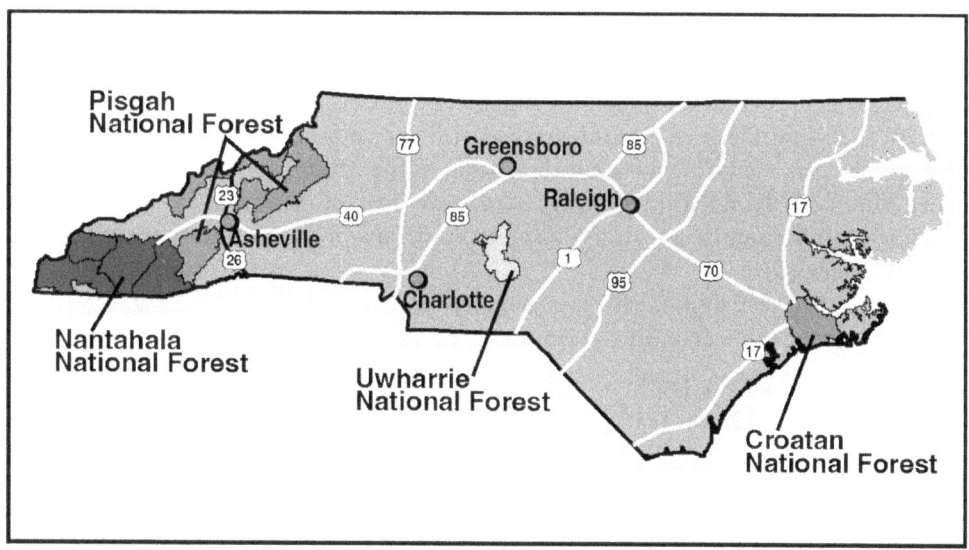

The locations of North Carolina's four national forests (U.S Forest Service).

Each national forest in North Carolina also contains designated wilderness areas and together these 11 areas total more than 102,000 acres. "By law, these lands are affected primarily by the forces of nature, where natural biological and physical processes are allowed to proceed with little to no human intervention and humans are considered 'visitors.'"[4] There are some trails in these wilderness areas, but you'll find they are minimally maintained. There are typically only signs at trail intersections and few if any trail blazes. Footbridges over creeks are not guaranteed. You're also more likely to find uncleared downed trees and overgrown trails during certain parts of the year. Motorized and wheeled vehicles (except for wheelchairs) are not allowed in these areas and groups are limited to 10 people. When hiking in a designated wilderness area you should come prepared with reliable navigation tools (not just electronic) and definitely carry the 10 Essentials.

Pisgah National Forest

Pisgah National Forest was the first of North Carolina's national forests to be established. A section of it was the first tract of land purchased under the 1911 Weeks Act which authorized the federal government to purchase and maintain land in the eastern United States as national forests. Prior to this, neither state nor federal governments owned substantial amounts of forested land east of the Mississippi River. More than 80,000 acres of the land that was first designated as part of Pisgah was bought from the Biltmore Estate after George Vanderbilt's death.[5] The forest is also home to the first school of forestry in the United States.

Pisgah National Forest includes more than 500,000 acres of land that stretch north, east, and west of Asheville. The land is included in 15 mountain counties and broken into three ranger districts—Grandfather, Appalachian, and Pisgah.[6] You'll find three designated wilderness areas in Pisgah: Linville Gorge Wilderness,[7] Middle Prong Wilderness,[8] and Shining Rock Wilderness.[9] While trails exist in all three wilderness areas, even some of shorter distance, they are almost all considered difficult. The terrain in these areas is known to be steep and rugged and the trails (and access roads) can be difficult to follow. Despite these things, several very popular trails exist in the three wilderness areas including a four-mile section of the Mountains-to-Sea Trail and the Green Mountain Trail (Middle Prong), Art Loeb Trail (Shining Rock Wilderness) and the Hawksbill Mountain, Shortoff Mountain, and Table Rock Mountain trails (Linville Gorge Wilderness).

Some other very popular hiking spots in the region are found in Pisgah National Forest, including (but certainly not limited to)[10]:

- Avery Creek Falls Trail
- Black Balsam Knob Trail
- Cat Gap Trail
- Courthouse Falls
- Craggy Pinnacle
- Frying Pan Lookout Tower
- Graveyard Fields Trail
- Looking Glass Rock Trail
- Moore Cove Falls Trail

- Mount Mitchell
- Mount Pisgah
- Pink Beds
- Skinny Dip Falls

Some of these trails are easily accessed via the Blue Ridge Parkway or other paved and maintained roads, while others are only accessible off forest service roads which can feature a variety of road conditions. All access points for these trails are subject to seasonal road closures, so be sure to do your research before choosing one to visit. Many of these trails also tend to be popular so you can expect busy trails and even difficulty parking on weekends and during the busiest times of year.

Some trails in Pisgah National Forest *do* offer a more accessible experience than those listed above. At the Cradle of Forestry Center located about an hour southwest of Asheville in Pisgah National Forest you'll find two accessible trails—the Forest Festival Trail, a wooded, paved, 1.3-mile trail that travels to visit a historic locomotive and a reconstructed sawmill, and the Biltmore Campus National Recreation Trail, which we'll discuss in detail below. There is a fee to visit the Cradle of Forestry which includes admission to the Forest Discovery Center Museum where restrooms and a café can be found. Be sure to check out the website for hours, current admission rates, and seasonal closures.[11]

In addition to the trails at the Cradle of Forestry facility, elsewhere in Pisgah National Forest you'll find the paved, half-mile Wiseman's View Trail that provides a beautiful view of Linville Gorge. There are some stairs to reach the final overlook, but views of the gorge can be seen without taking the stairs. (The mysterious Brown Mountain Lights can also sometimes be seen from Wiseman's View.) You also have the Roan Mountain Rhododendron Gardens Trail, a 1.0-mile paved trail found at 6,000 feet in elevation. This trail travels through native rhododendron and spruce-fir forest and provides views of the Black and Great Craggy mountains. There are picnic tables and restrooms at the trailhead.[12] In the past there have been several trails that started from the Linville Falls Visitor Center and, although they are not paved, they would be appropriate for many hikers and offer a variety of views of the falls.[13] Hurricane Helene caused extensive damage in the Linville Falls area and it remains to be seen which trails will be available after clean-up and repairs are completed. In Madison County between Marshall and Hot Springs, the 3.6-mile (one way) Laurel River Trail follows Big Laurel Creek, first passing through private property (with the owners' permission) before entering Pisgah National Forest. This trail is quite flat compared to most mountain trails, although there are some rocky sections that might be difficult or even impassable for those using adaptive hiking equipment. The first mile or so follows a gravel road, however, and still features the beautiful sights and sounds of Big Laurel Creek. The steepest grade on this trail is a very short section of 7 to 8 percent. The majority of the rest of the trail is under 5 percent.

Nantahala National Forest

Nantahala National Forest, established in 1920, is found in the southwestern corner of North Carolina. "'Nantahala' is a Cherokee word meaning 'land of the noon day sun,' a fitting name for the Nantahala Gorge, where the sun only reaches to the valley floor at midday."[14] It is the largest of the state's national forests with more than 530,000 acres and elevations in the forest range from 1,200 feet in Cherokee County near the Hiwassee River to 5,800 feet at Lone Bald in Jackson County. As in Pisgah National Forest, there are multiple ranger districts in Nantahala—Cheoah, Nantahala, and Tusquitee.

One of the giants of Joyce Kilmer Memorial Forest. To give you an idea of just how big some of these yellow poplar trees are, look carefully and you'll see my day pack and trekking poles at the bottom right of the tree's trunk.

Nantahala is world renowned for whitewater rafting, thanks in no small part to the Nantahala Outdoor Center location just south and west of Bryson City, but there are also lots of trails to be found—more than 600 miles worth that cater to hikers, mountain bikers, horseback riders, and off-highway vehicle drivers.[15] As much of this area sits on the Blue Ridge Escarpment, the terrain is often steep and rainfall is plentiful, with some regions receiving up to 90 inches per year. Tumbling streams and waterfalls are abundant in the region and area hikes often feature them. Be especially careful around waterfalls; unfortunately, people are injured and killed every year around them due to the swift currents, hidden obstacles and slick conditions. You should never walk out into a stream at the top of a waterfall, no matter the size. Also, when driving around Nantahala National Forest, expect roads that are as curvy and steep as many of the trails you'll find. There are not many straight(ish) two-lane highways to be found here!

One particular area to consider hiking in Nantahala National Forest is the Joyce Kilmer Memorial Forest in the Slickrock Wilderness Area. This area features old-growth forest with some trees more than 400 years old. You'll find giants here—yellow poplars—some of which are at least 100 feet tall and more than 20 feet in circumference. The memorial forest features an upper and a lower loop, and the biggest trees are found in the upper loop. The trail through both loops clocks in at just over 2.5 miles with decent elevation gain and is quite rocky and rooted. This is a designated wilderness area, so you won't find many signs or trail blazes, but you will find footbridges for the larger stream crossings, stairs on some inclines and flush restrooms and picnic facilities at the parking area. There are other trails in the area as well, but they are significantly more difficult and less developed than the memorial forest loop trails. Joyce Kilmer Memorial Forest is an out-of-the-way spot—not really on the way to anywhere—but it is inspiring and well worth the effort to find the location and complete the hike if doing so is within your capacity.

The Spirit Ridge Trail, also found in Nantahala National Forest, is a paved, out-and-back trail of less than a mile to some beautiful overlook views. You can also visit Whitewater Falls, one of my favorite hikes in a national forest. I'll share more about this hike at the end of this chapter.

Areas of Pisgah and Nantahala national forests were damaged during Hurricane Helene. Many areas of Nantahala National Forest reopened rather quickly, on October 11, 2024. The Pisgah Ranger District of Pisgah National Forest reopened one week later, while the Appalachian and Grandfather ranger districts remained closed for longer periods of time, opening trails and roads as they could be cleared.

Uwharrie National Forest

Uwharrie is the smallest of North Carolina's national forests, encompassing more than 51,000 acres in Davidson, Randolph and (mostly) Montgomery counties in the central part of the state. The land was first purchased by the federal government in 1931 and officially designated as a national forest in 1961, making it the youngest national forest in the state and the fifth youngest in the nation. As in the other national forests, there is an officially designated wilderness area in Uwharrie, but only one—Birkhead Mountains Wilderness.

The Uwharrie Mountains are some of the oldest in the world—definitely older than the Appalachians in the western part of the state—and if you hike in the area you might be surprised by some of the elevation changes, especially considering that you are in the Piedmont. You won't find any 6,000-foot peaks here, but you will find some just over

It's not hard to imagine Bigfoot coming around the bend on this stretch of the Uwharrie National Trail just north of the trail's southern terminus. These woods feel perfect for the hide-and-seek champion!

1,000 feet and they will feel much higher than that when the surrounding landscape can be as low as 200–300 feet.

Within the Uwharrie National Forest you'll find the 40-mile Uwharrie National Trail, the longest single-track footpath in central North Carolina. While plenty of people do backpack the trail over multiple days, there are also plenty of opportunities for shorter day hikes along this trail, as it crosses several roads and passes near several parking areas along the way. Shorter side trails that connect to the Uwharrie National Trail are available and the local trail-building group—the Uwharrie Trailblazers—is frequently working on building new trails and improving existing trails. In addition to the elevation changes, when hiking in the Uwharrie Mountains you'll find trails that can be quite rocky and sometimes muddy. Most trails in Uwharrie National Forest offer minimal, if any, facilities, and you should come prepared with your own water (or the ability and knowledge to treat creek water) and a reliable means of navigation. Ticks are abundant in the area during certain times of the year, so don't forget your repellent and other tick-mitigation measures. Also, the Uwharries are a hotbed of reported Bigfoot sightings in North Carolina, so you never know who you'll run into!

All kidding aside, don't let these things deter you from visiting the Uwharrie Mountains. The Uwharries are one of the few places in the Piedmont that you can feel like you are truly away from it all. The area offers fascinating natural and human history to discover and some beautiful hikes, especially in the winter when the lack of leaves allows one to appreciate the views from the tree-covered peaks.

Croatan National Forest

In July 1936, 77,000 acres that were owned by the federal government in Craven, Carteret and Jones counties were designated as the Croatan National Forest. For the three years prior, these lands had been used for reforestation experiments. The Croatan National Forest's current almost 161,000 acres are bordered by the Trent, Neuse and White Oak rivers on three sides and Bogue Sound on a fourth. There are also four designated wilderness areas in the forest that total more than 31,000 acres—Catfish Lake South, Pocosin, Pond Pine, and Sheep Ridge. These are primarily pocosin environments, peat-filled depressions in the landscape that contain thick growths of shrubs and small trees. These pocosins are typically difficult for people to traverse so the plants and animals that live in these areas tend to be undisturbed. Unlike in other national forests in the state, hiking trails are generally not available in the designated wilderness areas in Croatan.

Croatan National Forest is the only true coastal forest in the eastern part of the United States, and it features a wide variety of habitats including saltwater estuaries, fresh-water swamps, bogs, pocosins, hardwood forests, savannahs, evergreen forests, and woodlands. It's not surprising with all these different habitats that there's also a huge variety of terrestrial and marine animals and plant life. Black bear, bobcats, river otters and mink, among other mammals, call the forest home. Several kinds of snakes, turtles and alligators can be found as can many kinds of birds, including bald eagles, quail, osprey, and peregrine falcon. Plant life includes longleaf pine and bald cypress hardwoods and carnivorous plants such as Venus flytraps, sundew, and pitcher plants. The tannic-stained waters in the area, called "blackwater," are home to several varieties of sunfish as well as the swampfish. There is certainly a lot to see along these trails! Much of the habitat found in Croatan is fire-adapted and fire-dependent. Low-intensity fires play an important role in the plant diversity of the area. Prescribed fires managed by the Forest Service help to preserve the area and restore habitat. Before visiting the forest be sure to check online to see if any prescribed burns are happening in sections of the forest.[16]

Quite a few hiking trails of different lengths can be found in Croatan National Forest.[17] The 21-mile Neusiok Trail travels from the Neuse River to the Newport River, crossing through many of the habitat types mentioned above. It's also part of the Mountains-to-Sea Trail.[18] While 21 miles might be long for most people for a day hike, you could still have a wonderful experience hiking a shorter section of the trail. Many hikes of shorter lengths are available as well, including several five- to ten-mile trails and hikes of under three miles. For example, the Patsy Pond Nature Trails located between Morehead City and Cape Carteret range in length from .75 miles to 1.9 miles and can be combined for a hike of around three miles. These trails are flat but sandy, and there are restroom facilities at the nearby North Carolina Coastal Federation office during business hours.[19] Hunting is also allowed in this section of the forest from October to February and in April and May. Visitors are strongly encouraged to wear hunter orange vests or hats. The Coastal Federation office has vests available for loan during their normal hours. In the Flanners Beach section you'll find a trail system consisting of paved, natural surface and boardwalk trail treads. These trails can be enjoyed individually for shorter hikes starting at around a mile or combined for a lengthier hike of up to six miles.[20]

Hiking any of the trails in Croatan National Forest would be most enjoyable from October to May when the temperatures are more moderate, the brush growth is a bit thinner, and insects are not as prevalent. Also, be prepared to get your feet wet on any of these trails, even where there are boardwalks and bridges. In many ways, the presence of water defines Croatan National Forest. In addition to hiking, Croatan National Forest offers camping, biking, nature/wildlife viewing, hunting, boating, fishing and off-highway vehicle trails.

State Forests

The North Carolina Forest Service maintains Educational State Forests (ESF) specifically designed to teach the public about forest environments. Each forest features trails that include education exhibits.[21]

- *Clemmons ESF*: Located between Garner and Smithfield. Four trails ranging in length between .6 and three miles.
- *Holmes ESF*: Located between Brevard and Flat Rock. Five trails ranging in length between .1 and three miles.
- *Jordan Lake ESF*: Located at Jordan Lake, south of Raleigh and Chapel Hill. Four trails ranging in length between .5 and two miles.
- *Mountain Island ESF:* Located north of Charlotte. Currently no trails open to the public but there will be in the future.
- *Turnbull ESF:* Located just north of Elizabethtown and northwest of Wilmington. Six trails ranging from .25 to 4.5 miles.
- *Tuttle ESF:* Located between Lenoir and Morganton. Eight trails ranging in length between .1 and two miles.

13. National and State Forests

The North Carolina Forest Service also manages Bladen Lakes State Forest, Headwaters State Forest and Dupont State Recreational Forest. Each of these features many miles of hiking trails, often more challenging than those found in the Educational State Forests.

Top Recommended National Forest Hikes

Pisgah National Forest: Cradle of Forestry—Biltmore Campus Trail

Trail Location: 11250 Pisgah Highway, Pisgah Forest, NC 28768
Trail Type: Loop
Trail Length: 1.75 miles
Trail Elevation Change Description: Some hills but they are gentle by mountain standards with a maximum grade of around 5 percent. The trail has an overall elevation gain of 72 feet.
Trail Tread: Paved, asphalt
Finding the Trail: The trail starts behind the museum building, to the left as you face away from the museum.
Facilities: The Cradle of Forestry in America museum offers restrooms, a gift shop and a small café. You'll also find places to sit and lots of interesting exhibits to explore. There are quite a few disabled spaces available in the parking lot and the building is accessible via ramps. There are numerous benches along the trail for resting and restrooms located about half-way during the hike. Note: There is an entrance fee to access the Cradle of Forestry in America facility.
Favorite Feature: This lovely trail winds through a beautiful forest and features interesting buildings and exhibits from the days of the Biltmore Forestry School.

Nantahala National Forest: Whitewater Falls

Trail Location: On Whitewater Road (NC 281) south of Cashiers and just north of the South Carolina border
Trail Type: Out-and-back
Trail Length: .3 miles to the first overlook of the falls and another .1 down the steps to the viewing platform; .6–.8 miles total
Trail Elevation Change Description: Gentle incline to first overlook with a maximum grade of around 8 percent. The one-hundred fifty-five steps leading down to the viewing platform are much steeper.
Trail Tread: Paved asphalt to the first overlook and wooden steps with railings down to the viewing platform. There are a couple of breaks in the pavement where the trail has sunk a bit, creating a step up of a couple of inches. These occur at the beginning of the trail where the surrounding field is flat, so it is possible to avoid these steps by going off into the grass.
Finding the Trail: The entrance to the trail is located at the back of the parking area, away from the parking area entrance. It is clearly marked.
Facilities: There are several disabled parking spots in the parking area, as well as accessible restrooms. There are also picnic facilities available and a few benches

A wooded stretch of the Biltmore Campus Trail at the Cradle of Forestry in America.

located along the trail. Note that there is a parking fee for this area of $3 for vehicles with seven or fewer passengers and $1 per person for each additional person over seven. There are envelopes and drop boxes available for paying the fee. Please stay on trails when viewing the waterfall. Going off trail can lead to injury or even death; unfortunately, people die every year at North Carolina's waterfalls.

Favorite Feature: Of course, it's the waterfall. Whitewater Falls is quite impressive, and you can see it well from the first overlook, without walking down (and up) the stairs. You can hear the falls from the parking area. Also, partway up the paved trail there is a beautiful long-range view of the elevation change of the Blue Ridge Escarpment.

Whitewater Falls is the tallest waterfall east of the Mississippi River and beautiful views of it can be seen from this short trail nearby.

Uwharrie National Forest: Little Long Mountain via the Uwharrie National Trail from Joe Moffitt Trailhead

Trail Location: Joe Moffitt Trailhead, 998 Thayer Road, Troy, NC 27371 (on some maps the road is named King Mountain Road, and it connects to Thayer Road)
Trail Type: Out-and-back

Beautiful long-distance views of the Uwharrie Mountains can be seen from the summit of Little Long Mountain.

Trail Length: Approximately 2.0 miles

Trail Elevation Change Description: This trail is consistently but fairly gently uphill until you reach the summit of Little Long Mountain. There is one section just before the summit that is a little steeper than the rest, with grade of about 10 percent. The nice thing is that it's almost all downhill on the back half of your hike!

Trail Tread: Natural surface with plenty of rocks, roots and (potentially slippery) pine needles along the way. This is a single-track trail, but not terribly narrow until the last short climb just before the summit.

Finding the Trail: The small gravel parking area is found on Thayer Road (King Mountain Road on some maps) where the Uwharrie Trail crosses the road. There is parking for about six cars. The entrance to the trail is off the side of the parking area by the small rock monument dedicated to Joe Moffitt. Do not follow the old road behind the gate seen at the far edge of the parking area.

Facilities: There are no restrooms available at this location and the closest restrooms, gas, etc., would be at least 15 minutes away by car. Cell service can vary in this area, but I have had good coverage on this hike.

Favorite Feature: The top of Little Long Mountain provides wonderful long-range views of the surrounding areas as it is not tree covered like most of the other peaks in the Uwharrie Mountains. Along the way, you'll also see lots of milky quartz, including some pieces that are boulder size, and an unusually shaped tree affectionately known as the Dragon Tree.

A section of the boardwalks on the Cedar Point Tideland trail can be seen in the distance. These boardwalks allow for a much more up-close view of the saltwater marsh here.

Croatan National Forest: Cedar Point Tideland National Recreation Trail

Trail Location: Forest Route 153A, Swansboro, NC 28584

Trail Type: Loop

Trail Length: There are two loops—the shorter inner loop is approximately .7 miles, and the longer outer loop is about 1.4 miles.

Trail Elevation Change Description: These trails are essentially flat. There are a few very gentle inclines as the boardwalks go up and over the marshlands.

Trail Tread: Crushed gravel with some small roots and boardwalks. Some boardwalks involve metal grates to allow for better drainage.

Finding the Trail: The trail is located near the Cedar Point Campground which is off NC 58 about 1.5 miles north of the intersection of NC 24 and NC 58.

Facilities: Quite a few parking spaces and restrooms at the trailhead. Some benches for resting along the trail. Fairly good cell coverage throughout.

Favorite Feature: The boardwalks that crisscross the marshlands are wonderful and offer lots of opportunities to spot wildlife on land and in the air and water. (Visiting at low tide will allow for better viewing of some wildlife.) The views of the surrounding area are great and the sunset views are gorgeous.

14

The Blue Ridge Parkway

"The idea is to fit the Parkway into the mountains as if nature has put it there."

—Stanley Abbott, chief landscape architect of the Blue Ridge Parkway and first Parkway superintendent, 1937–1944

The iconic Blue Ridge Parkway, managed by the National Park Service, travels for 469 miles between Great Smoky Mountains National Park near Cherokee, through North Carolina, before entering Virginia and ending at Shenandoah National Park near Waynesboro, Virginia. It "travels the crests, ridges, and valleys of five major mountain ranges, encompassing several geographic and vegetative zones ranging from 600 to over 6,000 feet above sea level"[1] and is the longest road in the United States planned as a single unit.[2]

Blue Ridge Parkway History

The initial plan for the Blue Ridge Parkway—a park-to-park highway with recreational areas and preserved views along the way—was approved on November 24, 1933, and given a budget of $16 million (more than $370 million in 2024). The exact route of the road was not yet set, and a battle between Tennessee and North Carolina ensued, each campaigning mightily in Washington, D.C., for the non–Virginia section of the Parkway to pass through their state. Ultimately North Carolina prevailed and construction began on September 11, 1935, near Cumberland Knob.

The Civilian Conservation Corps (CCC), Emergency Relief Administration (ERA) and Works Progress Administration (WPA) were involved in building the Parkway, although most of the construction was completed by private contractors. By the beginning of World War II, approximately 170 miles were open to the public and an additional 160 miles were under construction. An accelerated plan to finish the Parkway by 1966—the 50th anniversary of the National Park Service—was introduced in the mid-1950s and all but 7.7 miles of the roadway were complete by this NPS milestone.[3]

This short, unfinished stretch included Grandfather Mountain. Grandfather's owner, Hugh Morton, did not agree with the proposed construction plan, citing the mountain's fragile ecosystem.[4] After much negotiation, the award-winning, 1,234-foot Linn Cove Viaduct was built to complete the Blue Ridge Parkway *and* protect the

Cumberland Knob, located just inside North Carolina from the border with Virginia, is the place where construction began on the Blue Ridge Parkway. Today there are two trails to enjoy at this location—the Cumberland Knob Trail of less than a mile and the much more challenging Gully Creek Trail.

ecology of Grandfather Mountain. Design began for this complex concrete bridge in the late 1970s and its construction was complete in 1982. Additional roadwork around the area took another five years and the last stretch of the Blue Ridge Parkway opened in 1987.[5]

Walking across the Linn Cove Viaduct is not allowed unless the Blue Ridge Parkway is closed to vehicular traffic in the area, but many people enjoy exploring the Viaduct by foot during the winter when the Parkway is closed due to snow and ice. This section of the Parkway was also closed during the Covid-19 pandemic, and I had the opportunity to walk the bridge. It's a unique feeling to stand on it and look out toward the mountains. You feel as if you're floating in space.

In September 2024, the Blue Ridge Parkway, especially the North Carolina section, suffered significant damage from Hurricane Helene. In the days following the storm the National Park Service shared that staff assessing the conditions of the Parkway had found "tens of thousands of trees across the roadway and nearly three dozen rock and mud slides."[6] Even as sections of the Parkway began to reopen after Helene, it became obvious that some portions of the roadway and even more trails would likely take months or even years to fully recover. Hikers should be prepared to encounter the impacts of Helene along trails for the foreseeable future.

The Linn Cove Viaduct is often featured in pictures of the Blue Ridge Parkway (courtesy Nathaniel Wallace).

Hiking and the Blue Ridge Parkway

The Blue Ridge Parkway in North Carolina provides direct access to many wonderful trails. These range from shorter paved trails, a half mile or less and rated as "easy," to longer, more strenuous trails and everything in between. (Remember: "easy" is a subjective term!) Sections of the Mountains-to-Sea Trail parallel the roadway and access to even more trails can be found not far off the Parkway in many areas. The National Park Service publishes a wonderful list of trails by milepost with basic descriptions of all trails listed and more detailed information (including maps) of some.[7] You can also search for hiking trails on the interactive Blue Ridge Parkway map found at blueridgeparkway.org or check out the list of trails[8] and list of Parkway resources by milepost on the Parkway Milepost Guide on virtualblueridge.net.

My favorite Parkway hiking locations have included:

- Sections of the Bluff Mountain Trail (between milepost 238.5 and 244.7)
- Various trails at Moses Cone Park (milepost 294)
- Boone Fork Trail (milepost 296.5)
- Jumpinoff Rock (milepost 260.3)

The northern half of the Parkway in North Carolina is definitely worth checking out if you haven't.

A section of the Bluff Mountain Trail around the Bluffs picnic area that is also part of the Mountains-to-Sea Trail. In the spring and summer this section of trail is filled with wildflowers (courtesy Nathaniel Wallace).

With all the amazing hiking, breathtaking views, and other attractions that can be found along the Parkway, it's no wonder that it's so popular; more than 16 million people visited in 2023 (in both Virginia and North Carolina).[9] During the most popular times of year and especially on weekends, the Parkway can get *very* busy. Traffic can back up, parking lots can fill, and popular trails can be packed with people. If you're planning to hike during one of these times, have a Plan B and even a Plan C in mind in case there's no parking available at your first-choice trailhead.

Sections of the Parkway can close in the winter for snow and ice and even during other seasons if high winds or heavy rains are expected. Sections that typically stay open aren't usually treated and scraped in the same way other state- and city-maintained roads are and can be quite icy even if traffic is allowed on them. Check out road conditions in advance if you think there's a chance for weather-related closings. If you are away from your car hiking and a decision is made to close the roadway, rangers will leave information on your windshield about how to exit the Parkway. It's also not unusual during the spring and summer to find sections of the road closed or reduced to one lane for paving or other road maintenance. Always allow yourself more time to drive on the Parkway than you would need for the same distance on other roads. Plus, when hiking near the Parkway, part of the fun is the drive there! Some locations along the Parkway have restrooms and other visitor services, but definitely not all, and cell service can be spotty, so plan ahead and be prepared.

The highest point on the Blue Ridge Parkway motor road is at Richard Balsam Overlook, mile marker 431.4. The forest here features red spruce and Fraser fir trees, more typical of Canada than the southern United States. The nearby Haywood-Jackson Overlook at mile marker 431 features a loop trail through this forest to the summit of Richard Balsam Mountain—the ninth highest peak east of the Mississippi River. This 1.5-mile hike involves an elevation gain of around 400 feet.

Top Recommended Blue Ridge Parkway Hike

Moses Cone Memorial Park: Flat Top Mountain Trail

Trail Location: Moses Cone Memorial Park, near Blowing Rock
Trail Type: Out-and-back
Trail Length: 5.5 miles, but you could do any amount of this trail and still have a beautiful, enjoyable hike.

It's rare to see a stretch of the Blue Ridge Parkway empty like this on a fall day. Many people from near and far head to the Parkway to check out the autumn leaves (courtesy Nathaniel Wallace).

One of the beautiful long-range views hikers are treated to along the Flat Top Mountain Trail at Moses Cone Memorial Park.

Trail Elevation Change Description: 600 feet for the entire trail. The trail features a steady but fairly gentle climb on the way out. The grade averages around 4 percent, with a maximum grade of 9 percent—if you don't count the optional fire tower climb at the top for the view!

Trail Tread: Wide, crushed gravel trail. No stairs if you don't opt to do the fire tower climb on top. The trail, a former carriage road, is very well maintained and clear.

Finding the Trail: Park at Moses Cone Manor at mile marker 294 on the Blue Ridge Parkway. Follow the trail through the tunnel under the Parkway and then upward toward Flat Top Mountain. This is a very popular trail, and you will likely see other hikers going the same direction.

Facilities: Restrooms are located at the manor house parking area.

Favorite Feature: The views are amazing throughout this hike and the trail is very well maintained. Also, there are lots of other trails worth checking out in Moses Cone Park.

15

State Park Sites

> First came the miners. All they wanted were a few minerals and there were plenty.
> Then came the lumberjacks. All they wanted were a few trees and there were plenty.
> Then came the railroad men. All they wanted was a little space to travel up the mountain and there was plenty.
> Then came the mill. Lumber was needed for construction and the mill made plenty.
> And then came the lumber camps, housing, and loggers by the hundreds. Lots of men were needed for labor and the camps provided plenty.
> The economy was booming. It was the land of opportunity. And everyone thought there was plenty—except for a few, who were afraid that soon there would be none.
> Trees were cut by the hundreds. Whole forests were destroyed. And the few became outraged and appealed to the governor who insisted that it stop, and he convinced the legislature to establish the first state park. And then there was one.[1]

The above is from an introduction to the history of the North Carolina State Parks system written in 2011, and the "one" was Mount Mitchell State Park, formed in 1915. Fort Macon State Park, all the way on the opposite side of the state, was the second park and was formed in 1924. These two parks have grown into a system of more than 40 state parks, recreation areas, natural areas, lakes, rivers and state trails that encompasses more than 250,000 acres of land and water across North Carolina.[2]

Different Types of State Park Sites

State parks are the primary unit of the state park system, and they strive to strike a balance between conservation and recreation. Parks may vary in the facilities available, but you will find most of the land in state parks left undisturbed and free from any kind of improvements except for trails. Outdoor recreation is the primary purpose of state recreation areas rather than conservation and preservation, although these are still important. These areas tend to be less sensitive to human impact and typically provide more recreation facilities than parks. Natural areas focus on protecting ecologically and scientifically valuable locations that are more sensitive to human impact. They typically offer fewer or no facilities and some are not open to the public.

The Balsam Nature Trail at Mount Mitchell State Park passes through a fairytale-like section of spruce-fir forest. The evergreen smell that surrounds you on this hike is also a treat.

The North Carolina State Parks system also includes a set of state trails.[3] These are considered separate from other local and regional trails, and each trail is sponsored by a partnership of federal, state, and local governments, nonprofit organizations and private landowners that build, maintain, and manage their section of trail. These state trails can

A view from the Pine Barrens Trail at Weymouth Woods Sandhills Nature Preserve, located 35 miles northwest of Fayetteville. Here hikers can spot several rare species including the fox squirrel, the red-cockaded woodpecker, and the purple pitcher plant among acres of longleaf pines, some of which are hundreds of years old. Longleaf pine forests once covered millions of acres of the southeastern U.S.

feature land-based hiking trails or paddle trails that follow local rivers and allow for canoeing or kayaking. While these trails are all longer than a day hike, they still offer some shorter sections that would make for a wonderful afternoon out. Many of these trails are still being developed so be sure to check out maps and current conditions. The North Carolina State Trails are:

- Dan River State Trail (paddle)
- Deep River State Trail (paddle and hike)
- East Coast Greenway State Trail (hike and bike)
- Fonta Flora State Trail (hike and bike)
- French Broad River State Trail (paddle)
- Hickory Nut Gorge State Trail (hike and bike)
- Mountains-to-Sea Trail (hike, bike and paddle; discussed in "Long-Distance Trails" chapter)
- Northern Peaks State Trail (hike)
- Overmountain Victory State Trail (hike and drive; discussed in "National Park Sites" chapter)
- Roanoke River State Trail (paddle)
- Wilderness Gateway State Trail (hike, bike, and paddle)
- Yadkin River State Trail (paddle)

Hiking at State Park Sites

State park sites are in all three geographical regions of North Carolina, and they are some of the most popular places to visit in the state. Each park offers a variety of activities but all offer hiking trails. You can find free detailed maps on each park's website and print versions available at the park offices and visitor centers. These maps offer general information as well as specific trail information including distances and difficulty levels. The maps show topographical lines, but you'll want to look the trails up on a hiking app or perhaps in a guidebook for more specific elevation profile information. Some parks offer multiple access points or even sections of park that are not attached to each other. If you're planning to hike at a state park, be sure you know the access point you'll need to visit for the trail you plan to hike.

A variety of trails are offered across the state parks, with some being quite difficult, so it pays to do your research in advance instead of just randomly picking a trail when you arrive at a park. Many parks have trails deemed "nature trails" or "Kids in Parks Track Trails."[4] These trails are *not* just for kids, so don't hesitate to check them out! They are typically shorter trails with less elevation gain and can provide a great introduction to the landscape, flora and fauna of the park. For example, in the mountains you'll find the Beech Tree Trail at Elk Knob State Park. This one-mile loop through beautiful forest has gentle inclines that add up to just over 100 feet of elevation gain and features an Art in Parks installation of wonderful pieces to discover along the way. In the piedmont, at Morrow Mountain State Park, the Quarry Trail is the "Kids in Parks" trail. This nice loop trail is less than a mile in length with less than 100 feet in elevation gain. A creek runs beside the trail, and you can visit the historic quarry site where the Civilian Conservation Corps quarried many of the rocks used in the construction of the park. There is now a small pond in the quarry, and you can often spot wildlife. At the coast, the Track Trail at Hammocks Beach State Park is the Live Oak Trail. This hike is less than a mile of sandy and boardwalk trail that highlights longleaf pines and a view of the Intracoastal Waterway. Many of the Track Trails in state parks are also located close to visitor centers, restrooms and other amenities.

I've had the joy of hiking at 29 of North Carolina's state parks, from the oldest— Mount Mitchell—to the youngest—Grandfather Mountain State Park—as well as in

This view shows part of the Hickory Trail at the U.S. 221 Access of New River State Park shortly after a prescribed fire (a.k.a. controlled burn). Fire has played an important ecological role across North Carolina for millennia and some species are even dependent on periodic fires. Natural and prescribed fires help return nutrients to the soil, control invasive plants that inhibit the growth of native ones, and reduce the fuel load, thus reducing the risk of uncontrolled wildfires. According to the North Carolina Division of Parks and Recreation, between 2018 and 2022, 35 state park system locations conducted prescribed burns (courtesy Nathaniel Wallace).

several recreation and natural areas and on several state trails. (Note: Mayo River State Park and Carvers Creek State Park were established before Grandfather Mountain but did not open to the public until after it, in 2010 and 2013, respectively. The 35th park to join the state park system, Pisgah View State Park, was slated to open in 2025, but the impacts of Hurricane Helene have likely altered that timeline. A new anticipated opening date has not been released as of this publication.) These spaces are amazing places to visit and appreciate the varied landscapes across this beautiful state. In addition to those discussed in detail below, here are some of my favorite hikes within state park locations.

- Carvers Creek State Park: Rockefeller Loop Trail and Cypress Point Loop Trail
- Dismal Swamp State Park: Boardwalk Trail and Supple Jack Loop
- Grandfather Mountain State Park: Nuwati Trail; lower section of Profile Trail
- Hammocks Beach State Park: Mainland trails—Live Oak Trail; Coastal Fringe Trail; Evergreen Trail; Hickory Bluffs Trail
- Hanging Rock State Park: Riverbluffs Trail
- Lake Norman State Park: Lakeshore Trail

- Lake Waccamaw State Park: Sand Ridge Nature Trail and section of Lakeshore Trail
- Lumber River State Park: Only trail at Princess Ann Access
- Mayo River State Park: Fall Creek Falls and Mayo River Trails
- Medoc Mountain State Park: Fishing Creek Loop Trail
- Merchants Millpond State Park: Coleman Trail and Cypress Point Trail
- Mount Mitchell State Park: Balsam Nature Trail
- New River State Park: River Run Trail
- Pilot Mountain State Park: Grassy Ridge and Mountain Trail loop; Pilot Knob Trail
- Raven Rock State Park: Raven Rock Loop Trail
- South Mountains State Park: Hemlock Nature Trail
- Stone Mountain State Park: Summit Trail as an out-and-back hike from the upper trailhead parking area
- Weymouth Woods Sandhills Nature Preserve: Pine Barrens Trail

If you plan to visit multiple state parks, consider getting a state park passport (free) and having it stamped at each park. It's a fun way to keep up with your visits and the booklet offers some "bucket list" activities in each park.

Several state park sites received damage from Hurricane Helene. In fact, all parks west of I-77 were closed for at least four weeks after the storm. Five of the 13 closed sites partially reopened on November 1, 2024, and another five reopened by the end of the month. Most of South Mountains State Park reopened by mid–2025, although some trails remained closed, and Chimney Rock State Park reopened in June 2025 with capacity limited by required advanced reservations. Mount Mitchell State Park remained closed until just 12 days shy of the year anniversary of the storm, reopening on September 15, 2025. It was truly a happy day to see North Carolina's first state park once again welcome visitors to enjoy its trails, views, and famous peak. The amazing work done to bring these parks back online is truly praiseworthy.

Top Recommended State Park Hikes

Mount Jefferson State Natural Area: Summit, Rhododendron, and Lost Province Trails Loop (Mountain Region)

Trail Location: Mount Jefferson State Natural Area, 1481 Mount Jefferson State Park Road, West Jefferson, NC 28694

Trail Type: Lollipop—the Summit section of the trail is an out-and-back and the Rhododendron and Lost Province trails form a loop that connects to the Summit Trail.

Trail Length: 2.5 miles if you complete all three trails. The Summit Trail is .6 miles as an out-and-back; the Rhododendron Trail is a 1.1-mile loop; and the Lost Province Trail is a .75-mile loop.

Trail Elevation Change Description: This hike begins with a climb from the parking area up to Mount Jefferson's summit. Inclines on this climb reach 12 percent so it can be a bit steep. The remainder of the trail includes a gentle

The amazing view of Ashe County and beyond from Luther Rock along the Rhododendron Trail at Mt. Jefferson.

downhill—and then back uphill—slope before the Summit Trail travels back downhill to the parking area.

Trail Tread: The Summit Trail is gravel, and the other trails are natural surface. The natural surface trails can be rocky and rooted in places and quite narrow in certain sections. A few stairs are included in certain spots.

Finding the Trail: This trailhead is found at the last parking area at the top of the main park road, where you'll find ample parking except, perhaps, on the busiest weekends. The trail begins at the top end of this parking lot where it passes by the picnic shelter and some picnic tables before bending to the right and beginning the climb up to the summit.

Facilities: Restrooms are available at the park office year-round as well as at the summit parking area seasonally.

Favorite Feature: This loop of trails features some beautiful wooded areas and amazing views of the surrounding landscape.

Hanging Rock State Park: Rock Garden and Upper Cascades Falls (Piedmont Region)

Trail Location: Hanging Rock State Park, 1790 Hanging Rock Park Road, Danbury, NC 27016; main park entrance and visitor center area

Trail Type: Out-and-back

Heading to the Upper Cascades Falls at Hanging Rock State Park.

Trail Length: .6 mile to the rock garden and 1.2 miles to the Upper Cascades Falls
Trail Elevation Change Description: 118 feet if you complete the entire trail, 16 feet if you stop at the rock garden. The trail to the rock garden has a gentle downhill slope on the way out, but the trail becomes much steeper closer to the falls with a 12 percent grade.

Trail Tread: Paved to the rock garden and then gravel to the falls with some wooden boardwalk and stairs near the falls.

Finding the Trail: From the park's visitor center parking lot, follow the trail across the main park road.

Facilities: Restrooms and disabled parking can be found at the park visitor center.

Favorite Feature: Both the cool rock formations and the waterfall are worth seeing on this hike.

Morrow Mountain State Park: Three Rivers Trail (Piedmont Region)

Trail Location: Morrow Mountain State Park, 49104 Morrow Mountain Road, Albemarle, NC 28001; boat launch and parking area on Yadkin River within the park boundaries

Trail Type: Lollipop

Trail Length: Approximately a mile

Trail Elevation Change Description: Around .8 mile of the trail is quite flat, although there are some larger steps up onto wooden bridges that cross creeks and wetlands. A short .2-mile section contains less than 100 feet of elevation gain as the trail climbs up to the top of a small ridge overlooking the river. Parts of this section can be fairly steep.

Trail Tread: Natural surface, including roots, with wooden bridges. The lower-lying sections of the trail near the river can be muddy after lots of rain or if the river is up and sections of the trail by the river are quite narrow.

Finding the Trail: From the park's visitor center parking lot, make a right onto the main park road, continuing to follow it to the right when the road forks. Park at the boat ramp parking area. The trail starts at the far end of the parking lot (away from the restrooms) and then crosses the main park road.

Facilities: Restrooms can be found at the park visitor center and at the boat ramp parking area. Picnic areas can be found throughout the park. There is limited cell service in parts of the park, including on this trail, for some carriers.

Favorite Feature: Seeing the exact spot where three North Carolina rivers come together—the Yadkin, Uwharrie and Pee Dee rivers —along with the wildlife that can be frequently found around the river.

Goose Creek State Park: Palmetto Boardwalk Trail (Coastal Plain Region)

Trail Location: Goose Creek State Park, 2190 Camp Leach Road, Washington, NC 27889

Trail Type: Out-and-back but does connect to other longer trails to form a loop if you'd like to add to the distance.

Trail Length: 1.3 miles

Trail Elevation Change Description: 13 feet. Very gentle downhill to get to the beginning of the boardwalk section, and gentle climb back up at the end.

You're likely to spot wildlife, especially different birds, along this section of the Three Rivers trail.

Trail Tread: Sandy natural surface for about .4 mile total and the rest is very nice wooden boardwalk with very small spaces between the boards.

Finding the Trail: From the park's visitor center parking lot, find the trail to the right of the building when facing the building.

The Palmetto Boardwalk Trail at Goose Creek State Park offers close views of the surrounding marshlands.

Facilities: Restrooms and disabled parking can be found at the park visitor center. Very quiet trail with limited road noise. Adequate cell coverage.

Favorite Feature: Beautiful views of the marsh and the chance to see many kinds of wildlife.

16

Land Trusts and Conservancy Organizations

> "The trademarked slogan of the Nature Conservancy is 'Protecting Nature. Preserving Life.' This wonderful sentiment also applies to the network of local unsung heroes preserving the best of North Carolina."
> —Tom Earnhardt, *Crossroads of the Natural World*

According to the Land Trust Alliance, "land trusts work in their communities to conserve habitat for wildlife and plants, secure water quality, ensure land is available for future generations, provide equitable access to nature, protect family farms and ranches, tackle climate change, build healthy communities and so much more."[1] Numerous such organizations in North Carolina work to conserve and protect natural spaces and family farms. To date, North Carolina's land trust organizations have conserved more than 1.5 million acres of land across the state.[2] A sampling of the largest such organizations include:

- *Blue Ridge Conservancy*: Alleghany, Ashe, Avery, Mitchell, Watauga, Wilkes and Yancey counties
- *Catawba Land Conservancy*: Catawba, Gaston, Iredell, Lincoln, Mecklenburg, and Union counties
- *Coastal Land Trust*: 31 counties of the Coastal Plain region
- *Conserving Carolinas*: Henderson, Polk, and Transylvania counties as well as part of other surrounding counties, including some lands in Upstate South Carolina
- *Davidson Land Conservancy*: City of Davidson area
- *Eno River Association*: Lands and waters along the Eno River and its tributaries
- *Foothills Conservancy*: Alexander, Burke, Caldwell, Catawba, Cleveland, Lincoln, McDowell, Rutherford, Cleveland counties
- *Mainspring Conservation Trust*: Little Tennessee and Hiwassee river basins in Cherokee, Clay, Graham, Jackson, Macon and Swain counties
- *New River Conservancy*: Lands and waters along the New River and its tributaries
- *Piedmont Land Conservancy*: Alamance, Caswell, Forsyth, Guilford, Randolph, Rockingham, Stokes, Surry and Yadkin counties
- *Southern Appalachian Highlands Conservancy*: Areas of the Western North Carolina mountains including areas adjacent to Asheville
- *Tar River Land Conservancy*: Tar River Basin and surrounding areas
- *Three Rivers Land Trust*: Anson, Cabarrus, Cumberland, Davidson, Davie,

Harnett, Hoke, Iredell, Montgomery, Moore, Randolph, Richmond, Rowan, Scotland and Stanly counties
- *Triangle Land Conservancy*: Areas around Raleigh, Durham and Chapel Hill

Some national and international conservation organizations, such as the Nature Conservancy, also work in North Carolina.

Most land conservancy organizations also strive to increase sustainable access to natural spaces for the public and they often partner with trail maintenance clubs, local governments or other organizations to develop and maintain trails. Even if another agency now oversees the trail you're on, you'll often find that a land conservancy organization was involved in the process of protecting the location and developing the trail. For example, Blue Ridge Conservancy is planning the Northern Peaks State Trail. It will be designated a North Carolina State Trail and will stretch from Boone to West Jefferson. They were also involved in the development of the 3.6-mile system of trails at Paddy Mountain Park in West Jefferson. This new park opened in early 2025 and features a lush, rich cove forest. As another example, Foothills Conservancy owns and operates the Oak Hill Community Park and Forest outside Morganton, where 11 miles of trails are already available. Future expansion of the trails at this location includes a .75-mile accessible trail designed to help hikers fully engage with the sounds, smells, and sights of the park as they travel through a sensory garden and orchard. (Sounds just like some of that mindfulness stuff we discussed before, huh?)

Hiking on Protected Lands

You can find trails of all lengths and difficulty levels on lands conserved by these organizations, some of which are maintained and managed by the organization themselves while others are maintained by partnering groups. These conservation organizations can also serve as great sources for trail information. One example is the Carolina Thread Trail network.

One of Catawba Land Conservancy's major projects is the Carolina Thread Trail, a network of trails located in a 15-county region of North and South Carolina that consists of natural surface trails, greenways, blueways, and other conservation corridors. It was launched in 2007 and is a partnership with local governments, businesses and other conservation organizations, and it currently boasts more than 300 miles of walking paths—trails of all kinds—and 170 miles of blueways, with many more planned. The Carolina Thread Trails website also offers detailed maps and information about each trail in the network; it's an awesome resource for hikers in the region.[3] One of my favorite Carolina Thread Trail hikes is the Forney Creek Trail in eastern Lincoln County near Denver. It features a beautiful forest and two waterfowl ponds at which you can spot wildlife. A 66-foot suspension bridge is located near the trailhead at the beginning of one of the other trails in this conservation area.

The Carolina Thread Trail is certainly not the only example. For example, Piedmont Land Conservancy partnered with the Piedmont Triad Regional Council to create Piedmont Legacy Trails, a trail collective for their 12-county region. They maintain a website with great trail guides and an interactive map. Coastal Land Trust maintains an interactive map with information about public preserves to visit. Triangle Land Conservancy and Conserving Carolina share detailed information about the trails available on protected

Carolina Thread Trails are marked with signs designating them as such. This sign appears at the beginning of the Carolina Thread Trail at Dan Nicholas Park near Salisbury. This trail circles Lake Murtis and then extends to include the Persimmon Branch loop trail for a total of around two miles of hiking. If you're looking for a shorter, less strenuous hike you can stick to the section of trail around the lake and enjoy lots of wildlife and two nice bridges.

land.[4] And there are many others.

Many land conservancy organizations also host events to encourage people to visit the areas under their conservatorship. For example, they might host guided hikes that focus on a particular subject like wildflowers, birding, or the unique geology of an area. Other organizations put forth "challenges" to encourage residents and visitors in their communities to get out and experience these natural spots. For example, Conserving Carolina offers two challenges, the White Squirrel Hiking Challenge and the Flying Squirrel Outdoor Challenge.[5] The specific hikes included in the White Squirrel Hiking Challenge change every couple of years, but the challenge generally involves completing eight hikes of varying levels of difficulty. The Flying Squirrel Outdoor Challenge offers more flexibility, however, making it more accessible to hikers of all kinds.[6] For this challenge you are required to submit logs of eight outings (out of a list of a possible 13) that can involve hiking or several other kinds of activities. Both challenges are free to enter, but you must be a member of Conserving Carolina to participate, which does involve a financial donation that goes toward their conservation activities. If you complete one of the challenges, you receive a challenge prize pack and completion certificate. Triangle Land Conservancy also offers a hiking challenge, encouraging folks to complete six hikes at six out of seven preserves. A membership is not required to participate.[7]

Some land conservancy organizations also prioritize creating accessible spaces for all people to enjoy. For example, the Nature Conservancy manages the Nags Head Woods Preserve in the Outer Banks. There are quite a few trails to enjoy at this preserve, including the ADA Trail. This trail is flat and comprised of wooden boardwalks with rails and concrete pathways. The trail is at least four feet wide, with wider passing areas, and it features a freshwater pond, a butterfly garden, a maritime swamp forest, and a marsh overlook.

Top Recommended Land Conservancy Hikes

Green Swamp Preserve (Coastal Plain Region)

Trail Location: 673 Green Swamp Road NW, Supply, NC 28462
Trail Type: Out-and-back
Trail Length: 2.6 miles
Trail Elevation Change Description: This trail is essentially flat with no steep sections.
Trail Tread: Natural surface with dirt, sand, grasses and some exposed roots. Parts of the trail can be muddy and mucky after periods of rain.
Finding the Trail: The trail continues directly from the parking area.
Facilities: There are no facilities available on this trail.
Favorite Feature: Being able to see several kinds of carnivorous plants, especially Venus flytraps, in their natural habitat.

Some of the most interesting things to see on this trail at Green Swamp Preserve are at your feet, so don't forget to look down!

Knight Brown Nature Preserve
(Piedmont Region)

Trail Location: 221 Waterfield Lane, Stokesdale, NC 27357
Trail Type: Trail system of seven different trails that can form multiple loops. My favorite route includes the Beechwood Bottom Loop, sections of the Leatherwood and Creekside loops along the creek and the Poet's Walk.

This wonderfully sturdy bridge makes crossing the stream at the intersection of the Beechwood Bottom, Fern, and Creekside trails at Knight Brown Nature Preserve a breeze. No wet feet required!

Trail Length: Up to five miles of hiking. The route I describe above is around two miles.

Trail Elevation Change Description: There is a good amount of elevation change between the parking area and the streams at the lowest points of the trail. The Beechwood Bottom trail probably has the gentlest approach to this change with switchbacks. The route described above involves about 125 feet of elevation change. Other trails available would add to this.

Trail Tread: Natural surface with lots of roots and rocks. In the fall lots of leaves cover the trail and they can be slick on the steeper sections of the trail. There are points where there are steep inclines on either side of a narrow, single-track trail.

Finding the Trail: The trailhead is easily spotted by the kiosk at the parking area. The parking area is a cul-de-sac at the end of Waterfield Lane. The trails are well marked, and trail intersection signs often feature maps.

Facilities: Picnic tables can be found at the trailhead, but no other facilities are available. I have had adequate cell coverage at this trail.

Favorite Feature: The forest and streams are beautiful here and it's very peaceful. Five wooden carved animals are placed on the trails (one per trail) and it is fun to try and find them. Piedmont Land Conservancy protects and manages this preserve and they do a great job maintaining and updating the trails.

17

County and Municipal Parks and Privately Owned Lands

"Trails provide opportunities for people to connect with nature and move their bodies. Studies show that as little as 30 minutes spent outside creates positive health outcomes, including improvement in mental health. Trails are free to use and there is a trail for everyone, regardless of age, ability, or background."
—North Carolina Great Trails State Coalition

The Benefits of Trails in Communities

With so many competing projects and limited budgets, why would counties, cities, towns, neighborhoods, land and business owners, and other types of non-conservation organizations want to invest in building, hosting, and maintaining trails? Many take on this work and expense because research has shown that trail availability benefits the economy, the environment, and the health of the citizens of a community. As we've already discussed, being active on trails can help improve mental health and promotes and encourages physical activity. Trails can also improve connections between individuals and communities. For example, the Emma and Stuart Thomas Memorial Trail, which opened in 2023 and is managed by the Crossnore Communities for Children in Winston-Salem on conserved farmland, was intentionally built, in part, to serve as a connection point between the majority Black Boston-Thurmond neighborhood and the mostly white Buena Vista neighborhood. It is intended to provide "equitable access to [a] place that has previously been a boundary" between these two communities.[1] This trail system of almost three miles across open fields and pasturelands features an amazing view of the downtown Winston-Salem skyline and has trailheads easily accessible to both neighborhoods. It is meant to be "a front porch where everybody's welcome," according to Brett Loftis, the CEO of Crossnore Communities for Children.[2] This is a wonderful trail that I recommend you check out if you're in the area.

Having trails available in communities also benefits the environment. Depending on their locations, trails can help preserve wildlife habitat, provide a buffer for creeks and streams thus protecting and improving water quality, and improve air quality by maintaining vegetation.

The Emma and Stuart Thomas Memorial Trail in Winston-Salem offers a peaceful hike through rolling farmland within just a few miles of downtown.

Lastly, trails have an economic impact. They promote tourism and have been shown to increase property values and enhance the ability to attract new businesses and retain the ones already in a location. For example, in 2022 the Institute of Transportation Research and Education at NC State University assessed the economic impact of six greenways and trails within the Carolina Thread Trail network (discussed in the last chapter). They found that each of the six trails studied supported at least $3 million in annual business sales and that one trail alone supported nearly 60 employees in the local community. Surveys and interviews they conducted with North and South Carolina business owners revealed that those individuals had "purposefully located their facilities next to trails, [had] made targeted capital investment decisions based on a trail's existence and [had] generated a substantial share of their revenue from patronage by trail users."[3]

Hiking at Local Parks and Privately Owned Lands

So many trails across the state fit into this category that listing them all here would be impossible. In addition to the typical hiking apps, local governments, land and business owners, and organizations will sometimes provide information about the trails they manage on their websites. Googling the name of a location and "trails" or "hiking" can even lead you to some great options. You truly never know where you'll find trails! Some of my favorite trails in the Piedmont are managed by the North Carolina Zoo. There's even a wonderful nature trail at the visitor center and rest area on NC 421 near Wilkesboro—a great leg-stretcher on a trip.

In addition to those described in detail below, here are some other examples of trails in this category to get you started.

Ridges Mountain Preserve is managed by the North Carolina Zoo. This two-mile trail with about 150 feet of elevation gain features interesting human history, natural history and geology with large rock outcroppings like those pictured here.

Mountains and Foothills

- Adawehi Trail (near Columbus; Adawehi Wellness Village)
- Ashley Ladd Trail (Yadkinville; Yadkin Memorial Park at Hampton Lake—County Park)
- Beaver Lake Bird Sanctuary and Perimeter Trail (Asheville; Lake View Park Commission)
- Boone United Trail (Boone; church)
- Brookshire Park Trail (Boone; Watauga County park)
- Carter Falls (public-private partnership near Elkin)
- Crab Orchard Falls (Valle Crucis; Valle Crucis Conference Center)
- Highlands Biological Station (Highlands; Western Carolina University)
- J. Douglas Williams Park (Sugar Mountain; village park)
- Otter Falls Trail (Seven Devils; town park)

Piedmont

- Bluestem Trails (Cedar Grove; conservation cemetery)
- Bog Garden at Benjamin Park Trail (Greensboro; city park)
- Boone's Cave Park, Cottonwood, Red Oak, and Wetlands and Woodlands trails (Davidson County Parks and Recreation Facility)
- Company Mill Preserve (Guilford County facility)
- Faith Rock Trail (Franklinville; town historical site)
- Fred and Alice Stanback Educational Forest and Nature Preserve (Spencer; town facility)
- Fred Stanback, Jr., Ecological Preserve (Salisbury; Catawba College)
- Hinson Lake (Rockingham; Richmond County Parks and Recreation facility)
- Lake Hickory Riverwalk (Hickory; city facility)
- Lake Thom-a-Lex (Lexington; Davidson County facility)
- Miller Park (Winston-Salem; city facility)
- Purgatory Mountain (Asheboro; North Carolina Zoo facility)
- Reynolda Gardens Trails (Winston-Salem; private organization)
- Ribbonwalk Nature Preserve (Charlotte; Mecklenburg County facility)
- Ridges Mountain Preserve (Asheboro; North Carolina Zoo facility)
- Rocky Face Mountain Recreational Area (Hiddenite; Alexander County facility)
- Salem Lake (Winston-Salem; city facility)
- Saxapahaw Island Trail (Saxapahaw; Alamance County park)
- Turnipseed Nature Preserve (Wake County park)

Coastal Plain

- Calico Creek Boardwalk (Morehead City; city facility)
- Emerald Isle Woods Park (Emerald Isle; town park)
- Fenwick Hollowell Wetlands Trail (Elizabeth City; community college campus)
- Howell Woods Environmental Learning Center trails (Four Oaks; community college campus)
- Ocean Isle Beach Nature Trail (Ocean Isle; town facility)

Top Recommended Local Park and Privately Owned Land Hikes

Forest Bathing Trail via Vineyard Trail
(Foothills Region)

Trail Location: Grassy Creek Vineyard and Winery, 235 Chatham Lodge Lane, State Road, NC 28676

Grassy Creek flows peacefully by the Forest Bathing Trail.

Trail Type: Lollipop
Trail Length: 2.1 miles
Trail Elevation Change Description: 160 feet. The trail travels downhill from the trailhead, up and over a small knoll in the loop and then back uphill to the trailhead to finish.
Trail Tread: Natural surface, dirt, gravel, some roots
Finding the Trail: Grassy Creek Vineyard and Winery allows hikers to park in the gravel lot behind the tasting room. The trail is to the right of the parking area as you are facing the building and is clearly marked.
Facilities: There are no restrooms available on the trail. There are a few benches along the way. Cell coverage is typically adequate, but hikers are encouraged to turn off their phones on the forest bathing trail. The trail is very peaceful with little road noise.
Favorite Feature: The forest bathing trail is especially pretty as it travels beside Grassy Creek. The mural that has been painted on the dam seen along the trail is also a nice treat.

Underground Railroad Tree Trail: Guilford College (Piedmont Region)

Trail Location: Guilford College campus, off Nathan Hunt Road
Trail Type: Out-and-back
Trail Length: Approximately 2.0 miles from parking behind field house. Around a mile if you park at the Nathan Hunt Road parking location (see below).
Trail Elevation Change Description: 100 feet. Most slope is under 6 percent grade but a couple of very short sections do have a steeper slope.
Trail Tread: Single track natural surface with roots, some rocks, and leaves
Finding the Trail: Please visit the Guilford College website about this hike for full information on location (and to complete the visitor form they request).[4] You'll find a small parking area on Nathan Hunt Road where the true trailhead is located, but if others are hiking, you'll likely need to park elsewhere. Visitor parking can be found in the gravel lot behind the Ragan-Brown Field House on campus. If you park in this location, you'll need to walk by the lake and then to the right up Nathan Hunt Road a bit to reach the trailhead on your left. Note: You do not want the trailhead located just before the lake on Nathan Hunt Road. This trailhead does lead to some nice trails that are worth exploring but will not easily lead you to the "Witness Tree." While there is a connector trail to the tree that can be accessed from this trailhead it is not marked well and involves a creek crossing.
Facilities: There are no permanent restrooms available at this location. The closest restrooms, as well as gas and food, are located close by, just a couple minutes' drive away on Friendly Avenue. Occasional road noise does filter through from Friendly Avenue, but it is not bad considering the proximity. Visiting this trail when the college is on break will likely result in a more peaceful, less busy hike. I had adequate cell coverage throughout this hike.
Favorite Feature: The huge "Witness Tree" and the story behind it are definitely the highlight of this trail, but there are other large, beautiful trees along the hike too that are certainly worth taking the time to admire.

The Underground Railroad "Witness Tree" is a tulip poplar that dates to before 1800. This giant tree dwarfs those around it and the overlook deck gives a wonderful spot to sit and reflect on all that happened in this area of Guilford Woods during the days of the Underground Railroad.

Four Seasons Trail-McDowell Nature Preserve (Piedmont Region)

Trail Location: McDowell Nature Preserve, 15222 York Road, Charlotte, NC 28278
Trail Type: Loop
Trail Length: .5 mile

Trail Elevation Change Description: Some gentle slopes but never greater than 4 percent grade.
Trail Tread: Paved
Finding the Trail: From the preserve nature center, continue to follow the road past two larger parking lots to where the road dead ends at a small parking lot.

Even on a rainy day like the one pictured here, the Four Seasons Trail at McDowell Nature Preserve is lovely and the creek flowing beside it is very peaceful.

Facilities: This trail is ADA compliant and there are several benches along the way for resting. Restrooms can be found at the preserve nature center. Cell phone coverage is adequate, and this is a very peaceful trail.

Favorite Feature: This trail travels beside a beautiful creek and through very peaceful woods. There are multiple places to access the creek to dip a toe in and the trail connects with several natural surface trails.

New Bern Battlefield Park (Coastal Plain Region)

Trail Location: 300 Battlefield Trail, New Bern, NC 28560

Trail Type: Figure-eight loop with several connector trails between sections

One of the wonderful bridges built on the trail at New Bern Battlefield Park. This one allows you to easily cross a wetlands area.

Trail Length: 1.5 miles

Trail Elevation Change Description: 40 feet. Some gentle hills throughout the hike. You are often actually hiking up and over earthworks built around the time of the battle.

Trail Tread: Natural surface, some gravel, some wooden bridges

Finding the Trail: The trailhead is clearly marked at the parking area.

Facilities: There are restrooms at the trailhead and some spots to stop and rest along the way. There is a bit of road noise and occasional train noise. I had adequate cell coverage on this hike.

Favorite Feature: This trail was created and is maintained by the New Bern Historical Society and the history of the Battle of New Bern shared on this hike is wonderful. There are informational signs throughout, a downloadable audio tour that you can listen to, and some great information online. This trail has been well built and is well cared for.

18

Long-Distance Trails

"The trail was designed to have no end, a wild place on which to be comfortably lost for as long as one desired. In those early days nobody fathomed walking the thing from beginning to end in one go."
—Ben Montgomery, author *Grandma Gatewood's Walk: The Inspiring Story of the Woman Who Saved the Appalachian Trail*

North Carolina is home to a number of longer distance trails—trails that would require multiple days (or weeks, or months) of backpacking and camping if one were going to hike them in one trip. Thankfully, some of them offer wonderful day hiking opportunities as well and we're going to discuss two of them here: the Appalachian Trail (AT) and the Mountains-to-Sea Trail (MST).

The Appalachian Trail

The complete Appalachian Trail runs more than 2,190 miles from Springer Mountain, Georgia, to Mount Katahdin, Maine, crossing through 14 states in the process. It is the longest hiking-only footpath in the world. The idea for the trail was developed in 1921 and the first section opened in 1923. The AT was completed in 1937 and became the first designated National Scenic Trail in 1968. It is now managed by the Appalachian Trail Conservancy alongside the National Park Service, U.S. Forest Service, and many state agencies, with the help of thousands of volunteers. More than three million visitors walk even a short portion of the AT each year, while more than 3,000 attempt a thru hike of the entire distance. Spoiler alert: Most don't complete the 2,190-plus miles. About 25 percent of those who start the journey finish it; this percentage has stayed consistent over time.[1]

Approximately 96 miles of the Appalachian Trail are exclusively in North Carolina and the trail runs along the North Carolina/Tennessee border for more than 200 additional miles. This section of the trail contains the highest peaks that hikers will find along the entire length, including several that are above 6,000 feet.

Thankfully, you don't have to thru hike the trail's entire length to experience some wonderful moments following the AT's iconic white blazes. There are lots of great day hikes available as well, many of which are very popular, so you'll likely encounter other day hikers—and even crowds—along the way. One such hike features the Max Patch Mountain summit. The Appalachian Trail crosses this summit, and you can hike this section as a part of the Max Patch Loop Trail in the Pisgah National Forest. This loop trail is around 1.5 miles with an elevation gain of just over 300 feet, which does include some rustic steps. The summit of Max Patch Mountain is a grassy bald where the lack of trees allows for amazing 360-degree views of the surrounding mountains. This is considered an iconic spot along the AT and is a very popular location for day hiking as well. This spot is so popular, in fact, that in July 2021 the Forest Service implemented new restrictions on the use of the area to protect the fragile ecosystem from overuse and even abuse. Camping and fires are no longer allowed, group sizes must be kept to no more than 10, pets must remain on-leash, and the area closes one hour after sundown and reopens one hour before sunrise. These restrictions have helped the area start to recover well.[2]

Another popular stretch of the Appalachian Trail for day hiking can be found starting at Carvers Gap along the North Carolina/Tennessee line. The trail in this section follows the state boundary and travels to three balds—Round Bald, Jane Bald and Grassy Ridge Bald—as an out-and-back hike. If you hike all the way to Grassy Ridge Bald, the furthest from the parking area, you'll cover just over five miles with around 1,000 feet of elevation gain. You can also stop at either of the other two balds for a shorter hike with less elevation but still amazing views. The hike to Round Bald would be around 1.5 miles and to Jane Bald just under three miles. As with Max Patch, each of these balds offers beautiful, long-range views of the surrounding mountains.

Near Franklin, a third popular area for day hiking on the AT offers a shorter trail of half a mile with 32 feet of elevation gain on a paved and stone-paver path. The Wayah Bald overlook and stone fire tower at the top of this trail offer gorgeous views of the surrounding area. (The fire tower view does require climbing some stairs.) An AT shelter for thru hikers is located nearby, so, especially during March and April, meeting some of those hikers in this area would not be unusual. This would be a great place to practice some of that "trail magic" we talked about in Chapter 10 if you visit during thru hike season!

The Mountains-to-Sea Trail

Whereas North Carolina's section of the Appalachian Trail sticks exclusively to the mountains, the Mountains-to-Sea Trail (MST) crosses the entire state and highlights the environment and people of each region. The MST stretches almost 1,200 miles, more than 700 of which are footpath—a distance that increases each year as volunteers continue to build trails and reduce the amount of road walking required to complete a thru hike. The MST begins at Kuwohi (formerly Clingmans Dome) in Great Smoky Mountains National Park and ends at Jockey's Ridge on the Outer Banks, with sections of the trail passing through 37 counties along the way. A thru hike of the MST also features four national parks, three national forests, two national wildlife refuges, ten state parks, three lighthouses, two ferry rides and countless other natural areas of the state. Especially outside of the mountains, the MST travels via trails that were already available in some areas, so you might see sections of the MST referred to by other names.

The Mountains-to-Sea Trail is broken into 18 segments ranging in length from 39.2 miles to 90.4 miles. There's even an alternate route for sections 11–16 that allows you to paddle the Neuse River rather than hiking.

18. Long-Distance Trails

These signs, alongside the classic Mountains-to-Sea Trail white circle blaze, let hikers know just how far they can go in either direction from this spot near Jumpinoff Rock along the trail in Ashe County. Clingmans Dome has been restored to its Cherokee name, Kuwohi, since this sign was created.

Segment Number	Segment Title	Segment Location
Segment 1	Peak to Peak	Kuwohi (formerly Clingmans Dome) to Waterrock Knob
Segment 2	The Balsams	Waterrock Knob to Pisgah Inn
Segment 3	The High Peaks and Asheville	Pisgah Inn to Black Mountain Campground
Segment 4	Gorges, Peaks and Waterfalls	Black Mountain Campground to Beacon Heights
Segment 5	The High Country	Beacon Heights to Devils Garden Overlook
Segment 6	The Elkin Valley	Devils Garden Overlook to Pilot Mountain State Park
Segment 7	The Sauratown Mountains	Pilot Mountain State Park to Hanging Rock State Park
Segment 8	Rivers, Railroads, and Lakes	Hanging Rock State Park to Bryan Park
Segment 9	Revolution and Textiles	Bryan Park to Eno River State Park
Segment 10	Eno River and Falls Lake	Eno River State Park to Falls Lake Dam
Segment 11	Neuse River Greenways and the Let'Lones	Falls Lake Dam to Howell Woods

Segment Number	Segment Title	Segment Location
Segment 12	Agricultural Heartland	Howell Woods to Suggs Mill Pond Game Land
Segment 13	Carolina Bay Country	Suggs Mill Pond Game Land to Singletary Lake State Park
Segment 14	Land of History	Singletary Lake State Park to Holly Shelter Game Land
Segment 15	The Onslow Bight and Jacksonville	Holly Shelter Game Land to Stella
Segment 16	Croatan and Neusiok Trail	Stella to Oyster Point Campground
Segment 17	Down East North Carolina	Oyster Point Campground to Cedar Island Ferry
Segment 18	The Outer Banks	Cedar Island Ferry to Jockey's Ridge State Park

Many wonderful day hikes are possible on the MST as well, and you can experience many of the joys of this state trail without attempting a thru hike. A terrific book titled *Great Day Hikes on North Carolina's Mountains-to-Sea Trail*, by Jim Grode, features 40 hikes from across the state ranging in distance from less than a mile to 8.4 miles and provides detailed information about each hike. The Mountains-to-Sea Trail website also contains a wealth of information about the trail including detailed section-by-section descriptions and a list of trail updates that is kept as current as possible.

I have thoroughly enjoyed hiking along several sections of the Mountains-to-Sea Trail. Some of these include:

- MST near Pisgah Inn (Segment 2)
- MST near Boone at Goshen Creek (Segment 5)
- Tomkins Knob Overlook to Cascades Falls (Segment 5)
- Raven Rock Overlook between Boone and Blowing Rock on the Blue Ridge Parkway (Segment 5)
- Cascades Preserve Loop (Segment 8)
- Great Bend Park/Haw River Trail (Segment 9)

Top Recommended Long-Distance Trail Hikes

Appalachian Trail: Fontana Dam

Trail Location: 1001 Fontana Dam Road, Fontana Dam, NC 28733
Trail Type: Out-and-back
Trail Length: If you wish to do only the section of the Appalachian Trail that crosses the dam, the hike is a mile or a little under as an out-and-back. If you wish to continue further, you can pass the end of the dam and travel further up Lakeview Drive, West. About 1.1 miles from the beginning of your hike on the visitor center side of the dam, the pavement will end and the Appalachian Trail will fork to the left and continue 22 miles before reaching Cades Cove. The Lakeshore Trail will

18. Long-Distance Trails

This MST blaze marks the end of segment 5 at Devils Garden Overlook on the Blue Ridge Parkway. From here, the trail drops more than 2,500 feet in elevation to Stone Mountain State Park.

head to the right for 6.6 miles before intersecting with additional trails. Both are natural surface trails with much more rugged conditions.

Trail Elevation Change Description: Essentially flat across the dam. Past the end of the dam, the road climbs steadily with grades up to 10 percent. The natural surface portions of the AT and the Lakeshore Trail mentioned above feature significant elevation gain.

Trail Tread: Paved sidewalk or road for the trail across the dam and about a half mile beyond. Natural surface beyond that.

Finding the Trail: From the lower section of the parking lot nearest the visitor center you'll need to climb a flight of stairs to get to the trail. You can access the trail across the top of the dam without climbing the stairs by parking in the upper section of the parking lot.

Facilities: Ample parking at the visitor center (open early May to late October) with a small gift shop, museum and restrooms.

The amazing view of the impounded Little Tennessee River and surrounding mountains from the middle of Fontana Dam. You can see the hydroelectric power station at the bottom right as well as the small parking area that gives a bottom-up view of the dam. The other side of the dam (not pictured) offers beautiful views of Fontana Lake.

Favorite Feature: This hike offers amazing views of the surrounding mountains, the Little Tennessee River, Fontana Lake and the dam itself. The AT across Fontana Dam is featured in the 2015 movie *A Walk in the Woods* starring Robert Redford and based on Bill Bryson's book of the same name.

Mountains-to-Sea Trail: Hines Chapel Preserve (Piedmont Region)

Trail Location: 4465 Hines Chapel Road, McLeansville, NC 27301
Trail Type: Out-and-back
Trail Length: Around three miles on the Grande Peninsula Trail which is also part of the Mountains-to-Sea Trail. (Other trails are planned for this area.)
Trail Elevation Change Description: 150 feet of gain; small hills throughout the hike but no slopes over 5 percent grade.
Trail Tread: Natural surface with quite a few roots and one wooden bridge over a creek.
Finding the Trail: The trailhead is well marked in the gravel parking area at the address listed above. The turnoff for the parking area from Hines Chapel Road can be a bit tricky to spot as there is only a small sign currently.

The Mountains-to-Sea Trail's white circle blazes can be seen here as the trail at Hines Chapel Preserve in McLeansville comes out of the woods to the edge of a restored grasslands and native wildflower meadow.

Facilities: There are no facilities at this trail. I had adequate cell coverage on this hike and the road noise is minimal after you get away from the parking area a bit.

Favorite Feature: Opened in 2023, this is one of the newer sections of the Mountains-to-Sea Trail to be moved off road in the Piedmont. This hike features a nice mix of woods and edge of restored grasslands and is a great area for birding. I saw or heard at least 20 different kinds of birds on this hike.

Epilogue

> "The path is made in the walking of it."
> —Zhuangzi

By the time this book was published I had completed more than 250 hikes. I had hiked on over 200 unique stretches of trail and visited 25 nature preserves, 15 named waterfalls, 20 named lakes, five national forests, and 30 city and county parks—all while hiking in 60 different counties, in four different states. I had also seen my only child graduate from high school and move out; moved twice; sold our house; gotten rid of more than half of what we owned; moved to a new town in a different part of the state; gone through four bouts of Covid-19; had a parent in the hospital more than once; totaled my car; reconnected with old friends, disconnected with others and made some brand new ones; welcomed a new nephew and niece; co-founded a local hiking group; and watched as the place where I spent the first 18 years of my life—home—was devastated by Hurricane Helene. All of the wonderful, beautiful, hard, heartbreaking, frustrating, angering, inspiring things that life can throw your way over a five-year period still happened. Hiking didn't change any of that.

What hiking did was give me a new lens through which to see it all. I routinely turn to the trail for challenge, solace, inspiration, and education. I have learned many things about myself, found confidence, confronted weaknesses and anxieties, and discovered peace and kindness in a world that more and more often experiences a lack of it. I have lost myself, found myself, forgiven myself and forgotten myself, sometimes all on the same trail. When nothing seems stable in the world, I look to the rock formations that are millions of years old that can be found on so many of the trails I've hiked. I look to the hundreds-year-old trees that tower above me. Sure, they are weathered and worn; aren't we all? But they still stand strong and offer comfort to those who come to spend time with them. When the world seems like it will never change in the ways it needs to, I look to the wildflowers blooming new each spring, the acorn sprouting in the dirt, the baby birds and tadpoles and bear cubs. Similarly, I watch as those same wildflowers die off each year, the fallen leaves disintegrate back into the soil and even the mighty trees are felled at the hand of the wind. Things are always changing and growing and dying around me on the trail—some quickly and some very, very slowly—but always. The only true constant in nature, as in our own lives, is change. Whether we like it or not.

If the statistics are to be believed, I'm not the only one who is looking for some peace, perspective, and joy through hiking. Ever-growing numbers of people are hitting the trail in North Carolina and beyond. More and more people are visiting and appreciating the amazing natural spaces in the Old North State, the land of the longleaf pine, the home to much beautiful diversity in its environment and its people. If you're one of them, I hope this book helps you along your journey, and, especially as you travel North Carolina's many special paths, I hope you discover what the North Carolina Great Trails State Coalition so eloquently expresses in their "Year of the Trail Anthem" (2023).

North Carolina Year of the Trail Anthem

In North Carolina we are the product of our environment. The people who can greet a sea breeze in the morning and tuck into a mountain chill at night. Who sprout from land that rolls across the hills of the piedmont. Who shape cities that hustle and bustle beside glistening rivers.

Across this vibrant stretch of Southern soil, a system of trails unfurls into limitless opportunity. These paths are a place of refuge and recreation. They connect us to the very essence of this state. To its natural splendor. To its storied, winding history. And—with our active use and care—to its future. Because we blaze and sustain trails together: those born and bred here, and those beckoned by its promise as the Great Trails State.

Down rugged trailheads and through city parks, there is a trail for each of us. An invitation for bikers, hikers, paddlers, and riders. For amblers, explorers, and commuters. Craving the inhale of impossibly crisp air, we meet mountains and look over the edge of the earth. The lull of Atlantic tides pulls us back to sandy paths. With the wind in our hair and a rush of adrenaline, we weave and bob alongside buildings that scrape the clouds.

Standing at the overlook at Jumpinoff Rock in Ashe County along the Mountains-to-Sea Trail, you can see over the Blue Ridge Escarpment to the North Carolina Piedmont and beyond. It was on this hike, at this view, in February 2021, that I first thought, "Maybe I should write a book about hiking." You are now holding that book. I hope you've enjoyed reading it as much as I enjoyed writing it.

Along these trails, we lead, and we follow. With kids on our shoulders, dogs trotting ahead, critters burrowing below and flying above. We march on our own and we build community. We find new purpose, generation after generation. We laugh and sweat and reflect. We take on epic adventures. Or we might just take a moment.

We need trails. To move, to play, to discover. Because North Carolina's trails are for all of us. To enjoy, to sustain, and to champion. Us, the products of the places where our feet are firmly planted—and the new growth where great trails lead.

Appendix I

Most Recommended Hikes by Region

There are so many fantastic trails to explore across North Carolina—many more than are mentioned in this book. In addition to the those already covered in detail in Part III, here you'll find information about the 15 trails I would most recommend in each region for the type of hiking we've discussed in this text. This was a hard choice to make, as there are so many good trails, but I hope that this list will serve as a starting point for a long and happy journey of engaging with North Carolina's amazing natural places.

Information about each trail is listed in the following format:

Trail name: location (closest town or city, county, etc.) / distance / elevation increase / other notes

Remember, you will want to do a lot more research on these trails before hiking any of them. You'll see an asterisk (*) beside the names of those trails I have personally completed. You'll find pictures and my summary of these starred hikes (and many others) on my Instagram account. Trails marked with a hash symbol (#) were likely significantly impacted by Hurricane Helene and may be rerouted, closed for a period of time or show significant tree damage, washouts or landslides. In reality, you can expect to see some evidence of Helene's damage on almost all mountain trails for the foreseeable future.

Mountain and Foothills Region Trails

Adawehi Trail: Adawehi Wellness Village near Columbus / 1.5 miles / 26 ft. / natural surface and gravel tread; lots of wildflowers and mushrooms; views of White Oak Creek; includes a stone walking labyrinth

Balsam Nature Trail*#: Mount Mitchell State Park / 1.25 miles / 155 ft. when trail to summit is included / a beautiful spruce-fir forest; weather is typically much cooler on Mount Mitchell; stairs involved on the trail

Bluff Mountain Trail Picnic Area Section*#: Doughton Park off the Blue Ridge Parkway, MM 241 / 2.2 miles / 250 ft. / the entire Bluff Mountain Trail is 8.4 miles (4.2 one way) but this is my favorite section; beautiful long range views; especially nice at sunset; access the trail from the visitor center or different points along the picnic area road for a shorter or longer hike; check out the Bluffs Restaurant nearby as well as the Brinegar Cabin homestead at the north terminus of the Bluff Mountain Trail

Carl Sandburg Home—Hiker's Lot to Goat Barn and House*#: Flat Rock / 1.4 miles / 72 ft. / hike follows a gravel road up to the house; restrooms and water available near the house; lots to see here and lots of other trails to explore

Carter Falls*: Near Elkin on Pleasant Ridge Road / 1 mile / 124 ft. / small parking lot at trailhead can become crowded; steepest section of the trail is right by the falls; beautiful falls with nice views; connects to the MST across street from the parking area

Crab Orchard Falls*#: Valle Crucis at Valle Crucis Conference Center / 1.3 miles / 324 ft. / fairly steep trail with beautiful falls at the end

Deep Creek Waterfall Loop: Great Smoky Mountains National Park near Bryson City / 2.4 miles / 426 ft. / parking pass required; can be very busy in season especially on weekends; visits three falls; instead of completing the loop you could start going counterclockwise and visit the first two falls for an easier out-and-back hike of 1.6 miles with slope grades under 5 percent; the entire loop has grades up to 17 percent

Joyce Kilmer Memorial Forest Upper and Lower Loop Trails*: Nantahala National Forest near Robbinsville / 2.75 miles / 350 ft. / steady climb to the top of the loops with grades up to 10 percent; beautiful, huge trees to see in the upper loop; some stairs

Jumpinoff Rock*: Blue Ridge Parkway, MM 260.3 / 1.1 miles / 203 ft. / grades up to 16 percent but only for short sections; beautiful overlook out to the east

Max Patch Loop Trail#: Pisgah National Forest west of Marshall and south of Hot Springs / 1.5 miles / 308 ft. / steady incline on first half of loop with slopes up to 17 percent grade; beautiful long-range views from the top; very popular hiking area

Moore Cove Falls Trail: Pisgah National Forest near Brevard / 1.2 miles / 154 ft. / steady incline up to falls with highest slope of 12 percent grade; 50-foot Moore Cove Falls at destination of trail; involves some stairs

MST at Goshen Creek*: Blue Ridge Parkway near Boone, south of MM 285.5 / 3.1 miles / 633 ft. / this out-and-back hike is a steady incline on the way out; this is a beautiful hike and worth doing any amount even if you don't feel like doing the entire 3.1 miles

Rhododendron Garden Trail#: Roan Mountain / 1 mile / 95 ft. / paved path through rhododendron forest; picnic tables and restrooms at trailhead; was closed in 2024 for renovations and improvements and is due to reopen in 2025

Spirit Ridge Trail: Nantahala National Forest near Robbinsville / 1 mile / 9 ft. / paved trail through the forest with observation deck at the end; view would be especially good in the winter

Tomkins Knob Overlook to Cascades Falls*: Blue Ridge Parkway between Boone and West Jefferson, MM 272.5 / 2.2 miles / 202 ft. / ability to see Jesse Brown Cabin and Cool Springs Baptist Church along with the beautiful Cascades Falls; lots of trillium and other wildflowers to see in the spring

Piedmont Region Trails

Bicentennial and Bog Gardens Trail*: Greensboro near Friendly Center / 1.1 miles / 29 ft. / mostly paved or boardwalk trail with some optional natural surface sections in the bog garden; lots of benches along the way; lots to see, including wildlife; ample parking and restrooms at trailhead

Bluestem Trails*: Bluestem Conservation Cemetery near Cedar Grove / 1.75 miles / 75 ft. / trails are located at a conservation cemetery; beautiful, peaceful trails in a sacred spot; this is an active burial ground so sections might be closed for services; visit the barn first to learn about Bluestem

Company Mill Preserve*: Southern Guilford County, near Pleasant Garden / 4.3 miles / 225 ft. / I completed this trail from the dam end trailhead rather than the Hagan Stone Park trailhead; lots to see along this trail including wildlife, large trees, wetlands, and an old cabin

Fall Creek Falls and Mayo River Trails*: Mayo River State Park, Deshazo Mill Access / 1.75 miles / 82 ft. / beautiful falls and trail beside the creek and river; some stone steps are required by the falls; you can extend your hike and follow the trail a bit into Virginia

Fred and Alice Stanback Educational Forest and Nature Preserve—Blue Path*: Spencer / 1.8 miles / 100 ft. / nice pond for wildlife and beautiful forest with lovely wildflowers in the spring; there is another trail, the red path, that goes the opposite direction that I don't recommend as much as the blue bath; no facilities on site

Hinson Lake*: Rockingham / 1.8 miles / 95 ft. / wide, sandy gravel trails with a few wooden walkways; very nice wooden boardwalk bridge across one end of the lake; nice lake views; restrooms at trailhead

Lake Hickory Riverwalk: Hickory / 2.3 miles / 216 ft. / paved and bridge boardwalk; travels through woodlands and along the Catawba River; includes the longest Fink truss bridge in the country

Lake Thom-a-Lex*: between Lexington and Thomasville / 2.3 miles / 90 ft. / nice lake views; easy to follow trail; lots of birds to see; restrooms at the trailhead

Meadow and Boulder Trail: Turnipseed Nature Preserve near Wendell / 2.4 miles / 111 ft. / crushed gravel and boardwalk tread; opportunity to see wildlife and wildflowers

Pilot Knob Trail*: Pilot Mountain State Park / 1 mile / 240 ft. / beautiful views of the surrounding area and the famous Pilot Mountain Knob; involves stairs including rock steps of tall and/or uneven height

Reed Gold Mine*: Midland; east of Charlotte / 2.5 miles / 197 ft. / lots to explore related to the discovery of gold in North Carolina, including a trail through an underground mine; restrooms at the visitor center

Ridges Mountain Preserve*: near Asheboro / 1.75 miles / 150 ft. / very peaceful; amazing large rock formations at the top of the trail; interesting human history in the area

Rocky Face Mountain Recreational Area—Grindstone Trail*: Hiddenite; near Taylorsville / 2.75 miles / 325 ft. / there are quite a few trails here, but all involve some amount of elevation gain; parts of some trails can be done without elevation gain; amazing views and cool rock formation; restrooms at the parking area

Salem Lake*: Winston-Salem / 7 miles / 236 ft. / wide gravel trail; popular area; multi-use trail that allows bikes; easy to do a shorter distance as an out-and-back hike rather than completing the entire seven-mile loop and still have a great experience; lots of wildlife to see around the lake; restrooms at the trailhead; suggest parking by the playground and hiking counterclockwise; hike to the first big cove is a nice out-and-back of about two miles

Saxapahaw Island Trail*: Saxapahaw; near Chapel Hill / 2.3 miles / 69 ft. / essentially flat with some little inclines to get closer to the river; lovely views of the Haw River; ability to see an American Indian fishing weir; restrooms at the parking area

Coastal Plain Trails

ADA Trail: Nags Head Woods Preserve at Kill Devil Hills / .5 mile from the trailhead, 1 mile from the non-disabled parking area / flat / paved and boardwalk trail that features views of the wetlands; lots of opportunities to see wildlife; two parking spaces for those with disabled placards at the trailhead that are van accessible, all others are asked to park at the main preserve parking area and walk a short distance down the road to access the trail

Boardwalk Trail*: Dismal Swamp State Park / .75 mile / flat / sandy path up to boardwalk; views of swamp forest and chance to see wildlife; restrooms available at visitor center

Buxton Woods Trail: Cape Hatteras National Seashore / 1 mile / 29 ft. / sand and dirt natural surface with some roots; boardwalks; fresh and saltwater ponds; live oak canopy; lots of opportunities to see wildlife; restrooms at trailhead; definitely wear effective insect repellent

Coleman Trail and Cypress Point Trails*: Merchants Millpond State Park / 2 miles / flat / natural surface and boardwalk trails; nice views of the forest and swamp land; trail is down the road from the main entrance

Fenwick Hollowell Wetlands Trail*: College of the Albemarle, Elizabeth City / 1 mile / flat / trail tread is paved and boardwalk; informational signs provided; beautiful views of the Pasquotank River

Flytrap and Sugarloaf Trails Loop: Carolina Beach State Park / 2.7 miles / 39 ft. / sand/dirt natural surface and boardwalk; lots to see along this trail including Venus flytraps growing in their native habitat; connects to several other trails; can do only the Venus Flytrap Trail for a shorter hike

Freedom Trail: Fort Raleigh National Historic Site / 2.4 miles / 13 ft. / brick paved and sand/dirt natural surface; leads to the sound; hike through a maritime forest with historical exhibits; restrooms on site

Hammocks Beach State Park mainland trails*: near Swansboro / 2.5 miles / 49 ft. / a loop of four trails that could be hiked in a different combination for a shorter hike; sandy natural surface trail tread; nice views of the water and beautiful coastal forest

History and Tarheel Trails: Moores Creek National Battlefield / 1.3 miles / 30 ft. / trail tread is paved, boardwalk or rubberized surface; lots of historical information provided along the trails; good views of the wetlands; chance to see Venus flytraps growing

Howell Woods Environmental Learning Center: Four Oaks / varies but all short / flat / many trails available at this location that all connect with each other; daily trail status is posted on the information board at the Learning Center; a variety of habitats to explore

Lake Wilson Loop Trail: near Wilson / 2 miles / 40 ft. / includes one bridge over a part of the lake and another over a creek; paved, sandy gravel and boardwalk trail tread; restrooms on site; beautiful views of the lake and good chances to spot wildlife

Lumber River State Park Princess Ann Access trail*: Lumber River State Park / 1 mile / 42 ft. / nice view of the Lumber River wetland area; quiet park; restrooms available on site; trail does include some stairs

Ocean Isle Beach Nature Trail*: Ocean Isle Beach / 1.4 miles / 10 ft. / sandy natural surface and boardwalk trail treads; views of the saltwater marsh and Intracoastal Waterway; some beautiful live oaks and lots of birds to see

Appendix I: Most Recommended Hikes by Region

Patsy Pond Nature Trail Loop: Croatan National Forest off NC 24 / 2.4 miles / 36 ft. / lots of trails to combine here for longer or shorter hikes; opportunities to see wildlife; sandy natural surface trails; some road noise closest to the parking area; hunting allowed in season

Sand Ridge Nature Trail and Lakeshore Trail Loop*: Lake Waccamaw State Park / 1.3 miles / 13 ft. / beautiful views of the lake including the pier; interesting trail through the sandy pine forest; this loop starts from the parking lot at the furthest end of the park road and includes a short section of the Lakeshore Trail in addition to the Sand Ridge Nature Trail and one of the boardwalk connectors; restrooms at the parking area and park visitor center

Appendix II

North Carolina Every Body Hiking Challenge

A few hiking challenges have already been mentioned in this text, and there are still more to consider. For example, Carolina Mountain Club administers several challenges, and many of them are … well … quite challenging![1] I have participated in several local and nationwide hiking challenges during my hiking journey. My favorite two have been the Hikerbabes 100 Hike Challenge and, especially, the 52 Hike Challenge. The 52 Hike Challenge encourages you to hike at least a mile, at least once a week, and these hikes can happen on any trail, anywhere—paved, gravel or natural surface—and pace doesn't matter. You can go as fast or as slow as you'd like! They also offer an adaptive option where a 30- to 45-minute outing in nature counts as a hike for the challenge if you are not able to complete a mile with or without adaptive hiking gear.

These challenges have motivated me and encouraged me to try new trails and new experiences. Below you'll find the North Carolina Every Body Hiking Challenge if you'd like to give it a try. You're allowed to write in your book! There is no time limit to complete the challenge, but I would love to know if you participate and what you enjoyed along the way. Feel free to reach out on social media or through my website[2] and share your experiences with me!

Challenge Item:	Date Completed:	Location:
Hiked in the Mountains		
Hiked in the Piedmont		
Hiked in the Coastal Plain		
Hiked in spring		
Hiked in summer		
Hiked in autumn		
Hiked in winter		
Used something I learned in this book		
Spotted a beautiful wildflower		
Listened to a unique birdsong		
Saw some cool wildlife		
Dipped a hand or foot in a stream or river		

Appendix II: North Carolina Every Body Hiking Challenge

Challenge Item:	Date Completed:	Location:
Noticed a small detail on the trail		
Saw something that made me smile		
Tried a new trail snack		
Took a picture to save a memory		
Visited a national forest		
Visited a state park		
Visited a national park site		
Visited a nature preserve		
Visited a trail in a city or county park		
Hiked on a greenway		

Chapter Notes

Chapter 1

1. "A History of Hiking: The Driving Force Behind Our Footprints," *Silverlight*, December 9, 2021.
2. *Ibid.*
3. Forest History Society, "Hiking in America," https://foresthistory.org/research-explore/us-forest-service-history/policy-and-law/recreation-u-s-forest-service/hiking-in-america/.
4. "A History of Hiking: The Driving Force Behind Our Footprints."
5. Yellowstone National Park, "Birth of a National Park," February 5, 2020, https://www.nps.gov/yell/learn/historyculture/yellowstoneestablishment.htm.
6. For example, see Tazbah Rose Chavez, "Nüümü Poya: A Story of Reclamation on a Well-Loved Trail," https://www.rei.com/blog/news/nuumu-poyo-a-story-of-reclamation-on-a-well-loved-trail.
7. Robert E. Manning, "Men and Mountains Meet: Journal of the Appalachian Mountain Club, 1876–1984," *Journal of Forest History*, vol. 28, no. 1 (January 1984): 24–33.
8. Peter M. Steurer, "History of the Carolina Mountain Club: Commemorating the 70th Anniversary 1923–1993," http://www.carolinamountainclub.org/view/assets/uploadedAssets//CMC%20History%2070th%20Anniversary.pdf.
9. Alan Eakes, Lewis Ledford, and Don Reuter, "History of the North Carolina State Park System," *NC Division of Parks and Recreation, NC Department of Cultural Environment and Natural Resources*, 2011, https://files.nc.gov/ncparks/37/-NC-State-Parks-History.pdf.
10. Steurer, "History of the Carolina Mountain Club."
11. "Stories: Creating a National Park," *NPS: Great Smoky Mountains National Park*, November 15, 2016, https://www.nps.gov/grsm/learn/historyculture/stories.htm#:~:text=In%20May%2C%201926%2C%20a%20bill,Park%20and%20Shenandoah%20National%20Park.
12. Steurer, "History of the Carolina Mountain Club."
13. "A History of Hiking: The Driving Force Behind Our Footprints."
14. "NC Year of the Trail: About," *Great Trails State Coalition*, https://greattrailsnc.com/about/.
15. For example, see Florence Williams, "Take Two Hours in a Pine Forest and Call Me in the Morning," *Outside Magazine*, updated June 30, 2021, https://www.outsideonline.com/health/wellness/take-two-hours-pine-forest-and-call-me-morning/, and Florence Williams, *The Nature Fix: Why Nature Makes Us Happier, Healthier and More Creative* (New York: W.W. Norton, 2018).
16. Qing Li, et al., "Phytoncides (Wood Essential Oils) Induce Human Natural Killer Cell Activity," *Immunopharmacology and Immunotoxicology*, vol. 28, issue 2 (2008): 319–333, https://www.tandfonline.com/doi/full/10.1080/08923970600809439.
17. "Good Sleep for Good Health: Get the Rest You Need," *NIH News in Health*, April 2021. https://newsinhealth.nih.gov/2021/04/good-sleep-good-health.
18. Julia Clarke, "How Hiking Helps You Sleep," *Advnture*, https://www.advnture.com/features/-hiking-sleep. Also see Emi Morita, et al., "A Before and After Comparison of the Effects of Forest Walking on the Sleep of a Community-Based Sample of People with Sleep Complaints," *BioPsychoSocial Medicine*, vol. 5, article 13 (2011); Stephanie Anzman-Frasca, et al., "Effects of a Randomized Controlled Hiking Intervention on Daily Activities, Sleep, and Stress Among Adults During the Covid-19 Pandemic," *BMC Public Health*, vol. 23, article 893 (2023).
19. U.S. Environmental Protection Agency, "Indoor Air Quality," https://www.epa.gov/report-environment/indoor-air-quality#.
20. Neil E. Klepis, et al., "The National Human Activity Pattern Survey (NHAPS): A Resource for Assessing Exposure to Environmental Pollutants," *Journal of Exposure Analysis and Environmental Epidemiology*, vol. 11, no. 3 (2001): https://escholarship.org/uc/item/1zg3q68x.
21. Michelle C. Kondo, et al., "Nature Prescriptions for Health: A Review of Evidence and Research Opportunities," *International Journal of Environmental Research and Public Health*, vol. 17, no. 12 (June 2020): 4213, https://www.ncbi.nlm.nih.gov/pmc/articles/PMC7344564/; Michael Precker, "Your Next Doctor's Prescription Might Be to Spend Time in Nature," *American Heart Association News*, October 19, 2021.
22. Michael Easter, "The '20-5-3' Rule Prescribes

How Much Time You Should Spend Outside," *Prevention*, July 12, 2021.

23. See this interesting article from Hiker University on hiking pace and what can influence it: Peter Brooks, "How Fast Does the Average Human Hike?" *Hikers University*, December 19, 2023, https://www.hikersuniversity.com/post/how-fast-does-the-average-human-hike.

Chapter 2

1. To see a slightly different view of the regions of North Carolina, check out this map from the EPA: https://gaftp.epa.gov/EPADataCommons/ORD/Ecoregions/nc/nc_eco.pdf. This map shows the different ecoregions of North Carolina. They vary slightly from the more well-known three regional distinctions we'll discuss in this chapter but give a more nuanced view of the natural divisions of the state. The North Carolina Wildlife Action Plan, developed by the North Carolina Wildlife Resources Commission, began using these ecoregion distinctions in 2015 to help better plan conservation efforts. The regions share common landscape settings and patterns which are influenced by climate, soil types, landforms, and natural vegetation.

2. If you're interested in learning more about the variety of natural communities found across North Carolina, I would highly recommend *Wild North Carolina: Discovering the Wonders of Our State's Natural Communities* by David Blevins and Michael P. Schafale.

3. For a more in-depth description of the habitats found in the Mountain region, see "Mountain Habitats," *North Carolina Wildlife Resources Commission*, https://www.ncwildlife.org/Conserving/Habitats/Mountain.

4. If you want to read lots more great information about the mountains of North Carolina, read *The Longstreet Highroad Guide to the North Carolina Mountains* by Lynda McDaniel. You can find the entire text of this guide at https://www.sherpaguides.com/north_carolina/mountains/index.html.

5. "Western North Carolina Physical Geography," https://www.hikewnc.info/areainfo/geography.

6. "Our State Geography in a Snap: The Mountain Region," *NCpedia*, https://www.ncpedia.org/our-state-geography-snap-mountain.

7. Nick Roberts, "Where to Trout Fish in Western North Carolina," *Garden and Gun*, May 9, 2023, https://gardenandgun.com/articles/where-to-trout-fish-in-western-north-carolina/.

8. For a (fictional) coming-of-age story that centers around fly fishing in the Brevard area, check out *Grandpa's Fish* by Don Harris.

9. For a list and brief description of North Carolina's rivers from all regions, see https://www.nps.gov/subjects/rivers/north-carolina.htm.

10. "Beyond the Exhibits: North Carolina Museum of History—North Carolina Mountain Region," https://files.nc.gov/dncr-moh/Mountain%20%28final%29.pdf.

11. For more information, see https://files.nc.gov/deqee/documents/files/french-broad-river-basin_0.pdf.

12. For more information, see https://files.nc.gov/deqee/documents/files/catawba-river-basin.pdf.

13. For more information, see https://files.nc.gov/deqee/documents/files/new-river-basin.pdf.

14. Robin Jarvis, "The One County in North Carolina with 250 Waterfalls to Visit," *Only in Your State*, April 19, 2022, https://www.onlyinyourstate.com/north-carolina/county-with-250-waterfalls-nc/.

15. To read more about Fontana Dam, the Road to Nowhere and some of the controversies surrounding the construction of the dam, see "Fontana Dam," *Western Carolina University*, https://dh.wcu.edu/index.php/2010/08/30/fontana-dam/.

16. "Beyond the Exhibits: North Carolina Museum of History—North Carolina Mountain Region," https://files.nc.gov/dncr-moh/Mountain%20%28final%29.pdf.

17. "Biodiversity," *Blue Ridge National Heritage Area*, https://www.blueridgeheritage.com/heritage/natural/biodiversity/.

18. *Ibid.*

19. Frank Graff, "Putting the Blue in the Blue Ridge Mountains," *PBS North Carolina*, https://static.pbslearningmedia.org/media/media_files/0d83ef92-65ad-4b54-bd77-2dd1b4b886c2/-239b6682-7944-4df8-bc28-548eda4d33eb.pdf.

20. "Hurricane Helene's Damage, Related Expenses in North Carolina Shattering Records, Estimated at $53 Billion," *CBS News*, October 24, 2025, https://www.cbsnews.com/news/hurricane-helenes-north-carolina-damage-53-billion-record/.

21. "N.C Forest Service Estimated Acres and Dollar Amount Damage by Hurricane Helene," *Watauga Online*, November 1, 2024, https://wataugaonline.com/n-c-forest-service-estimated-acres-and-dollar-amount-damaged-by-hurricane-helene/.

22. For a more in-depth description of different habitats found in the Piedmont region, see "Piedmont Habitats," *North Carolina Wildlife Resources Commission*, https://www.ncwildlife.org/Conserving/Habitats/Piedmont.

23. "Beyond the Exhibits: North Carolina Piedmont Region," *North Carolina Museum of History*, https://files.nc.gov/dncr-moh/Piedmont%20%28final%29.pdf.

24. "Reed Gold Mine," *North Carolina Historic Sites*, https://historicsites.nc.gov/all-sites/reed-gold-mine.

25. "Beyond the Exhibits: North Carolina Piedmont Region," *North Carolina Museum of History*, https://files.nc.gov/dncr-moh/Piedmont%20%28final%29.pdf.

26. Clarke Knight, "Drinkable, Fishable,

Swimmable: Yadkin Riverkeeper Promotes Water Usage for Everyone," *ESAL*, November 8, 2020, https://esal.us/yadkin-riverkeeper/.

27. "Lakes and Reservoirs: Piedmont Ecoregion," https://www.wrcuatweb.org/Portals/0/Conserving/documents/Piedmont/P_Lakes_and_reservoirs.pdf?ver=v5lVHLBpXU7BiiDx2_yu3Q%3d%3d.

28. Dennis P. Niemeyer, "Native Plants and Communities of the Piedmont of North Carolina," *Combined Proceedings International Plant Propagators' Society*, vol. 56 (2006): 566–568; "Forest Succession," *Duke Forest*, https://dukeforest.duke.edu/forest-environment/-forest-succession/#:~:text=Succession%20in%20the%20North%20Carolina%20Piedmont&text=Vegetation%20follows%20established%20patterns%20of,change%20is%20called%20plant%20succession.

29. "Coastal Region Appendix," *Green Growth Toolbox: North Carolina Wildlife Resources Commission*, https://www.ncwildlife.org/Portals/0/Coastal%20Region%20Appendix_2023.pdf?ver=RqPeb76EToIBSV_qpAttAQ%3D%3D#:~:text=These%20habitat%20types%20are%20associated,Fear%20and%20Lumber%20River%20watersheds.

30. For a more in-depth description of different habitat types found in the Coastal Plain, see "Coastal Plain Habitats," *North Carolina Wildlife Resources Commission*, https://www.ncwildlife.org/conserving/habitats/coast.

31. "Fall Line" is a bit of a misnomer here, as it's really the "Fall Zone." This geological boundary where the more sedimentary rock of the Coastal Plain overlaps the metamorphic rock of the Piedmont can range from a few feet wide to up to 20 miles wide. Raven Rock State Park lies in the Fall Zone and has an interesting display about it in their visitor center.

32. Corey Davis, "Our Curious Coast: Geography and Coastal Climate," *North Carolina State Climate Office*, July 13, 2022, https://climate.ncsu.edu/blog/2022/07/our-curious-coast-geography-and-coastal-climate/.

33. "Beyond the Exhibits: North Carolina Coastal Region," *North Carolina Museum of History*, https://files.nc.gov/dncr-moh/Coastal%20%28final%29.pdf.

34. "Beyond the Exhibits: North Carolina Coastal Region," *North Carolina Museum of History*, https://files.nc.gov/dncr-moh/Coastal%20%28final%29.pdf.

35. To read more about the Intracoastal Waterway in North Carolina, see "North Carolina Intracoastal Waterway," *CoastalGuide.com*, https://www.coastalguide.com/north-carolina-intracoastal-waterway.html and Philip Gerard, "Safe Passage on the Intracoastal Waterway," *Our State*, July 25, 2022.

36. William S. Powell, ed., "Carolina Bays," *Encyclopedia of North Carolina*, 2006 (revised 2023), https://www.ncpedia.org/carolina-bays.

37. "Mattamuskeet National Wildlife Refuge/Lake Mattamuskeet," *Visit North Carolina*, https://www.visitnc.com/listing/ay7Q/mattamuskeet-national-wildlife-refuge-lake-mattamuskeet.

38. "Beyond the Exhibits: North Carolina Coastal Region," *North Carolina Museum of History*, https://files.nc.gov/dncr-moh/Coastal%20%28final%29.pdf.

39. "Great Dismal Swamp," *Britannica*, https://www.britannica.com/place/Great-Dismal-Swamp.

40. "Tidal Swamp Forest and Wetlands: Mid-Atlantic Coastal Plain," *North Carolina Wildlife Resources Commission*, https://www.ncwildlife.org/portals/0/Conserving/documents/Coast/CP_Tidal_swamp_forest_and_wetlands.pdf.

41. For more information about bodies of water in the Coastal Plain region, see Corey Davis, "Our Curious Coast: Rivers and Wetlands," *North Carolina State Climate Office*, July 20, 2022, https://climate.ncsu.edu/blog/2022/07/our-curious-coast-rivers-and-wetlands/.

42. Corey Davis, "Our Curious Coast: Geography and Coastal Climate," *North Carolina State Climate Office*, July 13, 2022, https://climate.ncsu.edu/blog/2022/07/our-curious-coast-geography-and-coastal-climate/.

43. "Beyond the Exhibits: North Carolina Coastal Region," *North Carolina Museum of History*, https://files.nc.gov/dncr-moh/Coastal%20%28final%29.pdf.

44. Janna Sasser, "Amazing Coast: Flora of the Coastal Plain," *Sea Grant North Carolina Coastwatch*, Summer 2016, https://ncseagrant.ncsu.edu/coastwatch/previous-issues/2016-2/summer-2016/-amazing-coast-flora-of-the-coastal-plain/.

Chapter 4

1. For descriptions of many different cloud types, see "NOAA Cloudwise," https://www.noaa.gov/sites/default/files/2023-03/cloudchart-front.pdf.

2. Daniel Terrill, "Can You Predict the Weather by Observing Cloud Patterns While Camping?" *Outdoors*, August 3, 2023, https://outdoors.com/how-to-predict-the-weather-by-looking-at-clouds/.

3. For a more detailed explanation on reading clouds, see Brian Mertins, "How to Predict Weather with Clouds (8 Types of Clouds and What They Mean)," *Nature Mentoring*, https://nature-mentor.com/how-to-predict-weather-with-clouds/.

4. Kenneth Reece, "Seven Struck by Lightning at Grandfather Mountain," *Watauga Online*, August 13, 2021, https://wataugaonline.com/seven-struck-by-lightning-at-grandfather-mountain/.

5. "Becoming Severe Weather Ready in the Western Carolinas and Northeast Georgia: Lightning and Lightning Safety," *National Weather Service*, https://www.weather.gov/gsp/gspPreparc_8.

6. "U.S. Lightning Strike Deaths," *Centers for Disease Control and Prevention*, https://www.cdc.

gov/disasters/lightning/victimdata/infographic.html#:~:text=Florida%2C%20Texas%2C%20Colorado%2C%20North,June%2C%20July%2C%20and%20August.&text=Lightning%20strikes%20cause%20more%20deaths%20on%20weekends%2C%20mostly%20on%20Saturday.

7. "Becoming Severe Weather Ready in the Western Carolinas and Northeast Georgia: Lightning and Lightning Safety," *National Weather Service*, https://www.weather.gov/gsp/gspPrepare_8.

8. "Understanding Lightning: Thunder," *National Weather Service*, https://www.weather.gov/safety/lightning-science-thunder#:~:text=If%20you%20count%20the%20number,a%20safe%20place%20while%20counting.

9. "Lightning Safety," *American Hiking Society*, https://americanhiking.org/resources/lightning-safety/.

10. "The National Lightning Safety Council Reiterates Stance on Outdated Outdoor Safety Message," *EINPRESSWIRE*, April 1, 2025, http://www.lightningsafetycouncil.org/2025-Media-Release.pdf.

11. "Corey Buhay, "Everything Hikers Know About Lightning Safety Is Wrong," *Backpacker*, April 11, 2024, https://www.backpacker.com/survival/natural-hazards/lightning/lightning-safety-facts-for-hikers/.

12. "Beaufort Wind Scale," *National Weather Service*, https://www.weather.gov/mfl/beaufort.

13. For more information on weather patterns in North Carolina, see Peter J. Robinson and Gregory B. Fishel, "Climate and Weather: Part II Climactic Factors, Precipitation Patterns, and Seasonal Trends," *NCpedia*, 2006, https://www.ncpedia.org/climate-and-weather-part-2-climatic.

14. "North Carolina Traditional Weather Lore," https://www.ncnatural.com/wildflwr/fall/folklore.html.

15. *Ibid.*

Chapter 5

1. "1017 Trails," *U.S. Access Board*, https://www.access-board.gov/aba/chapter/ch10/#1017-trails.

2. "About the U.S. Access Board," https://www.access-board.gov/about/.

3. Kathleen Snodgrass, project leader, "Forest Service Trail Accessibility Guidelines (FSTAG) Pocket Version," *United States Department of Agriculture and the U.S. Department of Transportation Federal Highway Administration*, October 2015, https://www.fs.usda.gov/sites/default/files/FSTAG-Pocket-Guide.pdf.

4. *Ibid.*

5. "What Does 'Accessible' Mean?" *The Trail Access Project*, https://www.trailaccessproject.org/what-does-accessible-park-mean.html.

6. "Trackchair Program," *North Carolina Wildlife Resources Commission*, https://www.ncwildlife.org/outdoors/disabled-access/trackchair-program#HowtoReserve-623.

7. "Access for All: Park and Recreation Introduces New All-terrain Wheelchairs," *Mecklenburg County*, November 14, 2004, https://news.mecknc.gov/access-all-park-and-recreation-introduces-new-all-terrain-wheelchairs.

8. "Transit to Trails," https://www.partnc.org/414/Transit-To-Trails.

9. "Accessible Hiking Trails in Asheville," *Loyal Lifts*, https://loyallifts.com/blog/accessible-hiking-trails-in-asheville.

10. "Accessibility at State Parks," *North Carolina Department of Natural and Cultural Resources*, https://www.dncr.nc.gov/about/diversity-equity-accessibility-and-inclusion/accessibility/accessibility-state-parks.

11. "Blue Ridge Parkway Accessibility," https://www.blueridgeparkway.org/parkway-accessibility.

12. "Accessibility," *North Carolina Department of Natural and Cultural Resources*, https://www.dncr.nc.gov/about-us/office-cultural-engagement/accessibility.

13. "Great Adaptive Hiking Trails by State," *Trail Access Project*, https://www.trailaccessproject.org/trail-network.html.

14. "Describe Your Trail's Characteristics," *Trail Access Project*, https://www.trailaccessproject.org/tips-on-describing-a-trail.html.

Chapter 6

1. "Dehydration," https://www.mountsinai.org/health-library/diseases-conditions/dehydration#:~:text=A%20decrease%20in%20skin%20turgor,a%20late%20sign%20of%20dehydration.

2. Will Burkhart and Marcus Shapiro, "Tips to Avoid Bonking While Hiking and What to Do If You Hit the Wall," *Fit for Trips*, https://fitfortrips.com/tips-to-avoid-bonking-while-hiking/.

3. *Ibid.*

4. "Hiking Boots vs. Trail Runners: The Great Debate," https://www.rei.com/learn/expert-advice/hiking-boots-vs-trail-runners-the-great-debate.html.

5. "How to Choose Hiking Socks," https://www.rei.com/learn/expert-advice/backpacking-socks.html; Amber King, "How to Choose Hiking Socks," August 8, 2022, https://www.outdoorgearlab.com/topics/shoes-and-boots/best-hiking-socks/buying-advice.

6. Hypothermia," *Mayo Clinic*, April 16, 2024, https://www.mayoclinic.org/diseases-conditions/hypothermia/symptoms-causes/syc-20352682.

7. Nancy East, "Hypothermia: The Sneakiest Danger You'll Face on a Hike (in Every Season)," https://www.hopeandfeathertravels.com/hypothermia-the-sneakiest-danger-youll-face-on-a-hike-in-every-season/.

8. "Sunlight: Solar Radiation," *Britannica*, updated September 27, 2023, https://www.britannica.com/science/sunlight-solar-radiation.

9. "Sun Safety," *Johns Hopkins Medicine*,

https://www.hopkinsmedicine.org/health/-wellness-and-prevention/sun-safety#:~:text=The%20earth%27s%20atmosphere%20absorbs%20UVC,including%20skin%20cancer%20and%20cataracts.

10. "The States with the Highest Melanoma Rates May Surprise You," *City of Hope Cancer Centers*, https://www.cancercenter.com/community/blog/2023/05/skin-cancer-rates-by-state.

11. Steven Q. Wang, MD, "Ask the Expert: Does a High SPF Protect My Skin Better?" *Skin Cancer Foundation*, May 1, 2023, https://www.skincancer.org/blog/ask-the-expert-does-a-high-spf-protect-my-skin-better/.

12. Ali Venosa, "Breaking Down Broad-Spectrum Protection: Why Your Sunscreen Needs to Have It," *Skin Cancer Foundation*, https://www.skincancer.org/blog/broad-spectrum-protection-sunscreen/.

13. Priyanka Vedak, MD, "Do People of Color Need Sunscreen?" *UNC Health Talk*, May 4, 2022, https://healthtalk.unchealthcare.org/do-people-of-color-need-sunscreen/.

14. "Hyperthermia: Too Hot for Your Health," *National Institutes of Health*, June 27, 2012, https://www.nih.gov/news-events/news-releases/-hyperthermia-too-hot-your-health-1.

15. For example, see Joey Holmes, "Homemade Simple Fire Starter: 18 Simple Methods," https://coolofthewild.com/homemade-fire-starter/.

16. Andrew Engelson, "How to Build a Hiker's First Aid Kit," *Washington Trails Association*, https://www.wta.org/go-outside/trail-smarts/like-your-life-depends-on-it-building-your-first-aid-kit.

17. https://www.roadid.com.

18. AMC Staff, "How to Build an Emergency Tarp Shelter," *Be Outdoors: Appalachian Mountain Club*, https://www.outdoors.org/resources/amc-outdoors/outdoor-resources/how-to-build-an-emergency-tarp-shelter/.

Chapter 7

1. Diego Alonso San Alberto, et al., "The Olfactory Gating of Visual Preferences to Human Skin and Visible Spectra in Mosquitoes," *Nature Communications*, vol. 13, article 555 (2022), https://www.nature.com/articles/s41467-022-28195-x.

2. Michael Waldvogel and Charles Apperson, "Insect Repellent Products," *NC State Extension*, September 30, 2022, https://content.ces.ncsu.edu/insect-repellent-products.

3. "'Fight the Bite!' Prevent Mosquito and Tick Bites," *Centers for Disease Control and Prevention*, May 9, 2023, https://www.cdc.gov/ncezid/dvbd/media/fight-the-bite.html.

4. "Using Insect Repellents Safely and Effectively," *Environmental Protection Agency*, July 6, 2023, https://www.epa.gov/insect-repellents/-using-insect-repellents-safely-and-effectively.

5. Rachel Shoemaker, "How to Treat Your Hiking Clothes with Permethrin," *The Trek*, November 3, 2022, https://thetrek.co/how-to-treat-your-clothes-with-permethrin/.

6. Want to see a funny version of this necessary post-hike activity turned into a romantic interlude? Check out Brad Paisley's song "Ticks." Seriously, though, frequent tick checks are really important and one of the best things you can do to prevent getting tick-borne illnesses.

7. Ashley L. Hawke and Randall L. Jensen, "Are Trekking Poles Helping or Hindering Your Hiking Experience? A Review," *Wilderness and Environmental Medicine*, vol. 31, issue 4 (2020), https://journals.sagepub.com/doi/full/10.1016/j.wem.2020.06.009.

8. Nicola Giovanelli, et al., "Do Poles Really 'Save the Legs' During Uphill Pole Walking at Different Intensities?" *European Journal of Applied Physiology*, vol. 123 (2023): 2803–2812, https://link.springer.com/article/10.1007/s00421-023-05254-9.

9. Hawke and Jensen, "Are Trekking Poles Helping or Hindering Your Hiking Experience? A Review."

10. Josette Deschambeault, "How to Use Trekking Poles and Hiking Staffs," *REI*, https://www.rei.com/learn/expert-advice/how-to-use-trekking-poles.html#:~:text=Baskets%20are%20generally%20round%20and,and%20keep%20your%20poles%20clean).

11. Clay Bonnyman Evans, "How to Keep Yourself Safe from Chafe," *The Trek*, August 29, 2019, https://thetrek.co/how-to-prevent-treat-chafing-while-backpacking/.

12. Joe Pasteris, "How to Save Phone Battery Life in the Backcountry," *GAIA GPS Blog*, February 8, 2023, https://blog.gaiagps.com/save-phone-battery-life/.

13. "NC Wildlife Recommends Wearing Orange," *The Transylvania Times*, December 6, 2021, https://www.transylvaniatimes.com/outdoors/n-c-wildlife-recommends-wearing-orange/article_272437f3-4985-5638-b8d4-2c3fbb01c7a9.html.

14. "SAM Splint," *SAM Medical*, https://www.sammedical.com/products/sam-splint?variant=32444250423405.

15. "Fox 40: Whistles," https://fox40shopusa.com/collections/pealess-whistles.

16. "Daypack vs Backpack: What's the Difference?" *The Pedal Project*, https://thepedalproject.org/daypack-vs-backpack-the-difference/.

17. Valerie Loughney Stapleton, "How to Choose Daypacks," *REI*, https://www.rei.com/learn/expert-advice/daypack.html.

18. Koala 2.0, https://www.hangtimegear.com.

19. "REI Co-op Membership," https://www.rei.com/membership.

Chapter 8

1. Thank you to Bill Sanderson for sharing this information about the 30–60–90 Walk. He is co-director of Carolina Mountain Club's Search

and Rescue team and a volunteer with Haywood County Search and Rescue. He includes this information in his navigation course for Carolina Mountain Club and in training for new search and rescue volunteers. As he shared with me, "This is something that I really try to drive home to everyone that goes into the woods, for even a short hike."

2. Ryan Dotson, "Statistics of Getting Lost and Found," *Survival Dispatch*, June 30, 2023, https://survivaldispatch.com/statistics-of-getting-lost-and-found/.

3. *Safe and Found*, Jester Wallis Productions, January 21, 2024, https://www.youtube.com/watch?v=mL2UeIMm9Xo&list=PLskxZDq_L8NRq7gkMQdNYkYwbfeAPs5LR&index=1.

Chapter 9

1. "Arboviruses," *North Carolina Department of Health and Human Services—Epidemiology*, https://epi.dph.ncdhhs.gov/cd/arbo/figures.html.

2. "Important Updates on Locally Acquired Malaria Cases Identified in Florida, Texas, and Maryland," *Centers for Disease Control and Prevention*, August 28, 2023, https://emergency.cdc.gov/han/2023/han00496.asp.

3. Berton, et al., "Common Ticks of North Carolina: An Identification Guide," *NC State University Department of Entomology and Plant Pathology*, https://pdic.ces.ncsu.edu/wp-content/uploads/2023/04/NC_Tick_Guide_v1.0_April_14_2023.pdf?fwd=no.

4. "Ticks and Tick-Borne Diseases," *NC State Extension*, https://content.ces.ncsu.edu/ticks-and-tick-borne-diseases.

5. "Alpha-gal Syndrome," *Centers for Disease Control and Prevention*, https://www.cdc.gov/ticks/alpha-gal/index.html; "Alpha-gal Syndrome," *Mayo Clinic*, https://www.mayoclinic.org/diseases-conditions/-alpha-gal-syndrome/symptoms-causes/syc-20428608#:~:text=Overview,alpha%2Dgal%20into%20the%20body.

6. "Ticks and Tick-Borne Diseases," *NC State Extension*, https://content.ces.ncsu.edu/ticks-and-tick-borne-diseases.

7. Julie Edgar, "FAQ: Tick-Borne Diseases," *WebMD*, https://www.webmd.com/skin-problems-and-treatments/faq-tick-borne-diseases; "Lyme Disease: Transmission," *Centers for Disease Control and Prevention*, https://www.cdc.gov/lyme/transmission/index.html#:~:text=In%20most%20cases%2C%20a%20tick,chances%20of%20getting%20Lyme%20disease.

8. "Arachnids of North Carolina," *North Carolina State Parks*, https://auth1.dpr.ncparks.gov/arachnid/index.php. (Be sure to see the map at the bottom of the page where you can click to see the different spider species reported in each county.)

9. Ibid.

10. Ibid.

11. "Africanized Honey Bees: Where Are They Now, and When Will They Arrive in North Carolina?" *NC State Extension*, https://content.ces.ncsu.edu/africanized-honey-bees-where-are-they-now-and-when-will-they-arrive-in-north-carolina.

12. "The Bees of North Carolina: An Identification Guide," *NC State Extension*, https://content.ces.ncsu.edu/the-bees-of-north-carolina-identification-guide.

13. "Non-Honey Bee Stinging Insects in North Carolina," *NC State Extension*, https://content.ces.ncsu.edu/non-honeybee-stinging-insects-in-north-carolina.

14. "Hornets in Turf," *NC State Extension*, https://www.turffiles.ncsu.edu/insects/hornets-in-turf/.

15. "Reptiles and Amphibians in Your Backyard," *NC State Extension*, https://content.ces.ncsu.edu/reptiles-and-amphibians-in-your-backyard#:~:text=Indeed%2C%20more%20than%20100%20species,roles%20in%20North%20Carolina%27s%20ecosystems.

16. See this informative handout that features all the snakes native to North Carolina from the North Carolina Wildlife Resources Commission and North Carolina Partners in Amphibian and Reptile Conservation: https://ncparc.org/wp-content/uploads/Snake-ID-Guide-Final-2021.pdf?fbclid=IwZXh0bgNhZW0CMTEAAR3YhY730Oropg4TsfGDjxkfk16pJuXhcdN7rCR4-oXSjgvRFtaTSh0021U_aem_ZmFrZWR1bW15MTZieXRlcw.

17. Tarek Mohamed Abd El-Aziz, Antonio Garcia Soares, and James D. Stockand, "Snake Venoms in Drug Discovery: Valuable Therapeutic Tools for Life Saving," *Toxins*, vol. 11, no. 10 (October 2019): 564, https://www.ncbi.nlm.nih.gov/pmc/articles/PMC6832721/; The Rattlesnake Conservancy, "Breast Cancer Awareness Month," October 1, 2018, https://www.savethebuzztails.org/single-post/2018/10/01/breast-cancer-awareness-month.

18. "The Venomous Snakes of North Carolina," *North Carolina Poison Control Center*, https://cdn.atriumhealth.org/-/media/nc-poison-center/documents/snakebrochure_final.pdf?rev=cf719fee3e08419093d78ef4fc27dec4&hash=A8A0384F76FA9A7AB3F9D8A103AA85A0.

19. Ibid.

20. "Eastern Coral Snake," *North Carolina Wildlife Resources Commission*, https://www.ncwildlife.org/Learning/Species/Reptiles/Eastern-Coral-Snake#:~:text=The%20Eastern%20Coral%20Snake%20is%20venomous.,failure%2C%20paralysis%20and%20possibly%20death.

21. "The Venomous Snakes of North Carolina," *North Carolina Poison Control Center*, https://cdn.atriumhealth.org/-/media/nc-poison-center/documents/snakebrochure_final.pdf?rev=cf719fee3e08419093d78ef4fc27dec4&hash=A8A0384F76FA9A7AB3F9D8A103AA85A0.

22. Ibid.

23. "Wildlife Commission Provides Tips to Coexist with Alligators," *North Carolina Wildlife Resources Commission*, May 12, 2023, https://www.ncwildlife.org/Connect-With-Us/-

wildlife-commission-provides-tips-to-coexist-with-alligators-17; "American Alligator," *North Carolina Wildlife Resources Commission*, https://www.ncwildlife.org/Learning/Species/Reptiles/Alligator#81131874-have-a-problem.

24. "Protected Wildlife Species of North Carolina," *North Carolina Wildlife Resources Commission*, https://www.ncwildlife.org/Portals/0/Conserving/documents/Protected-Wildlife-Species-of-NC.pdf.

25. "Checklist of the Mammals of North Carolina," https://emammal.si.edu/system/files/ncmammalchecklist.pdf.

26. "Black Bear," *North Carolina Wildlife Resources Commission*, https://www.ncwildlife.org/Learning/Species/Mammals/Black-Bear#2498420-overview-brbr.

27. See the BearWise website for more information, https://bearwise.org.

28. "Elk," *North Carolina Wildlife Resources Commission*, https://www.ncwildlife.org/Learning/Species/Mammals/Elk#:~:text=Currently%2C%20the%20Wildlife%20Commission%20estimates,Great%20Smoky%20Mountain%20National%20Park.

29. "Forest Service Warns of Coyote Attack on Uwharrie Trail," *U.S. Forest Service*, April 28, 2024, https://www.fs.usda.gov/detail/nfsnc/news-events/?cid=FSEPRD1173842.

30. "Coyote," *North Carolina Wildlife Resource Commission*, https://www.ncwildlife.org/Learning/Species/Mammals/Coyote2#44771363-overview.

31. "Eastern Cougar," *North Carolina Wildlife Resources Commission*, https://www.ncwildlife.org/Portals/0/Learning/documents/Profiles/Mammals/Eastern-Cougar-Update-FINAL.pdf.

32. For example, see Robert Rehder, "Return of the Carolina Cougar," *Wrightsville Beach Magazine*, https://wrightsvillebeachmagazine.com/-return-of-the-cougar/; "Man Says He Saw a Cougar Deemed 'Extinct' in NC," *Charlotte Observer*, May 18, 2019; Carrie Hodgin, "Winston-Salem Woman Has Wild Problem in Her Backyard," *WFMY*, July 30, 2021, https://www.wfmynews2.com/article/news/local/could-cougars-be-on-the-prowl-winston-salem-woman-says-she-has-one-big-wild-problem/83-88eeb18d-0323-43cd-b132-3a591cdab5b1.

Chapter 10

1. "The 7 Principles," *Leave No Trace*, https://lnt.org/why/7-principles/.

2. Whitewater Off Leash, https://center.whitewater.org/off-leash/.

Chapter 11

1. Selin Kesebir and Pelin Kesebir, "A Growing Disconnection from Nature Is Evident in Cultural Products," *Perspectives on Psychological Science*, vol. 12, issue 2 (March 2017): 258–269.

2. Wonder what's on my playlist? Check it out on my website: https://northcarolinadayhikingforeverybody.com/hiking-playlist/.

3. For example, see "Seven Key Attitudes of Mindfulness," https://www.sc.edu/about/offices_and_divisions/housing/documents/resiliencyproject/7keyattitudesofmindfulness.pdf; "What Are the Seven Principles of Mindfulness," *The American Institute of Stress*, https://www.stress.org/what-are-the-seven-principles-of-mindfulness; "9 Attitudes of Mindfulness by Jon Kabat-Kinn," *Mindfulness Based Stress Reduction Training*, https://mbsrtraining.com/attitudes-of-mindfulness-by-jon-kabat-zinn/.

Chapter 12

1. "Park Statistics: Great Smoky Mountains National Park," *National Park Service*, https://www.nps.gov/grsm/learn/management/statistics.htm.

2. "Hiking: National Seashore-Cape Lookout," *National Park Service*, https://www.nps.gov/calo/planyourvisit/hiking.htm.

3. "Hiking: National Seashore-Cape Hatteras," *National Park Service*, https://home.nps.gov/caha/planyourvisit/hiking.htm.

4. "Things to Do: National Historic Site-Fort Raleigh," *National Park Service*, https://www.nps.gov/fora/planyourvisit/placestogo.htm.

5. "Outdoor Pursuits and Trail Maps: National Historic Site-Carl Sandburg Home," *National Park Service*, https://www.nps.gov/thingstodo/outdoor-pursuits.htm.

6. "Moores Creek National Battlefield," *National Park Service*, https://www.nps.gov/mocr/index.htm.

7. "Plan Your Visit: Guilford Courthouse National Military Park," *National Park Service*, https://www.nps.gov/guco/planyourvisit/index.htm.

8. "Self Guided Walking Tour: Guilford Courthouse National Military Park," *National Park Service*, https://www.nps.gov/guco/self-guided-walking-tour.htm.

9. "Kings Mountain," *American Battlefield Trust*, https://www.battlefields.org/learn/revolutionary-war/battles/kings-mountain.

10. "Horn in the West," *Southern Appalachian Historical Society*, https://www.horninthewest.com/about-horn-in-the-west.

11. "Places: Overmountain Victory National Historic Trail," *National Park Service*, https://www.nps.gov/ovvi/planyourvisit/places.htm.

12. "Trail of Tears National Historic Trail," *National Park Service*, https://www.nps.gov/trte/index.htm.

13. Heather L. Whittaker, "'This, Then, Is America!': *Unto These Hills* and Appropriation of Native American History," senior thesis, *University of Georgia*, 2007, https://getd.libs.uga.edu/pdfs/whittaker_heather_l_201008_ma.pdf; "Unto

These Hills," *Cherokee Historical Association*, https://cherokeehistorical.org/unto-these-hills/.

14. "Trail of Tears: North Carolina Map and Guide," *National Park Service*, https://www.nps.gov/trte/planyourvisit/upload/North-Carolina-Trail-of-Tears-Brochure-508.pdf.

15. "Accessibility: Wright Brothers National Memorial," *National Park Service*, https://www.nps.gov/wrbr/planyourvisit/accessibility.htm.

16. "Plan Your Visit: Wright Brothers National Memorial," *National Park Service*, https://www.nps.gov/wrbr/planyourvisit/index.htm.

17. "Park Statistics: Great Smoky Mountains National Park," *National Park Service*, https://www.nps.gov/grsm/learn/management/statistics.htm.

18. "Great Smoky Mountains Trail Map and Guide," *National Park Service*, https://www.nps.gov/grsm/planyourvisit/upload/GSMNP-Trail-Map_JULY21.pdf.

19. "Hiking: Great Smoky Mountains National Park," *National Park Service*, https://www.nps.gov/grsm/planyourvisit/hiking.htm.

20. "Indian Creek and Tom Branch Falls," *National Park Service*, https://www.nps.gov/grsm/planyourvisit/indian-creek-toms-branch-falls.htm.

21. "Juney Whank Falls," *National Park Service*, https://www.nps.gov/grsm/planyourvisit/juney-whank-falls.htm.

22. "Great Smoky Mountains National Park and Partners to Expand Adaptive Programs in 2024," *National Park Service*, April 17, 2024, https://www.nps.gov/grsm/learn/news/great-smoky-mountains-national-park-and-partners-to-expand-adaptive-programs-in-2024.htm.

Chapter 13

1. "This Is Who We Are," *USDA Forest Service*, March 2019, https://www.fs.usda.gov/sites/default/files/This-is-Who-We-Are.pdf.

2. "Go Wild: 4 North Carolina National Forests to Explore," https://www.visitnc.com/story/TCDD/go-wild-4-north-carolina-national-forests-to-explore.

3. For a list of day hiking locations in the four national forests, see "Day Hiking," *U.S. Forest Service*, https://www.fs.usda.gov/activity/nfsnc/recreation/hiking/?recid=48112&actid=50.

4. "Wilderness Areas in North Carolina," *U.S. Forest Service*, https://www.fs.usda.gov/detail/nfsnc/specialplaces/?cid=fseprd561546.

5. Michael Bonner, "Pisgah National Forest," *NCPedia*, 2021, https://www.ncpedia.org/pisgah-national-forest.

6. *Ibid.*

7. "Linville Gorge Wilderness," *U.S. Forest Service*, https://www.fs.usda.gov/detail/nfsnc/specialplaces/?cid=fseprd561553.

8. "Middle Prong Wilderness," *U.S. Forest Service*, https://www.fs.usda.gov/detail/nfsnc/specialplaces/?cid=fseprd561554.

9. "Shining Rock Wilderness," *U.S. Forest Service*, https://www.fs.usda.gov/detail/nfsnc/specialplaces/?cid=fseprd561555.

10. "Top 18 Pisgah National Forest Hiking Trails," *Blue Ridge Mountain Life*, https://blueridgemountainlife.com/top-18-pisgah-national-forest-hiking-trails/.

11. "Cradle of Forestry," https://gofindoutdoors.org/sites/cradle-of-forestry/; "Cradle of Forestry," *U.S. Forest Service*, https://www.fs.usda.gov/recarea/nfsnc/recarea/?recid=48230.

12. "Short Hikes on National Forests and Grasslands: North Carolina," *U.S. Forest Service*, https://www.fs.usda.gov/managing-land/national-forests-grasslands/accessibility/forests-grasslands.

13. "Linville Falls Hiking Trails," *National Park Service*, https://www.nps.gov/blri/planyourvisit/-linville-falls-trails.htm.

14. "Nantahala National Forest," *U.S. Forest Service*, https://www.fs.usda.gov/recarea/nfsnc/recarea/?recid=48634

15. Nantahala and Pisgah National Forest map, https://www.fs.usda.gov/Internet/FSE_DOCUMENTS/stelprdb5425096.pdf; see also the list of trails under the expandable "Hiking" tab at the bottom of this page—https://www.fs.usda.gov/recarea/nfsnc/recarea/?recid=48634.

16. "Croatan National Forest," *U.S. Forest Service*, https://www.fs.usda.gov/Internet/FSE_DOCUMENTS/stelprdb5188168.pdf.

17. "Croatan National Forest-Maps and Publications," *U.S. Forest Service*, https://www.fs.usda.gov/detail/nfsnc/maps-pubs/?cid=stelprdb5193038.

18. "Neusiok Trail," *U.S. Forest Service*, https://www.fs.usda.gov/Internet/FSE_DOCUMENTS/stelprdb5366095.pdf.

19. "Patsy Pond Nature Trail Guide," *North Carolina Coastal Federation*, https://www.nccoast.org/uploads/documents/Media%20Room/Trail%20Maps/PP_trailguide_web.pdf.

20. "Neuse River Trails," *U.S. Forest Service*, https://www.fs.usda.gov/recarea/nfsnc/recreation/natureviewing/recarea/?recid=48506&actid=64.

21. North Carolina Forest Service, https://www.ncforestservice.gov.

Chapter 14

1. "325.5 Million Visits to National Parks in 2023, 16.7 Million Visits to the Blue Ridge Parkway," *National Park Service*, February 23, 2024, https://www.nps.gov/blri/learn/news/325-5-million-visits-to-national-parks-in-2023-16-7-million-visits-to-the-blue-ridge-parkway.htm.

2. "History and Culture," *National Park Service*, https://www.nps.gov/blri/learn/historyculture/index.htm.

3. "Construction of the Parkway," *National Park Service, Ridge Parkway*, February 9, 2017,

https://www.nps.gov/blri/learn/historyculture/construction.htm.
  4. *Ibid.*
  5. "Linn Cove Viaduct-Milepost 304," *National Park Service*, December 26, 2022, https://www.nps.gov/blri/planyourvisit/linn-cove-viaduct.htm.
  6. "Hurricane Helene Recovery," *National Park Service,* October 15, 2024, https://www.nps.gov/blri/planyourvisit/hurricane-helene.htm.
  7. "North Carolina Hiking Trails," *National Park Service,* https://www.nps.gov/blri/planyourvisit/nc-trails.htm.
  8. "Blue Ridge Parkway Hiking," https://www.blueridgeparkway.org/hiking/.
  9. "325.5 Million Visits to National Parks in 2023, 16.7 Million Visits to the Blue Ridge Parkway."

Chapter 15

  1. Alan Eakes, Lewis Ledford, and Don Reuter, "History of the North Carolina State Park System," 2011, https://files.nc.gov/ncparks/37/NC-State-Parks-History.pdf.
  2. North Carolina Division of Parks and Recreation, https://www.ncparks.gov.
  3. "State Trails," *NC Trails: North Carolina State Parks,* https://trails.nc.gov/state-trails#Whatisastatetrail-444.
  4. "Kids in Parks: Track Trails Map," *Kids in Parks,* https://www.kidsinparks.com/map?keys=.

Chapter 16

  1. "What Is a Land Trust?" *Land Trust Alliance*, https://landtrustalliance.org/why-land-matters/land-conservation/about-land-trusts.
  2. "North Carolina," *Land Trust Alliance*, https://landtrustalliance.org/land-trusts/gaining-ground/north-carolina.
  3. Carolina Thread Trail, https://www.carolinathreadtrail.org.
  4. "Hiking Challenge," *Triangle Land Conservancy,* https://triangleland.org/explore/hiking-challenge; "Get Outside," *Conserving Carolina,* https://conservingcarolina.org/get-outside/.
  5. "White Squirrel Hiking Challenge 7," *Conserving Carolina*, https://conservingcarolina.org/white-squirrel-hiking-challenge-7/.

  6. "Flying Squirrel Outdoor Challenge," *Conserving Carolina*, https://conservingcarolina.org/flying-squirrel-challenge/.
  7. "Hiking Challenge," *Triangle Land Conservancy,* https://triangleland.org/explore/hiking-challenge.

Chapter 17

  1. David Ford, "A New Trail in Winston-Salem Preserves 93 Acres Bridging Two Communities Long Divided by the Land," *WFDD: NPR*, April 20, 2023, https://www.wfdd.org/story/new-trail-winston-salem-preserves-93-acres-bridging-two-communities-long-divided-land.
  2. *Ibid.*
  3. "Trail Benefits: Evaluating the Economic, Physical Health and Environmental Impacts of Completing Six Key Segments of the Carolina Thread Trail," *Institute of Transportation Research and Education,* December 2022, https://www.carolinathreadtrail.org/wp-content/uploads/2022/12/CTT-Econ-Impact-Report_Dec2022_Final.pdf.
  4. "Visiting the Underground Railroad Tree," *Guilford College*, https://library.guilford.edu/undergroundrr/tour.

Chapter 18

  1. "Media Room," *Appalachian Trail Conservancy,* https://appalachiantrail.org/our-work/about-us/media-room/#:~:text=Known%20as%20the%20"A.T."%2C,footpath%20in%20a%20single%20year.
  2. "How Max Patch Bald Is Finally Healing," *The Appalachian VOICE*, December 13, 2023, https://appvoices.org/2023/12/13/max-patch/.

Appendix II

  1. Carolina Mountain Club Challenges, https://www.carolinamountainclub.org/index.cfm/do/pages.view/id/49/page/Challenges.
  2. Instagram: @WhitneyGoesHiking; Facebook: Whitney Goes Hiking; Website: northcarolinadayhikingforeverybody.com.

Additional Resources

North Carolina Hiking Guidebooks

Adkins, Leonard M. *Hiking and Traveling the Blue Ridge Parkway, Revised and Expanded Edition.* Southern Gateways Guides. University of North Carolina Press, 2018.

Childrey, Don. *Uwharrie Lakes Region Trail Guide: Hiking and Biking in North Carolina's Uwharrie Mountains.* Earthbound Sports, 2014.

Davis, Jennifer Pharr, and Johnny Molloy. *Best Charlotte Hikes: The Greatest Views, Wildlife, and Forest Strolls.* Falcon Guides, 2018.

de Hart, Allen. *North Carolina Hiking Trails, 4th Edition.* Appalachian Mountain Club, 2005.

Grode, Jim, and Friends of the Mountains-to-Sea Trail. *Great Day Hikes on North Carolina's Mountains-to-Sea Trail.* Southern Gateways Guides. University of North Carolina Press, 2020.

Jeffries, Stephanie B., and Thomas R. Wentworth. *Exploring Southern Appalachian Forests: An Ecological Guide to 30 Great Hikes in the Carolinas, Georgia, Tennessee, and Virginia.* Southern Gateways Guides. University of North Carolina Press, 2014.

Johnson, Randy. *Hiking North Carolina: A Guide to More Than 500 of North Carolina's Greatest Hiking Trails.* Falcon Guides, 2020.

Molloy, Johnny. *Best Hikes Asheville, North Carolina.* Falcon Guides, 2024.

Molloy, Johnny. *Best Hikes Raleigh, Durham, and Chapel Hill: The Greatest Views, Wildlife and Forest Trails.* Falcon Guides, 2020.

Molloy, Johnny. *Hiking North Carolina's National Forests: 50 Can't-Miss Trail Adventures in the Pisgah, Nantahala, Uwharrie and Croatan National Forests.* Southern Gateways Guides. University of North Carolina Press, 2014.

Molloy, Johnny. *Hiking North Carolina's State Parks: The Best Trail Adventures from the Appalachians to the Atlantic.* Southern Gateways Guides. University of North Carolina Press, 2022.

Setzer, Lynn. *Tar Heel History on Foot: Great Walks Through 400 Years of North Carolina's Fascinating Past.* Southern Gateways Guides. University of North Carolina Press, 2013.

Watson, Melissa. *Hiking Waterfalls North Carolina: A Guide to the State's Best Waterfall Hikes.* Falcon Guides, 2019.

Williams, Robert L., Elizabeth W. Williams, and Robert L. Williams, III. *50 Hikes in the Mountains of North Carolina.* The Countryman Press, 2012.

Other Books

Arvidson, Chris, Scot Pope, and Julie E Townsend, eds. *Reflections on the New River.* McFarland, 2015.

Barker, Jerry. *Discovering North Carolina's Mountains-to-Sea Trail: A Companion for Hikers and Armchair Explorers.* Southern Gateways Guides. University of North Carolina Press, 2024.

Barnwell, Tim. *Blue Ridge Parkway Vistas: A Comprehensive Identification Guide to What You See from the Many Overlooks.* Numinous Editions, 2018.

Bernstein, Danny. *The Mountains-to-Sea Trail Across North Carolina: Walking a Thousand Miles Through Wildness, Culture, and History.* Natural History Press, 2013.

Bessette, Alan, Arleen R. Bessette, and Michael W. Hopping. *A Field Guide to the Mushrooms of the Carolinas.* Southern Gateways Guides. University of North Carolina Press, 2018.

Blevins, David, and Michael P. Schafale. *Wild North Carolina: Discovering the Wonders of Our State's Natural Communities.* University of North Carolina Press, 2024.

Bolen, Eric G., and James F. Parnell. *An Abundance of Curiosities: The Natural History of North Carolina's Coastal Plain.* University of Georgia Press, 2022.

Bryant, David, George Davidson, Terri Kirby Hathaway, and Kathleen Angione. *North Carolina's Amazing Coast: Natural Wonders from Alligators to Zoeas.* University of Georgia Press, 2013.

Cameron, Cortney, and Natalia Clarke. *Nature Therapy Walks: 22 Sensory Activities to Enjoy in Nature for Wellbeing.* Independently Published, 2020.

Cassebaum, Anne Melyn. *Down Along the Haw: The History of a North Carolina River.* McFarland, 2011.

Catlin, David T. *A Naturalist's Blue Ridge Parkway.* University of Tennessee Press, 1984.

Additional Resources

Clark, Robert C., and Tom Poland. *Carolina Bays: Wild, Mysterious and Majestic Landforms.* University of South Carolina Press, 2020.

Cooper, Leland R., and Mary Lee Cooper. *The People of the New River: Oral Histories from the Ashe, Alleghany and Watauga Counties of North Carolina.* McFarland, 2001.

Corey, Tommy. *All Humans Outside: Stories of Belonging in Nature.* Mountaineers Books, 2025.

Duncan, Barbara R., and Brett H. Riggs. *Cherokee Heritage Trails Guidebook.* Southern Gateways Guides. University of North Carolina Press, 2003.

Dungy, Camille, ed. *Black Nature: Four Centuries of African American Nature Poetry.* University of Georgia Press, 2009.

Earnhardt, Tom. *Crossroads of the Natural World: Exploring North Carolina with Tom Earnhardt.* University of North Carolina Press, 2013.

Ellison, George. *Mountain Passages: Natural and Cultural History of Western North Carolina and the Great Smoky Mountains.* The History Press, 2005.

Frankenberg, Dirk. *Exploring North Carolina's Natural Areas.* University of North Carolina Press, 2000.

Frankenberg, Dirk. *The Nature of North Carolina's Southern Coast: Barrier Islands, Coastal Waters and Wetlands.* Southern Gateways Guides. University of North Carolina Press, 2012.

Frankenberg, Dirk. *The Nature of the Outer Banks: Environmental Processes, Field Sites, and Development Issues, Corolla to Ocracoke.* Southern Gateways Guides. University of North Carolina Press, 2012.

Garriety-Blake, Barbara, and Karen Willis Amspacher. *Living at the Water's Edge: A Heritage Guide to the Outer Banks Byway.* Southern Gateways Guide. University of North Carolina Press, 2017.

Gooley, Tristan. *How to Read Nature: Awaken Your Senses to the Outdoors You've Never Noticed.* The Experiment, 2017.

Gooley, Tristan. *The Natural Navigator: The Rediscovered Art of Letting Nature Be Your Guide.* The Experiment, 2020.

Gooley, Tristan. *The Secret World of Weather: How to Read Signs in Every Cloud, Breeze, Hill, Street, Plant, Animal and Dewdrop.* The Experiment, 2023.

Hosier, Paul E. *Seacoast Plants of the Carolinas: A New Guide for Plant Identification and Use in the Coastal Landscape.* Southern Gateways Guides. University of North Carolina, 2018.

Kain, Christopher. *Rugged Access for All: A Guide for Pushikng America's Diverse Trails with Mobility Chairs and Strollers.* Rowman & Littlefield, 2022.

Keefe, Susan E., ed., with the Junaluska Heritage Association. *Junaluska: Oral Histories of a Black Appalachian Community.* McFarland, 2020.

Kenward, Louise, ed. *Moving Mountains: Writing Nature Through Illness and Disability.* Footnote Press, 2023.

Kimmerer, Robin Wall. *Braiding Sweetgrass: Indigenous Wisdom, Scientific Knowledge and the Teachings of Plants.* Penguin, 2020.

Lynch, Ida Phillips, and Margaret Fields. *North Carolina Afield: A Field Guide to Nature Conservancy Projects in North Carolina.* Blair, 2003.

Manning, Phillip. *A Foot in the South: Walks in the Natural Areas of North Carolina.* Blair, 1993.

McIntyre, Palmer, and Hollis Oberlies. *Trails and Treats: A Hiker and Runner's Guide to Great Trails and Good Eats in North Carolina.* NC Trailblazers, 2024.

Meyer, Peter. *Nature Guide to the Carolina Coast: Common Birds, Crabs, Shells, Fish, and Other Entities of the Coastal Environment.* Avian-Cetacean Press, 1991.

Michaud-Skog, Summer. *Fat Girls Hiking: An Inclusive Guide to Getting Outdoors at Any Size or Ability.* Timber Press, 2022.

Moor, Robert. *On Trails: An Exploration.* Simon & Schuster, 2016.

Morgan, Adam. *North Carolina's Wild Piedmont: A Natural History.* History Press, 2015.

Munroe, Doug. *The Trees of Ashe County, North Carolina.* McFarland, 2017.

Oliver, Mary. *Devotions: The Selected Poems of Mary Oliver.* Penguin, 2020.

Pegram, Tim. *The Blue Ridge Parkway by Foot: A Park Ranger's Memoir.* McFarland, 2007.

Pilkey, Orrin H., Tracy Monegan Rice, and William J. Neal. *How to Read a North Carolina Beach: Bubble Holes, Barking Sands, and Rippled Runnels.* Southern Gateways Guides. University of North Carolina Press, 2004.

Roe, Charles E. *North Carolina Wildlife Viewing Guide.* Falcon, 1992.

Rogers, Floyd, and Douglas L. Rights. *Yadkin Passage: A Voyage Down the Yadkin-Great Peedee River.* Winston-Salem Journal, 1983.

Scanlon, Dr. Rob. *Surviving the Trail: Five Essential Skills to Prepare Every Hiker for Adventure's Most Common Perils.* Falcon Guides, 2025.

Simpson, Bland, Ann Cary Simpson, Scott D. Taylor, and Tom Earnhardt. *North Carolina: Land of Water, Land of Sky.* University of North Carolina Press, 2021.

Sorrie, Bruce A. *A Field Guide to Wildflowers of the Sandhills Region: North Carolina, South Carolina, and Georgia.* Southern Gateways Guides. University of North Carolina Press, 2011.

Spira, Timothy P. *Wildflowers and Plant Communities of the Southern Appalachian Mountains and Piedmont: A Naturalist's Guide to the Carolinas, Virginia, Tennessee and Georgia.* Southern Gateways Guides. University of North Carolina Press, 2011.

Stewart, Kevin G., and Mary-Russell Roberson. *Exploring the Geology of the Carolinas: A Field Guide to Favorite Places from Chimney Rock to Charleston.* Southern Gateways Guides. University of North Carolina Press, 2007.

Tekiela, Stan. *Trees of the Carolinas Field Guide.* Adventure Publications, 2020.

Webb, David Rahahę·tih. *Indigenous Carolinians: A History from Original Peoples to Present-Day Tribes.* McFarland, 2025.

Wells, B.W., Dorothy Wilbur-Brooks, Lawrence S. Earley, and James W. Hardin. *The Natural Gardens of North Carolina.* University of North Carolina Press, 2002.

Wickert, Kristen. *The Plants of the Appalachian Trail: A Hiker's Guide to 398 Species.* Timber Press, 2024.

Williams, Florence. *The Nature Fix: Why Nature Makes Us Happier, Healthier and More Creative.* W.W. Norton, 2017.

Websites (in addition to those listed in the Chapter Notes)

Appalachian Trail Conservancy, https://appalachiantrail.org.
Catalyst Sports, https://www.catalystsports.org.
Friends of the Mountains-to-Sea Trail, https://mountainstoseatrail.org.
The Great Trails State, https://greattrailsnc.com.
HikeWNC, https://www.hikewnc.info.
National Park Service: North Carolina, https://www.nps.gov/state/nc/index.htm.
North Carolina Division of Parks and Recreation, https://www.ncparks.gov.
North Carolina Master Naturalists (specifically the information found in the classes linked under "Classes" on the homepage and the books listed under "Books" on the homepage). https://ncmasternaturalists.org.
NC Trails, https://trails.nc.gov/state-trails.
North Carolina Waterfalls, https://www.ncwaterfalls.com.
Sherpa Guides: The Longstreet Highroad Guide to the North Carolina Mountains, https://www.sherpaguides.com/north_carolina/mountains/index.html.
Survival Med, https://survivalmed.org.
Trail Access Project, https://www.trailaccessproject.org.
U.S. Forest Service—National Forests in North Carolina, https://www.fs.usda.gov/nfsnc.
University of Utah School of Medicine, Wild Med U. https://www.awls.online.
Waypoint Adventure, https://nc.waypointadventure.org/adventures/hiking/.

Other Media

AWLS: Advanced Wilderness Life Support (Podcast)
Bird Watching N.C. (Facebook Group)
Carolina Critters (Facebook Group)
Carolina Wildlife Identification and Appreciation Forum (Facebook Group)
Geology of North Carolina (Facebook Group)
iNaturalist (App)
Merlin Bird ID (App)
National Snakebite Support (Facebook Group)
NC Wild Snake ID and Education Group (Facebook Group)
Piedmont Discovery (App)
Plus Sized Hikers (Facebook Group)
Seek (App)
Southern Piedmont Natural History (Facebook Page

Index

Numbers in ***bold italics*** indicated pages with illustrations

access trail 57
accessibility 55–56, 56, 69–74, 127, 131, 145, 154, 159, 165, 190, 191, 220
Action Trackchair 72
ADA Trail (Nags Head Woods Preserve) 192, 220
adaptive hiking 12, 56, 69, 71–73, 127, 154, 159, 222
Adawehi Trail 198, 217
Alamance County 31, 189, 198, C2
alcohol 46, 87
Alexander County 31, 189, 198
Alleghany County 25, 27, 189
alligators 121–122, 163
AllTrails 53–55, 60, 73, 84, 97, 114, 133, 154
Alpha-gal syndrome 114–115
American dog tick 114
amphibolite mountains 30
Appalachian Mountain Club (AMC) 12
Appalachian Mountains (range) 25–27
Appalachian Ranger District 158
Appalachian Trail (AT) 13, 15, 29, ***106***, 127, 146, 153, 205–206, 208–211
apps 53, 57, 84–85, 97–98, 129
arachnids 113–116, ***C10***
Art in Parks 181
Ashe County 4, 25, 27, 30, 184, 189, ***207***, ***214***; *see also* Jefferson; West Jefferson
Asheboro 118, 198, 219, C10
Asheville 1, 11–13, 27, 73, 102–103, 123, 158–159, 189, 198, 207, 213
Ashley Ladd Trail 198
asthma 45
Atlantic and Yadkin Greenway 53–54
Atlantic Ocean 27, 37–38, ***40***–41, 215

backcountry trail 22, 27, 57, 104, 153–154
backpack 15, ***76***–77, 90–91, 95, 97, 100–103, 105, 108, 116, ***160***; plus-size 103
balance 17–18, 46, 94–95
Bald Mountains 26, 160
balds ***1***, 65, 127, 206
Balsam Mountains 26
Balsam Nature Trail ***179***, 183, 217, C7
bandana 78, 99, 108
Banner Elk 60, 67, 80, 103
barrier islands 36–38, ***40***–41, 146–148
Bass Pro Shop 102
Beaufort (city) 146
Beaufort Wind Scale 66–67
beaver 36, 61, 122
Beaver Lake Bird Sanctuary ***11***, 198
Beech Tree Trail 181
bees 116–118
benefits of hiking 6, 8, 15–21, 44, 136
Benjamin Park Trail 198
Bicentennial Gardens 218
Biltmore Campus National Recreation Trail 159, ***165***–***166***
Biltmore Forestry School 165
Birkhead Mountain Wilderness 161
black bear 41, 117, 122–124, 133, 155, 163, 213
Black Dome Mountain Sports 102
blacklegged tick 114
Black Mountain (town) 27, 72, 103, 207
Black Mountains 26–27, 159
black widow 115–116
blackwater river 36, ***39***, 163
Bladen Lakes State Forest 165

blaze orange clothing 99, 164
blisters 47, 81–82, 92
Blowing Rock 80, 103, 128, 175, 208
Blue Ridge Conservancy 189–190
Blue Ridge Escarpment ***26***–27, 161, 167, ***214***
Blue Ridge Mountains 25–27, 29
Blue Ridge Parkway 2, 7, 13, 16, 30, ***50***, 64, 73, 146, ***155***–156, 159, 171–177, 183, 208–***209***, 217–218, C1, C2, C8, C11
Bluestem Conservation Cemetery Trails 198, 218–219
Bluff Mountain Outfitters 102
Bluff Mountain Trail ***7***, ***64***, ***128***, 173–***174***, 217, ***C1***
Bluffs Restaurant 217
Boardwalk Trail (Dismal Swamp State Park) 182, 220
boardwalk trails (general) 11, 55, 69, 70, 131, 148, 150, 164, ***169***–170, 181, 186–***188***, 192, 198, 218–221
Bodie Island 37, 147
Bog Garden Trail 198, 218
Bogue Banks 41
Bogue Sound 38, 163
"bonking" 78–79
Boone 1, 50, 80, 102–103, 150, 190, 198, 208, 218
Boone Fork Trail ***16***, 173
Boone United Trail 198
Boone's Cave Park 198
breaks 49, 54, 82, 97, 128, 135, 137–138
Brevard 164, 218
Brinegar Cabin 217
Brookshire Park Trail 198
brown dog tick 114
brown recluse 115–116
Brushy Mountains 26–27
Bryson City 102–103, 154, 161, 218
Bryson City Outdoors 102

239

Index

bug net 113
Buxton Woods Trail 148, 220

cairn 107, 132
Caldwell County 25, 151, 189
Calico Creek Boardwalk 198
Cape Carteret 164
Cape Fear River 34, 37, 40
Cape Hatteras National Seashore 147–148, 220
Cape Lookout National Seashore 146–*147*
Carl Sandburg Home 148–*149*, 218
Carolina bays *38*–39, 121, 208
Carolina Beach State Park 220
Carolina Mountain Club (CMC) 12–13, 15, 109–110, 222
Carolina Thread Trail 190–*191*, 197
Carter Falls *19*, 198, 218
Carteret County 36, 163
Carvers Gap 206
Cascades Falls 208, 218
Cascades Preserve 107, 208
Cashiers 165
Catalyst Sports 72–73, 154
Catawba College 198
Catawba County 31, 35, 189
Catawba Land Conservancy 189–190
Catawba River 27, 34, 219
Catfish Lake South Wilderness Area 163
Cedar Grove 198, 218
Cedar Point Tidelands National Recreation Trail *169*–170
Chapel Hill 164, 190, 219
Charlotte 1, 4, 61, 102, 118, 135, 140, 164, 198, 201, 219
Cheoah Ranger District 160
Chimney Rock State Park 183
Chimney Run Trail *142*
chafing 96–97
Cherokee (people) 29, 151–152, 159, 207
Cherokee (city) 152, 154–155, 171
Cherokee County 25, 152, 160, 189
Clemmons Educational State Forest 164
Clingmans Dome *see* Kuwohi
clothing 82–83, 86, 93–94, 96, 99; extended sizes 103
clouds *64*–65
Coastal Fringe Trail 182
Coastal Land Trust 189–190
Coastal Plain (region) 25, 36–41, 114–115, 119, 122, 157, 186, 189, 192, 198, 203, 220–222
Coleman Trail 183, 220
College of the Albemarle 220
Columbus 198, 217

Company Mill Preserve 198, 219
compass 85, 108–110
connector trail 57, 200, 203
Conserving Carolinas 189–191
Cool Springs Baptist Church 218
coordination 17, 46
copperhead 119–*120*, *C12*
cottonmouth 119
cougar *125*–126
coyote 36, 124–125
Crab Orchard Falls 198, 218
Cradle of Forestry 159, 165–*166*
Craven County 36, 163
Croatan National Forest 157, 163–164, *169*–170
Croatan Sound 148
cross slope 55–57, 70
Crossnore Communities for Children 195
Crowders Mountain 31
Cumberland Knob 171–*172*
Cypress Point Loop Trail (Carvers Creek State Park) 182
Cypress Point Trail (Merchants Millpond State Park) 183, 220

Davidson County 31, 33, 131, 164, 189, 198
Davidson Land Conservancy 189
daypack *see* backpack
Deep Creek Waterfall Loop 154, 218
Deep River State Trail 181
deer 23, 36, 122, 138
deer tick *see* blacklegged tick
DEET 93
definition (of hiking) 10–12
dehydration 46, 77; *see also* drinking water
dewpoint 62–64
diabetes 79, 91
Diamond Brand Outdoors 102
Dismal Swamp State Park 182, 220
Doughton Park *64*, *128*, 217, *C1*
drinking water 20, 46, 49, 61, 64, 75, 77–78, 101, 106, 108, 128, 130, 135, 137, 140, 147, 155, 163, 218
Dry Falls Trail 73
duct tape 92
Dupont State Recreational Forest 165
Durham 190, C12

East Coast Greenway State Trail 181
eastern box turtle 2, *118*
Eastern Continental Divide 27

eastern coral snake 119–120, 126
eastern diamondback rattlesnake 119
eastern equine encephalitis 114
eastern hellbender 132
Educational State Forests (ESF) 164
electrolyte drinks 78, 89
elevation profile 55, 57, *59*–60, 181
Elizabeth City 198, 220
elk 124, 153, 155–156
Elk Knob Mountain 30
Elk Knob State Park 181
Elk River Falls 60, *62*
Elkin 19, 48, 198, 207, 218
Emerald Isle Woods Park 198
emergency blanket 91
Emma and Stuart Thomas Memorial Trail 195–*196*
Eno River 189, 207
Eno River Association 189
Eno River State Park 207
Evergreen Trail 182
eyeglasses 101

Faith Rock Trail 198
Fall Creek Falls Trail 183, 219
fall line 37
fatigue 47
Fenwick Hollowell Wetlands Trail 198, 220
ferry 146, 206, 208
52 Hike Challenge 222
fire: campfires 75, 88–89, 130, 206; naturally occurring and prescribed 36, 164, *182*
fire road 57
first aid kit 75, 79, 89–90
Fishing Creek Loop Trail 183
Flanner's Beach 164
flashlight 88
Flat Rock 164, 218
Flat Top Mountain Trail *128*, 175–177
flies 113
Flying Squirrel Outdoor Challenge 191
Flytrap and Sugarloaf Trails Loop 220
Fonta Flora State Trail 181
Fontana Dam *28*–29, 152, 208–211
food *see* nutrition
Footsloggers 80, 103
footcare 81–82
Foothills Conservancy 189–190
Foothills Gear Garage 102
footwear 56, 80–82, 121
Forest Bathing Trail via Vineyard Trail *199*–200
Forest Discovery Center Museum 159

Forest Festival Trail 159
Forest Service Trail Accessibility Guidelines (FSTAG) 69–70
forest therapy 136, 141
Fort Macon State Park **40**, 178
Fort Raleigh National Historic Site 148
Four Oaks 198, 220
Four Seasons Trail 201–203
Fox 40 whistle 100
Franklinville 198
Fred and Alice Stanback Educational Forest and Nature Preserve 198, 219
Fred Stanback, Jr., Ecological Preserve 198
FreeWheel Wheelchair Attachment 72
Freedom Trail 148, 220
French Broad River 27, 181

Gaia GPS 84
Garmin InReach 85, 104
Garner 164
Gaston County 31, 119, 189
Gear Goat Xchg 102
gnats *see* flies
Goose Creek State Park 186–**188**
Goshen Creek 208, 218
grade 56–57, 60, 69–70, 73, 159
Grande Peninsula Trail 211
Grandfather Mountain 65, 125–126, 171–172, C9, C10
Grandfather Mountain State Park 16, 106, 181–182
Grandfather Ranger District 158, 161
Grassy Creek Vineyard and Winery 199–200
Grassy Ridge and Mountain Trail Loop 183
Grassy Ridge Bald 206
gratitude 138–140
Great Bend Park 208
Great Craggy Mountains 159
Great Dismal Swamp 39
Great Outdoor Provision Co. 102
Great Smoky Mountains National Park 13–15, 29, 66, 72, 85, 88, 124, 146, 152–156, 171, 206, 218
Great Trails State Coalition 15, 195, 214
Green Swamp Preserve **192**, *C3*
Greensboro 53, 150, 198, 218
greenways 15, 21, 45, 53–54, 70, 84, 151, 181, 190, 197, 223
Gregory Pack 103
Grindstone Trail 219
GRIT Freedom Chair 71, 154
Guilford College 200–**201**

Guilford County 31, 142, 189, 198
Guilford Courthouse National Military Park 150

Hammock Beach State Park 105, 181–182, 220
Hammock Hills Trail 148
Hampton Lake 198
Hanging Rock 31–**32**
Hanging Rock State Park 32, 182, 184–186, 207
Harkers Island 146
Hatteras Island 37, 40
Haw River Trail 208
headlamp 75, 88
Headwaters State Forest 165
heat illness 87
Hemlock Nature Trail 183
Hickory (city) 103, 198, 219
Hickory Bluffs Trail 182
Hickory Nut Gorge State Trail 181
Hickory Trail (New River State Park) **182**
Hiddenite 219
High Country 26–27, 207
High Point 23, 70, C4
Highlands Biological Station 198
Hike Passport journal 98
hiking boots 56, 80–81, 116, 121
hiking challenges 191, 222
hiking groups 12, 20, 23, 66, 72, 89, 128–129, 131
hiking poles *see* trekking poles
Hiking Project 84
hiking speed 23, 54
Hines Chapel Preserve 211–212
Hinson Lake 198, 219
history (of hiking)10, 12–15
History Trail 220
Hiwassee Reservoir 152
Hiwassee River 27, 160, 189
Holmes Educational State Forest 164
honey bees 116–117
hornets 116–118
horses 57–**58**, 127, 129, 133, 146–**147**
horseshoe trail 57
Hot Springs 103, 159
Howell Woods Environmental Learning Center 198, 207–208, 220
humidity 62–64, 67
hunter orange clothing *see* blaze orange clothing
hunting 99, 132, 157, 164, 221
hurricanes 25, 40–41
Hurricane Helene 30, 102, 159, 161, 172, 182–183, 213, 217
hydration bladder 77, 101

hyperthermia *see* heat illness
hypoglycemia 79
hypothermia 47, 83–84, 88, 91

illness 6, 18, 44, 46, 114–115
I'M SAFE 46–47
immune system 18, 86
Indian Creek Falls 154
Indigenous peoples 12, 67, 132, 148, 219; *see also* Cherokee (people)
insect repellent 93–94
Intracoastal Waterway 38, 124, 139, 181, 220
interpretive trail 57
Iredell County 31, 35, 189–190
Iron Mountains 26

J. Douglas Williams Park 198, C9
Jackson County 25, 160, 189
Jane Bald 206
Jesse Brown Cabin 218
Jesse Brown's Outdoors 103
Jockey's Ridge 37, 206, 208
Joëlette Adventure chair 72
Jordan Lake Educational State Forest 164
Jones County 37, 163
Jones Falls 60, **62**
journal 98–99
Joyce Kilmer Memorial Forest **160**–161, 218
Jumpingoff Rocks (Uwharrie National Forest) 56
Jumpinoff Rock (Ashe County) 173, 207, **214**
Junaluska Memorial **151**–152
Juney Whank Falls 154

Kernersville 107
Kids in Parks Track Trails 181
Kill Devil Hills 152, 220
Kinsa Active 103
knife 51, 75, 92
Knight Brown Nature Preserve **193**–194
Koala phone harness 102
Kula Cloth 132
Kuwohi 206–207

La Crosse encephalitis 114
Lake Brandt 53–**54**
Lake Hickory Riverwalk 198, 219
Lake James State Park 151
Lake Loop Trail (U.S. National Whitewater Center) 135
Lake Mattamuskeet 39
Lake Norman 34–**35**
Lake Norman State Park 35, 119, 182
Lake Thom-a-Lex 198, 219
Lake Waccamaw **38**–39

Lake Waccamaw State Park 38, 183, 221
Lake Wilson Loop Trail 220
Lakeshore Trail (Lake Norman State Park) 35, 182
Lakeshore Trail (Lake Waccamaw State Park) 38, 183, 221
Land Trust Alliance 189
layering 82
Leave No Trace 130–133
Lenoir 164
Leukotape P 81, 89, 92
Lexington 1, 63, 198, 219
lightning 64–*66*
Lincoln County 31, 35, 189–190
Linn Cove Viaduct 171–*173*
Linville Falls 27, 159
Linville Gorge 27, 159
Linville Gorge Wilderness 158
Liquid IV 78
Little Long Mountain *141*, 168–169
Little Tennessee River 27, 29, 189, *210*–211
Live Oak Trail *105*, 181–182
Lone Bald 160
lone star tick 114–115
longleaf pine 41, 163, *180*–181, 213
loop trail 40, 48, 53, 57, 107, 135, 146, 150, 154, 165, 170, 175, 181–184, 186, 191, 193, 201, 206, 208, 218–221
Lost Province Trail 183–184
Loyal Lifts 73
Lumber River *39*, 40
Lumber River State Park 39, 183, 220
Luther Rock (Mt. Jefferson) *184*
Lyme disease 114–115

Mainspring Conservation Trust 189
mammals 117, 122–126, 163
Manteo 148
maps 47, 53, 55, 58–62, 73, 84–85, 98, 104–106, 173, 181, 190
marbled salamander 118
maritime forest 41, 148, 192, 220
Marshall 159, 218
Mast General Store 103
Max Patch Loop Trail 205–206, 218
Mayo River State Park 182–183, 219
Mayo River Trail 183, 219
McDowell County 25, 27, 30, 189
McDowell Nature Preserve 201–203
Meadow and Boulder Trail 219

Mecklenburg County 31, 35, 72, 189, 198; *see also* Charlotte
medical alert bracelet 91
medication 45–46, 87, 89, 91, 119
Medicine Wheel Trail 152
meditation 20, 22
Medoc Mountain State Park 183
memory 18, 21
mental health 18, 21, 73, 195
Merchants Millpond State Park 183, 220
microspikes 99
Middle Prong Wilderness 158
Midland 32, 219
Miller Park 198
mindful walking 140
mindfulness 136–143
monadnocks 31–*32*
Montgomery County 31, 37, 161, 190
Moore County 31, 37, 190
Moore Cove Falls Trail 158, 218
Moores Creek National Battlefield 148–149, 220
Morehead City 164, 198
Morganton 102, 164, 190
Morrow Mountain State Park 31, 181, 186–*187*
Moses Cone Memorial Park *128*, 173, 175–177
mosquitoes 93–94, 113–115, 148
Mount Jefferson 30
Mount Jefferson State Natural Area 183–*184*, C5
Mount Mitchell 12, *14*, 24, 27, 30, 159, *179*
Mount Mitchell State Park *14*, 178–*179*, 183, 217, C7
Mount Pisgah 159
Mountain Farm Museum 156
Mountain Island Educational State Forest 164
Mountains (region) 25–30, 157, 183, 217–218
Mountains-to-Sea Trail (MST) 15, 37, 50, 130, 148, 158, 164, 173, *174*, 181, 206–*209*, *211*–212, 214, 218, C11
multi-tool 92
multi-use trail 57–*58*, 127, 129, 133, 219
mushrooms 115, 136, 217, *C4*
music 129, 137

Nags Head 37
Nags Head Woods Preserve 191, 220
Nantahala Gorge 159
Nantahala Mountains 26
Nantahala National Forest 27, 30, 73, 157, 159–161, 165–*167*, 218

Nantahala Outdoor Center 103
Nantahala Ranger District 160
Nat Greene Trail 53–54
National Park Service 66, 124, 146, 148, 153, 171–173, 205
National Weather Service 62–63, 66
nature connection 1, 4–5, 10, 136, 140, 143
Nature Conservancy 189–191
nature trails 57, 181
Neuse River 34, 37, 40, 117, 163–164, 206–207
Neusiok Trail 164, 208
New Bern Battlefield Park *203*–204
New River 27, 189
New River Conservancy 189
New River State Park *70*, *182*–183
Newfound Mountains 26
Newport River 164
North Carolina Coastal Federation 164
North Carolina Department of Natural and Cultural Resources 73
North Carolina Poison Control 119, 121
North Carolina State Trails 179–182
North Carolina Trail Days 48
North Carolina Wildlife Resources Commission 72, 124
North Carolina Zoo 20, 32, 126, 197–198
Northern Peaks State Trail 181
nutrition 47, 78–79
Nuwati Trail 182

Oak Hill Community Park and Forest 190
Ocean Isle Beach Nature Trail *17*, *139*, 198, 220
Oconaluftee River Trail 153, *155*–156
Oconaluftee Visitor Center 152–156
Ocracoke Island 37, 147
Open Ponds Trail 148
Osprey packs 103
Otter Falls Trail 198
out-and-back trail 47–48, 57, 60, 154–155, 161, 165, 168, 175, 183–184, 186, 192, 200, 206, 208, 211, 218–219
Outdoor Supply Company 103
Outer Banks 37, 41, 147, 152, 191, 206, 208
Overmountain Victory National Historic Trail 150–151, 181

pace *see* hiking speed
Paddy Mountain Park 190
Palmetto Boardwalk Trail 186–*188*
Palmetto Trail 53–54
Pasquotank River 22, 220
Patsy Pond Nature Trail Loop 164, 221
Pee Dee River 34, 186
Permethrin 93–94, 99
pets 122, 133–135, 206
phones 21, 104, 110, 129, 137, 155; battery use 97–98, 111; phone tether 101–102
phytoncides 18
Picaridin 93
Piedmont (region) 24–25, 30–36, 198, 218, 222
Piedmont Environmental Education Center 23, C4
Piedmont Land Conservancy 189–190, 194
Piedmont Legacy Trails 190
Piedmont Plus Size Hikers 20
Piedmont Triad Regional Council 190
pigmy rattlesnake 119
Pilot Knob Trail *32*, 183, 219
Pilot Mountain 31–*32*
Pilot Mountain State Park 183, 207, 219
Pine Barrens Trail *180*, 183
Pisgah Inn 207–208
Pisgah Mountain 26, 159
Pisgah National Forest 2, 30, 151, 158–159, 161, 165–*166*, 206, 218
Pisgah Ranger District 158, 161
Pisgah View State Park 182
Play It Again Sports 102
Pleasant Garden 219
pocosin (environment) 36, 41, 163
Pocosin Wilderness Area 163
poison ivy *83*
Pond Pine Wilderness Area 163
power bank 97
precipitation potential percentage 62–63
Profile Trail 16, 106, 182
Propel 78
proprioception 17–18
Purgatory Mountain 20, 198
Purple Martin Trail 151

Quarry Trail 181
questing 114

rail trail 57, 84
Rails-to-Trails Conservancy 84
Raleigh 164, 190
Randolph County 31, 161, 189–190
Raven Rock Overlook 208

Raven Rock State Park 183
red wolves 41
Reed Gold Mine 32, 71, 219
Regear Outdoors 102
REI 80, 85, 103
Reynolda Gardens Trails 198
rhododendron 2, 67, 159, 218
Rhododendron Trail (Mt. Jefferson State Natural Area) 183–184
Rhododendron Garden Trail (Roan Mountain) 159, 218
Ribbonwalk Nature Preserve 198
Richmond County 31, 37, 190, 198
Ride the Triad 73
Ridges Mountain Preserve 118, *197*–198, 219
right-of-way 127–128
River Run Trail *70*, 183
Riverbluffs Trail 182
ROAD iD 91
Roan Highlands *1*, 127
Roan Mountain 26, 159, 218
Roanoke Island 148
Roanoke River 34, 37, 40, 181
Robbinsville 151–152, 218
Rock Garden Trail 184–186
Rockingham (city) 198, 219
Rocky Face Mountain Recreation Area 198, 219
Rocky Mountain spotted fever 114–115
Roots Outdoor NC 103
rough green snake 119, *C12*
Round Bald 206
Rowan County 31, 134, 190
Rutherfordton 151

Safe and Found 111
Salem Lake 127, 198, 219
Salisbury 191, 198
Sand Ridge Nature Trail 183, 221
Sandhills 37, 180, 183
Sauratown Mountains 31–*32*, 207
Saxapahaw Island Trail 198, 219, C2
Scotland County 37, 190
sea oat 41
search and rescue (SAR) 43, 51, 75, 79, 104, 111
Second Gear 102
second-hand gear 75, 102–103
self-defense 51–52
self esteem 18
sensory experiences 5, 19–20, 23, 129, 140, 159, 179, 190
Seven Devils 198
Shackleford Banks *147*, C6
Sheep Ridge Wilderness Area 163

shelter 12–13, 29, 65, 75, 91, 106, 206
Shining Rock Wilderness 158
shoes 56, 80–82, 99, 121
shovel 100, 132
single-track trail 57, 84, 127–*128*, 163
sit spot 141–143
Skinny Dip Falls 159
sleep 18, 46–47
slope *see* grade
Smart Wool 103
Smithfield 164
snacks *see* nutrition
snakes 112, 119–121, 126, 133, 148, 155, 163, *C12*
Sniffspot 135
Snowbird Mountains 26
socks 80–82, 94
sounds (bodies of water) 25, 37–41, 148, 163
Soundside Loop Trail 146
South Mountains 27
South Mountains State Park 183
Southern Appalachian Highlands Conservancy 189
Southern Appalachian Mountains *see* Appalachian Mountains
Southern Tick Associated Rash Illness (STARI) 115
Southwest Park *142*
Spencer 198, 219
spider *see* arachnids
Splash Dam Falls 60, *62*
splint 99–100
Spirit Ridge Trail 161, 218
SportivaPlus 103
spruce-fir forest 29, 159, 175, *179*, 217
stairs 45, *48*–49, 60, 73, 154, 159, 161, 206
Stanly County 31, 190
state forests 164–165
state parks 12, *14*–15, 20–21, 30, 32, 35, 37–*40*, 46, *48*, *70*, 73, 85, 99, *105*–106, 117, 119, 127, 132, 151, 178–188, 206–209, 217, 219–221, 223, C7
state parks passport 183
state recreation areas 178
state natural areas 178
Statesville 103
Stokesdale 193
Stone Mountain 31, 48, 183, 209
Stone Mountain State Park 48, 183, 209
strength 15–18
stress 18–21, 45–46, 91, 105, 136–137
succession 34–36
Sugar Mountain 198, C9
Summit Trail (Mount Jefferson

State Natural Area) 183–184, *C5*
Summit Trail (Stone Mountain State Park) 183
sun protection 86–87
Superfit Hero 103
Supple Jack Loop Trail 182
Supply (town) 192
swamp *see* wetlands
Swansboro 170, 220
switchbacks 57, 60, 131, 194

Take a Hike Mountain Outfitters 103
Tar-Pamlico River 40
Tar River 37, 189
Tar River Land Conservancy 189
Tarheel Trail 149, 220
tarp 91
Taylorsville 219
tea 78, 140–*141*
10 essentials 75–92, 158
Thicket Adventure 103
37 Minutes 103
30-60-90 Walk 108–*110*
Thomas Hariot Trail 148
Thomasville 219
Three Rivers Land Trust 189
Three Rivers Trail 186–*187*
ticks 93–94, 114–115, 119, 193
tides 37, 39, 170, 215
Tidewater 37
timber rattlesnake 119
Tom Branch Falls 154
Tomkins Knob Overlook 208, 218
topographical maps 58–60, 181
Trail Access Project 73
trail blazes *105*–107, 138, 158, 161, 205, *207*, *209*, *211*
"trail creep" 131
trail ducks 107
trail etiquette 127–130
trail magic 130, 206
Trail of Tears National Historic Trail 151–152
trail reviews 55, 57, 61, 72, 86, 106, 133
trail runners 56, 80–81; *see also* hiking boots
trail system 57, 164, 190, 193, 195, 214
trail tread 55–57, 69–*70*, 105, *128*, 148, 150, 154, 164
TrailLink 73, 84
Transit to Trails 73
transportation 15, 72–73
Transylvania County 25–27, 189

trash *see* waste disposal
trash bags 100
trekking poles 7, 17, 56, 88, 94–*95*, 99, *160*
Trent River 163
Triangle Land Conservancy 190–191
Turnbull Educational State Forest 164
Turnipseed Nature Preserve 198, 219
Tusquitee Ranger District 160
Tuttle Educational State Forest 164
20/5/3 Nature Pyramid 21–*22*
Tyvek sheeting 91

Unaka Mountains 26
Underground Railroad Tree Trail 200–*201*
Upper Cascades Falls Trail 184–186
U.S. Access Board 69
U.S. Forest Service 30, 69, 157, 159, 164, 205–206
U.S. National Whitewater Center 135
used gear *see* second-hand gear
UV rays 86–87
Uwharrie Mountains 31, *141*, 162–163, *168*–169
Uwharrie National Forest 32, *58*, 157, 161–163, *168*–169
Uwharrie National Trail *56*, 124, *141*, *162*–163, 168–169
Uwharrie River 186
Uwharrie Trailblazers 163

Valle Crucis 133, 198, 218
Venus flytrap 41, 163, 192, 220, *C3*
Venus Flytrap Trail 220

Wake County 31, 198
Washington (North Carolina) 186
wasps 115–*117*
waste disposal 100, 122, 130–132, 135
Watauga County 25, 30, 189, 198
Watauga River 27
waterfalls 16, *19*, 26–27, 32, 48–49, 55, 57, 60, *62*, 73, 133, 154, 158–159, 161, 165–*167*, 183–186, 198, 218–219
Wayah Bald 206
Waypoint Adventure NC 72
Waypoint Outfitters 103

weapons 51–52
weather forecast 62–64
Wendell 219
West Jefferson 1, 50, 80, 103, 183, 190, 218
West Nile virus 114
wetlands *39*, 121, 148, 163, 186, 192, 198, 203, 219–220
Weymouth Woods State Natural Area *180*, 183
wheelchair 15, 55–56, 69–73, 129, 154, 158
whistle 100, 110
White Oak Creek 217
White Oak River 40, 163
White Squirrel Hiking Challenge 191
Whitewater Falls 26–27, 165–*167*
Whitewater Off-leash 135
Whitewater River 27
Wikiloc Outdoor Navigation GPS 84
wilderness areas (in national forests) 158, 161, 163
Wilderness Gateway State Trail 181
wildflowers 3, 5, 19–20, 29, 140, 174, 191, 211, 213, 217–219, 222, *C1*, *C2*, *C9*
wildlife 25, 34, 36, 107, 112–126, 130–133, 135, 142, 155, 164, 170, 181, 186–191, 195, 206, 218–222, *C4*, *C10*, *C12*
Wilkes County 25, 151, 189, 197
Wilkesboro 197
Willow Pond Trail 146
Wilmington 41, 120, 148, 164, C3, C12
Wilson 220
wind 30, 34, 41, 52, 62, 66–68, 82–83, 174
Winston-Salem 1, 127, 195–196, 198, 219
Wiseman's View Trail 159
woolly worm 67–68
Works Progress Administration 171
Wright Brothers National Memorial 152

Yadkin Memorial Park 198
Yadkin River *33*, 134, 186
Yadkin River Greenway 151
Yadkin River Park 134
Yadkin River State Trail 181
Yadkinville 198
Year of the Trail 15, 214
Yellow Mountain Gap Trail 151
yellowjackets 117